Those Fabulous Philadelphians

THOSE FABULOUS PHILADELPHIANS

The Life and Times of a Great Orchestra

HERBERT KUPFERBERG

London · W. H. Allen · 1970

120841   785.062748

To Barbara

ACKNOWLEDGMENTS

This book was not commissioned by the Philadelphia Orchestra, but it could not have been written without its co-operation. I would like to thank the directors of the Orchestra Association for their many courtesies. Specifically, they permitted me access to the orchestra's scrapbooks, a set of meticulously-kept volumes of clippings containing, seemingly, every word written in the public press about the orchestra from the year 1900 to the present. They also made available to me other records and mementos of the orchestra, and invited me to interview as many members of the administration and staff as I wished. I am grateful to Mr. Eugene Ormandy and Mr. Leopold Stokowski for the many hours of time they gave me; some of their conversations are given in transcript form, other of their information is embodied more generally in the pages that follow.

I especially appreciate the opportunity I had of spending several weeks living among members of the orchestra at the Skidmore College dormitories during the Saratoga summer festival of 1968. Again, some of the fruits of my talks with the musicians are scattered throughout the book, but a great deal is concentrated in the final section called "The Life of the Orchestra." The soul and psyche of the American orchestral musician is a subject hitherto largely neglected, and I hope that this chapter may at least serve to direct the interest of other investigators into this area.

I would like to thank the scores of other persons connected with the orchestra in the past and present who kindly shared their time and memories with me. The names of most of them will be apparent to the reader, and although some quotations are not ascribed to individuals by name, I offer my assurance that every line is given exactly as spoken.

In addition to those named in the book, I would like to thank, for assistance well beyond the call of duty, Mr. Wayne Shilkret, the orchestra's director of publicity; Miss Audrey Michaels, its New York press representative; and Mrs. Mae Bowler, the custodian of that last remnant of a great institution, the library of the New York *Herald Tribune.*

Dr. Johnson wrote that a man would turn over half a library to make one book. He might also have noted that the same process could throw an entire family into upheaval. I would like to express deepest appreciation to my mother, Mrs. Augusta Kupferberg, for her long and patient encouragement; to my children, Seth, Joel and Natalie, for active assistance in various chores and also simply for disappearing discreetly at the right moments; and, not least, to my wife, to whom, in a small measure of gratitude, this book is dedicated.

HERBERT KUPFERBERG

Forest Hills, N.Y.

CONTENTS

Illustrations follow pages 86 and 150

Those Fabulous Philadelphians

CHAPTER I

The City and the Orchestra

"One is continually affronted in Philadelphia social life by a forthright
Philistinism, and then surprised by a hidden connoisseurship."
—Nathaniel Burt, *The Perennial Philadelphians.*

Every Friday afternoon at 2 o'clock in the city of Philadelphia a
multitude of women descends upon a dignified building in the center
of town. At first glance they appear to be almost as old as the structure
itself, which is called the Academy of Music and was opened in the
year 1857. It is only upon further examination that one notices that,
interspersed among the elderly ladies, some of whom actually need
help to climb the few steps in front of the Academy, there is a goodly
sprinkling of younger women, as though a newer generation was already being groomed to replenish the ranks of the older, and to receive from it the torch of tradition.

Although these ladies are going to a concert, their talk is not of
music. Rather they discuss their gardens, their clubs, their social
affairs—and each other. For they know each other very well, having
followed the same ritual in the same surroundings with the same com-
panions for as many years as they can remember.

3

Within the hall, a beautifully ornate, gracefully curved auditorium whose proscenium is crowned with a medallion of Mozart, a symphony orchestra is on the stage, tuning its instruments. The lights are dimmed, the chatter ceases, a short, pleasant-looking man walks to the podium, there is a polite round of applause—never more than that on a Friday afternoon—and another concert by the Philadelphia Orchestra has begun.

For seventy years now, Philadelphia audiences have been trooping into the Academy to hear the orchestra. The Friday afternoon concerts have been unshakably feminine since the start, with subscriptions for them handed down like the family jewels from mother to daughter or daughter-in-law. Many have been in the same family since the orchestra's inception. In fact, at the beginning of the 1968–'69 season there still remained in the audience a Miss Lena Hale, ninety-seven years old, who had been regularly attending Friday matinees since the first one, and who had just contributed to the Academy a fitting tribute to old ladies everywhere—a brand-new elevator.

Other audiences at the concerts during the week are equally loyal, considerably younger, and more outwardly responsive to the music they are hearing. On Saturday nights the hall is crowded with young people, students, and musical enthusiasts in general, as well as the wives of the orchestra members, who are afforded the privilege of hearing their husbands play at half price. On Monday nights doctors, lawyers, college professors and other professionals predominate; a largely masculine audience, though not as overwhelmingly as Friday afternoons are feminine. There also are new Thursday night, Friday night, and Saturday night subscriptions, which have had the effect of apparently opening up a brand-new audience to the Philadelphia Orchestra of people who were previously unable to get a place on the crowded subscription lists. The Academy on those nights is filled with unfamiliar faces; one Philadelphia newspaperman tells of an old subscriber, somehow finding himself in the house on one of the new Friday nights, looking around the crowded hall and testily demanding: "Where *is* everybody?" One of the attributes of the new audiences is enthusiasm; during their first year the Thursday nighters even applauded between movements, which of course, no proper Philadelphia audience does.

Between the orchestra on the stage and the audience in the hall a rapport exists such as few other cities can match. Even those Philadelphians who have never been to a concert in their lives—and there are some—know perfectly well that the orchestra exists and that it reflects glory on their city. Their attitude is perhaps not unlike—to quote an old Philadelphia joke—that of the two old Philadelphians who enter their social club to find that it has been draped in black crepe. "What's that for?" says one. "Don't know," replies the other, "but it certainly brightens the old place up." In like manner the Philadelphia Orchestra makes the town a better place even for those who enjoy its acquaintance only by reputation.

Sometimes in its programs and activities the orchestra has been thoroughly representative of the spirit of its tradition-minded, conservative home city. At other times, it has departed from it in unexpected and exciting ways. But wherever it has traveled, in the United States or abroad, it has become known as Philadelphia's most successful envoy to the world since Benjamin Franklin, and its most universally admired export of the twentieth century. Not, it should be added, that all Philadelphians are glad to see the orchestra go abroad. Its music director, Eugene Ormandy, tells of an elderly lady—a Friday matinee lady—who was not at all pleased by the success of the Philadelphia on its first tour of Europe. "*We* know that we have the greatest orchestra in the world," she told him. "Why should we have to go *there* to prove it to *them?*"

Whether the Philadelphia Orchestra is *the* greatest orchestra in the world is one of those unanswerable questions which serve little purpose except to provoke a lively discussion among music lovers. Few Philadelphians will come right out and say so, any more than they will buttonhole you and declare that the United States is the greatest country on earth. In Philadelphia, as elsewhere, certain facts are universally known and incontrovertible, and there is no need to proclaim them publicly.

Yet there is no doubt that for at least fifty years the Philadelphia Orchestra has provided a standard against which other orchestras are

measured. The modern symphony orchestra probably is the most
sensitive, flexible and expressive musical instrument yet devised by
man, and through some curious combination of circumstances it has
reached its highest gloss of perfection in the city of Philadelphia, Pa.
Other American orchestras have had, and are having, their flings at
glory and greatness. Boston and Chicago were the two leading American orchestras at the start of the twentieth century, but as the years
went by each oscillated between periods of brilliance and mediocrity.
The New York Philharmonic was rescued from a long decline by
Arturo Toscanini in the 1920s and '30s, then slipped once again until
Leonard Bernstein restored its prestige in our own day. After years
of existence as merely a good provincial organization the Cleveland
Orchestra attained national stature in the post-war era under the brilliant George Szell. Yet through all these changes, through the rise
and fall of other contenders for eminence, the Philadelphia Orchestra
has maintained its pace and its place steadily for half a century. It
may have had to share its pedestal, but it has never vacated it.

Why this great orchestra has grown and flourished in Philadelphia is a question that has often puzzled outside observers. One
school of thought holds that it was sheer accident—that had Leopold
Stokowski and Eugene Ormandy pursued their consecutive careers
on the podium of another orchestra in another city—*any* other city—
the outcome in terms of orchestral perfection would have been absolutely the same. In fact, one or two admittedly disgruntled observers
of the scene, including a former member of the board of directors,
have been known to contend that Philadelphia doesn't even deserve
its orchestra, let alone appreciate it.

On the other hand, there are those who maintain that the Philadelphia Orchestra could have arisen *only* in Philadelphia, that only
there did an audience exist which was patient enough to sit quietly
while first, Stokowski shaped the orchestra, experimented with it, and
led it through some of the most exciting and bewildering adventures
any American musical group has ever undertaken, and later, while
Ormandy honed and polished and refined its sound until it became
perhaps the sleekest vehicle of musical expression ever created—what
musicologist Paul Henry Lang once referred to as "the solid gold
Cadillac of the eastern orchestras."

It's likely, as a Philadelphia lawyer might conclude, that there is merit in both arguments. Chance certainly played its part in the evolution of a second-rate provincial orchestra into one of the world's foremost musical institutions. If Leopold Stokowski, a slim, ambitious stripling of thirty, hadn't happened along when he did; if Arthur Judson, a brilliant ex-critic just starting his managerial career, hadn't entered the picture at the same time; if such solid citizens as the publisher Edward Bok and the patrician Alexander Van Rensselaer hadn't been on hand to provide social, moral and financial support; if a band of determined women, with the seeds of Friday matinees already coursing through their bloodstreams, hadn't been waiting and watching and working, none of it would have happened as it did. But it was only in Philadelphia that all these factors could have come together.

That Philadelphia is a sedate and conservative city is a fact celebrated in dozens of anecdotes and jokes. None of these in the least bit bothers Philadelphians. Those who find the pace too quiet can easily travel ninety miles to New York, there to spend either an evening or a lifetime. But with a population of 4,000,000 in the metropolitan area, the city seems in no danger of going out of business. In fact, recent years have seen a striking resurgence of its vitality, with an imaginative urban renewal program in the center city that far outstrips in scope and grandeur anything going on in New York, and a refurbishing and beautification project that is restoring Independence Hall and its historic surroundings to their ancient glory.

Although people more and more are returning to the center city area, most of the orchestra's subscribers and other patrons come from the suburbs, notably from the towns that make up the famous "Main Line"—that lie along the main tracks of the Pennsylvania Railroad stretching westward. Some cite the beauty and comfort of Philadelphia's suburbs as the main reason for the relative placidity of the city's night life. Why stay out late in Philadelphia, the argument runs, when the comfort and security of an evening at home in Radnor, Bryn Mawr, or Paoli beckons?

A similar conservatism pervades the city's business life. It is not a town, on the whole, for new enterprises, sudden innovations, or dazzling departures. It has a solid base of industry, a thriving navy yard, an abundance of fine shops and department stores. But its main business, to a casual visitor strolling down Broad Street, seems to be banking. Just as Byron's Childe Harold could stand in Venice with "a palace and a prison on each hand," so can a modern pilgrim in Philadelphia stand with a bank and an insurance company on each side. At Broad and Chestnut Streets there are no fewer than four banks on four corners, and perhaps it is no coincidence that only a block or two away stands the Academy of Music, home of the Philadelphia Orchestra.

But Philadelphia's conservatism is not a matter of business interests or political belief; it is a general approach to life. Wealth, worth and achievement are all highly prized, but too much outward manifestation of them is frowned upon. That Friday matinee crowd at the Academy of Music may consist of some of the most affluent and aristocratic women in America, but it is certainly not one of the most fashionably or opulently dressed assemblages in the land. Just being there is symbol enough of one's belonging; there is no need to prove the point by over-dressing or ostentation.

Much of this feeling of inner worth and solid substance is embodied by the Philadelphia Orchestra. The orchestra is world-famous for its uniquely ripe and resonant sound, but this is no surface attribute, for the "Philadelphia sound" is neither flashy nor glittering. Like the town itself, it is rich rather than brilliant, solid rather than showy. It's the way the Philadelphia Orchestra *should* sound.

Through almost countless recordings and almost innumerable travels that sound has become famous throughout the musical world. The Philadelphia has never been strictly a home-town orchestra. Even its first two conductors, a pair of German-speaking kapellmeisters named Fritz Scheel and Karl Pohlig, were quick to take it on visits to such nearby centers as New York, Boston and Washington, and both Stokowski and Ormandy consistently insisted, in so many words, that Philadelphia must share its musical treasure with the rest of the world.

Consequently those Academy of Music subscription audiences are matched by subscription audiences in other cities. The Philadelphia Orchestra gives a series of "five Mondays" in Washington, "eight Tuesdays" in Baltimore, and "ten Tuesdays" in New York. In each of these cities it is virtually sold out. In addition, it tours frequently and widely; it was the first orchestra in the land to have a fifty-two week contract for its musicians, and it keeps them busy throughout. It will play anywhere within reason as long as a local sponsor will pay its fee of $12,500 a concert. It consistently logs more miles, visits more countries, gives more concerts, and makes more recordings than any other American orchestra.

Does this compulsion to travel, to perform in other cities, for other audiences and other critics, fill some deep-seated psychological need for Philadelphians? Beneath that surface of contentment and confidence is there a yearning for reassurance which can only be satisfied by the approbation of outside experts? Does it take the New York or Boston reviews to convince Philadelphia it has a great orchestra? It seems doubtful, but even if it were so, the orchestra can revel in the knowledge that it has received a full measure of acclaim and adulation wherever it has gone. And since 1949, when it made its first overseas voyage to the British Isles, it has gone practically everywhere a symphony orchestra can go, crisscrossing the world until there is hardly an important city from Moscow to Tokyo which has not heard and admired its unique sound. Speaking for them all, Harold C. Schonberg recently wrote in the *New York Times*—those New York critics again!—that the Philadelphia Orchestra was "the greatest virtuoso orchestra active today, and probably the greatest virtuoso orchestra of all time."

But it wasn't easy.

CHAPTER II

The Early Years

"In Boston they ask, How much does he know? In New York, How much is he worth? In Philadelphia, Who were his parents?"
—Mark Twain, *What Paul Bourget Thinks of Us.*

♭ A MUSICAL CAPITAL

For a city which in its early years was the nation's cultural as well as political capital, Philadelphia was a remarkably long time begetting its orchestra. New York gave birth to the Philharmonic in 1842 (and to the New York Symphony in 1878); Boston and St. Louis created symphonies in 1880; Chicago began its musical operations in 1891; and even Pittsburgh, the western metropolis of Pennsylvania, formed an orchestra in 1895, though it disbanded temporarily after only fifteen years of existence. Not until 1900 did the present Philadelphia Orchestra come into being.

But there was music in Philadelphia almost from the start. The city may have been founded, planned and named by William Penn and his Society of Friends, but it was populated largely by German and Swedish settlers who did not share the Quakers' distaste for things musical, and who brought with them their own hymnals and instruments. Moravian settlers made their influence felt throughout the state, turning Bethlehem into a center of musical activity which persists to this day in the famous Bach Festival. In Philadelphia, Penn's Friends may not have cared for music themselves, but they generally tolerated it in others, as they tolerated so many other human peculiarities, so that both vocal and instrumental works flourished in the city's Lutheran, Presbyterian and Roman Catholic churches. Eventually English immigrants with a taste for music began to arrive. In 1730, a certain Miss Ball, "lately arrived from London," announced that she taught "singing, playing on the spinet, and all sorts of needle-work," and in 1750 a Londoner named John Beals advertised in the *Pennsylvania Gazette* that he was ready to teach "Violin, Hautboy, German Flute, Common Flute, and Dulcimer by note" at his home in Fourth Street.

One imagines that these ancient music masters found eager pupils, for others soon began to advertise their expertise. In 1750, Philadelphia had a population of around 40,000; not only was it the largest town in North America, it was second only to London among the cities of the British Empire. Such culture as America could boast was largely concentrated there. The first recorded public concert was held in the Assembly Room in Lodge Alley on January 25, 1757; when a second was given on March 17 the audience included a young bachelor colonel named George Washington.

The two most famous names associated with Philadelphia music in the eighteenth century were Benjamin Franklin and Francis Hopkinson. Had there been a Philadelphia Orchestra in those days, both Franklin and Hopkinson would surely have been among its most ardent supporters. Franklin enriched virtually every branch of human activity from literature to science, and music was no exception. Nor was he a dabbler or dilettante. He knew his Handel; he inveighed against cluttering up pristine folk tunes with ornate accompaniments or incongruous harmonies; he published music in his printing establishment; he played the guitar and the harp. Moreover, he actually invented an instrument, the famous glass-harmonica or "Glassychord" —a set of musical glasses which emitted a haunting, harmonious sound when their edges were stroked. Several variants of this instrument existed when Franklin, around 1762, devised an ingenious mechanism which permitted the glasses to be rotated by pedal; it was essentially this device for which Mozart wrote his Quintet for harmonica, flute, oboe, viola and cello, K. 617, and his Adagio for harmonica solo, K. 356.

Franklin, as the colonies' foremost spokesman abroad, of necessity spent much of his time away from home, but Francis Hopkinson was Philadelphia-born and -bred and, though he visited England as a young man, found his world in his native city. Hopkinson, a lawyer by training, claimed to be the first American composer, and was the only avowed musician among the signers of the Declaration of Independence. A small, bright, convivial young man, he played the harpsichord and organ expertly; he wrote songs and keyboard works, and eventually composed a massive "oratorical entertainment" entitled *The Temple of Minerva.* He dedicated his *Seven Songs for the Harpsichord* in 1788 to George Washington, noting: "However small the Reputation may be that I shall derive from this Work I cannot, I believe, be refused the Credit of being the first Native of the United States who has produced a Musical Composition." Washington, who liked music tolerably well though he played no instrument, accepted the dedication gracefully, though he noted ruefully: "I can neither sing one of the songs nor raise a single note on any instrument to convince the unbelieving."

On June 12, 1787, Washington, then a delegate to the Constitutional Convention, attended a concert given by Alexander Reinagle, a new figure in Philadelphia music. Washington, for all his ignorance of the art, evidently had good taste in music, or at least knew where to get some good advice, for he engaged Reinagle to give lessons to his adopted daughter Nellie Custis. Reinagle seems to have been the first musician of major caliber to have emigrated from the Old World to the New. An Englishman of Austrian descent, he knew personally at least two of the famous sons of Bach, Karl Philipp Emanuel and Johann Christian, and he created some stir as a composer in London. For obscure reasons, whether personal or professional, he decided at the age of thirty to set sail for America. Like many a subsequent musician he headed for New York, but when he got there he found that for all its commerce, the city was little interested in culture. So few pupils appeared for the instructions he announced himself ready to give on the pianoforte, harpsichord and violin that he quickly removed himself to Philadelphia, where a more favorable musical climate was said to exist.

By 1792 Reinagle was practically running musical affairs in Philadelphia. Handsome, cultivated, vigorous, he became impresario as well as featured performer at the city's principal series of concerts. He teamed up with an actor named Thomas Wignell to form a joint theatrical-musical enterprise, and supervised the building of the New Theater in Chestnut Street, one of the first and finest auditoriums in the United States. It opened February 17, 1794 with a contemporary opera, *The Castle of Andalusia,* by the then celebrated English composer Samuel Arnold, and remained in active use until 1855. One contemporary observer, quoted by Gilbert Chase in his book *America's Music,* has left this picture of Reinagle, suggesting that even at that early date the Philadelphia pattern of genteel, mannerly patronage of the arts was firmly established:

> Such was Reinagle's imposing appearance that it awed the disorderly of the galleries, or the fop of annoying propensities and impertinent criticism of the box lobby, into decorum. . . . It was truly imposing to behold the polished Reinagle saluting from his seat (before the grand square pianoforte in the orchestra) the highest respectability of the city, as it entered into the boxes to take seats. It was a scene before the curtain that suggested a picture of the master of private ceremonies receiving his invited guests at the fashionable drawing-room.

In 1824 the city opened another celebrated auditorium, Musical Fund Hall at Eighth and Locust Streets. This edifice was erected by the Musical Fund Society, one of the city's most active artistic organizations in the nineteenth century. The Fund's charter gave as its two-fold objectives "the relief of decayed musicians and their families and the cultivation of skill and diffusion of taste in music." Today the building, long since disused (its last reincarnation was as a tobacco warehouse) still stands, and attempts are being made to raise funds to restore it to its original purpose.

Whatever the Fund may have done to arrest musicians' decay, it certainly enhanced the city's cultural life. It maintained an orchestra and chorus, it operated a conservatory, it produced concerts, often with foreign artists, it introduced to Philadelphia such works as Beethoven's symphonies and Mendelssohn's *Midsummer Night's Dream*. Its operatic wing gave the first local performance of Mozart's *The Magic Flute* in 1841.

By mid-century Philadelphia could honestly claim a status of respectability, and even eminence, among the world's music centers. It had produced another important composer in the person of William Henry Fry (1813–1864), though he spent much of his musical life in New York; it was visited by numerous foreign artists and operatic troupes (such works as Weber's *Der Freischütz*, Rossini's *Cenerentola*, Bellini's *Norma*, Verdi's *Il Trovatore* and Gounod's *Faust* all had their American premieres in Philadelphia); it had begun to produce excellent musicians of its own. Foremost among these was a symphonic group called the Germania Orchestra, which was founded in 1856 and remained for forty years the city's best orchestra, fading from existence on the eve of the Philadelphia Orchestra's formation—and contributing most of its personnel to it. The Germanians, incidentally, had an interesting custom, and one which sheds some light on the state of musical development in Philadelphia in the late 1880s and 1890s. They would play a different movement of a symphony each week for four weeks, and then play the entire work the fifth week.

Two other events also were to play a major part in the formation of a great orchestra in the years to come. In 1857 the Academy of Music, officially the American Academy of Music, was built on Broad and Locust Streets at the cost of $250,000, opening first with a grand ball and then with *Il Trovatore*, then only four years old. It became the city's most brilliant musical center immediately and has remained so ever since. The Philadelphia Orchestra gave its first concert there and has never known another permanent home.

In 1876 the city celebrated the 100th anniversary of the signing of the Declaration of Independence with a Centennial Exposition.

Music was assigned a far more prominent role than it was to receive at many a subsequent American exposition, and no less imposing a figure than the great Theodore Thomas was engaged as musical director of the fair.

Thomas, who had been brought to America from Germany as a child of ten, was the first great conductor this country had ever produced. Although his eventual base was Chicago, where he founded the Chicago Symphony in 1891, he was a national figure traveling throughout the country with the Theodore Thomas Orchestra, whose itinerary jokingly became known as the Thomas Highway. One of its frequent stops had been Philadelphia, and the city eagerly invited him to preside over the musical festivities of 1876. Thomas, in turn, gave of his best. He even commissioned Richard Wagner to compose a special *Grand Centennial Inaugural March* dedicated to the Women's Centennial Committee, which paid the tidy sum of $5000 for the piece. Wagner sent over a piece of musical trash, but cannily accompanied it with a letter saying: "I have given my friends to understand that in some of the more delicate portions of the composition I picture to myself the beautiful and vivacious women of America in their festival attire."

Thomas's symphonic concerts, although they started well, soon began playing before dwindling Centennial audiences, as did a subsequent series which he was invited to give five years later. But memories of the quality and authority of his concerts persisted among a small number of influential Philadelphians, and their longing was increased when the Boston Symphony began making regular appearances in Philadelphia, under the direction first of Wilhelm Gericke and then of Arthur Nikisch. Gradually the conviction grew that Philadelphia, too, merited its own orchestra and its own conductor.

THE FIRST CONDUCTOR

The name of Fritz Scheel is largely forgotten today, but it was widely respected in its own time. A German like most of the nineteenth century musicians who traveled to America, he was born in

Lübeck in 1852 and followed the footsteps of his father and grandfather in becoming a conductor. This was the era of Hans Richter,
Felix Mottl, Anton Seidl and others; the conductor's trade was as competitive then as it is now. Scheel, a tall, imposing man with a fine
handlebar moustache, was forty-one when he first came to the United
States. His initial stop was New York, where he gave several concerts, but his first major job was in Chicago, where he conducted the
Trocadero Concerts at the Columbian Exposition in 1894. Later that
year he went to San Francisco, where he remained until 1899, conducting both orchestral and operatic performances with considerable
success.

His appearance in Philadelphia came as conductor of a series of
summer concerts at Woodside Park, an amusement area, given by a
group grandiosely called "The New York Orchestra." The programs
were solid, including Beethoven symphonies and Wagnerian orchestral excerpts, and a good many musical Philadelphians, including a
dentist named Dr. Edward Keffer, speculated that Scheel might be
a good man to organize that full-sized, permanent, professional orchestra which the city, for all its cultural pretensions, still lacked. An
attempt to raise the necessary guarantee fell through, but at the very
least it was decided to keep Scheel in Philadelphia. To accomplish
this an intricate scheme was worked out by three groups of amateurs,
the Philadelphia Symphony Society, which rehearsed regularly and
gave three public performances a year; the Opera Class, a chorus
which gathered once a week at the home of the wife of the president of the Pennsylvania Railroad; and an association devoted to
staging a special one-week series of concerts in West Philadelphia.
Under the arrangement, Scheel agreed to conduct each of these
organizations, which would pay him $1000 apiece. Scheel, who evi-
dently was equal to the task of conducting negotiations with Philadelphia lawyers, insisted on one further proviso: that at the end of
the season he be permitted to conduct two concerts with an orchestra
of professional musicians.

Arranging this last detail proved to be a considerable perplexity,
but it was solved with such brilliance that the Philadelphia Orchestra
came into being as a result. The Spanish-American War had ended

a little more than a year before, and all through 1899 American troops had fought a guerrilla army led by Emilio Aguinaldo with heavy casualties. Why not arrange a pair of concerts benefitting the widows and orphans of the brave conquerors of the Philippines and also discharging the contractual obligation to Scheel? The idea was welcomed enthusiastically, and the "Philippines Concerts," as they came to be known in Philadelphia's annals, were a brilliant success. They were held on Thursday afternoons March 29 and April 5, 1900, with the pianist Vladimir de Pachmann as soloist at the first and the basso Edouard de Reszke at the second. The concerts were advertised as follows:

Our Soldiers and Sailors.
Academy of Music
Thursday, March 29th and April 5th, 3.30 P.M.
Two Orchestral Concerts under the direction of Mr. Fritz Scheel will be given for the Relief of Families of the Nation's Heroes killed in the Philippines.
Soloist for the first Concert: *M. Vladimir DePachmann*
Programme

Weber	Overture "Euryanthe"
Goldmark	Symphony, "A Rustic Wedding"
Chopin	Concerto in F minor
Schumann	"Abendlied"
Bizet	Scherzo, Suite Roma
Liszt	Rhapsodie Ongroise, No. 2

Second Concert by an Orchestra of Eighty
Philadelphia Musicians
Under the Direction of *Mr. Fritz Scheel*
Mr. Edouard de Reszke, the famous Basso, will sing.
Programme

Beethoven	Symphony "Eroica"
Meyerbeer	Aria, "O Jours Heureux" (from L'Etoile du Nord)
Wagner	Vorspiel, "Lohengrin"
Hofmann	"Im Sonnenschein"
Verdi	Aria, "Infelice" (Ernani)
Liszt	First Hungarian Rhapsody

Scheel displayed as much determination in recruiting his musicians as in devising his programs. In the entire Philadelphia Symphony Society, the amateur group he had conducted all year, he found only one player who met his standards for his professional organization. But he took over to a man another group called the Thunder Orchestra—named not for its sound, but for its conductor, one Henry Gordon Thunder, who had formed his band largely of members of the old Germania Orchestra. In addition, Scheel haunted the theaters that had pit orchestras, pad and pencil in hand, jotting down his impressions of various instrumentalists.

So successful were the Philippines Concerts (they netted $10,000 for the widows and orphans and were excellently reviewed) that everyone agreed that the orchestra which played them could not be permitted to disband permanently. Accordingly a committee was established which quickly issued an appeal for a public subscription of $10,000 in "any amount not less than five dollars." The idea was to transform the "resident players" of the Philippines Concerts into "a permanent Philadelphia Orchestra." So enthusiastic was the response that within six months the necessary sum was raised. On November 16, 1900, a Friday night, Scheel raised his baton at the Academy of Music over the "permanent Philadelphia Orchestra" which has been playing there ever since. And its inaugural program was one that could have very well turned up in any subsequent Philadelphia season including the present one: Goldmark's Overture *In Spring,* Beethoven's Symphony No. 5 in C minor, Tchaikovsky's Piano Concerto No. 1 in B-flat (with Ossip Gabrilowitsch as soloist), Weber's *Invitation to the Dance,* and Wagner's Entrance of the Gods into Valhalla from *Das Rheingold.* Almost simultaneously, the first board of directors was being set up; it drew upon the city's business, financial, and social leaders, and was headed by Alexander Van Rensselaer of Drexel and Company, who provided the board with singularly enlightened leadership until his death in 1933.

In this first season and those that followed, Fritz Scheel established himself not only as a resourceful organizer but as an exacting and accomplished musician. The local press, while noting some imbalance among sections of the orchestra, had nothing but approval for "Herr"

Scheel. "The sheer effect of his personality," his "extensive dynamic range," and his "rich palette of color" all were praised. It was felt on the whole that Scheel had achieved "really amazing results" in a remarkably short time. To these Philadelphia encomiums was added out-of-town approval, for when Scheel led the orchestra to Carnegie Hall for the first time on November 26, 1902, Richard Aldrich described it in the *New York Times* as "one of uncommon excellence."

"It is large and well-balanced," the *Times* critic wrote, "and is composed of excellent material. The strings have a fine and compact body of tone, brilliant and flexible; the woodwind choir is euphonious and of good quality. The tone of the orchestra is solid and well-knit, rich and warm. There is very little in its playing to indicate that it is of so recent establishment."

With succeeding years the new conductor began to emerge as something of a personality as well as a musician. He could be tough and scornful, but he had a sense of humor, and, most important of all, he knew his business. After playing a Bach concerto with him, Eugene Ysaÿe, the great Belgian violinist, was reputed to have declined to play the same piece with the Boston Symphony, remarking: "Not after the Philadelphia Orchestra will I play the Bach Concerto." That, at least, is how the story was told in Philadelphia. In 1903, the *Musical Courier* of New York compared the Philadelphia's performance of Beethoven's *Coriolanus* Overture to the New York Philharmonic's to the detriment of the latter: "The Filharmonic (sic) Fathers should have been provided with free transportation to Philadelphia in order to learn how one conductor can mar and another make the same composition. . . . Scheel's graphic characterization made the Philharmonic performance appear in the memory almost like a travesty." Since in music, as in other matters, nothing is more reassuring than praise from the rival camp, Philadelphians became more convinced than ever of the excellence of their new orchestra and its leader.

Scheel's English was less than perfect at the start, though it improved considerably as the years went on. But it was good enough to let him establish quickly that he meant to run things his own way. After a time the novelty appeal of the orchestra had begun to wear off and attendance took an alarming drop, with consequent financial problems. Several of the business men on the executive committee called on the conductor to express the view that unrelenting programs of Beethoven, Wagner and the like were "too high class for the people" and ought to be changed. Waltzes and similar light numbers should be scheduled, it was urged. Scheel listened closely and then, professing some difficulty in understanding the language, asked that the statement be repeated. Then, as an early chronicler of the orchestra recalled his words, he said in an English no less emphatic for its heavy Teutonic accent: "Gentlemen, I am the head of the department of music of this association. I am elected by you. You represent the business end of this association; I stand for art. I cannot allow anyone to interfere with my programs. If my programs and my management of the music side of the association does not meet with your approval, you may get another conductor; but as long as I am conductor of the Philadelphia Orchestra, waltzes will not be played on a symphony program."

This was the first time, but not the last, that the directors of the Philadelphia Orchestra Association encountered a strong-willed conductor. The executive committee, much abashed, departed and went about its business, while Scheel did likewise. No waltzes were played while he was conductor, although in later years the Philadelphia Orchestra did get around to them.

⸹ GUESTS AND GALAS

By the end of Scheel's third year, the board of directors of the Philadelphia Orchestra Association, pursuing their eternal hunt to make up the annual deficit (then around $70,000) felt emboldened enough to address themselves "to the people of Philadelphia" in the following terms:

> The management of the Philadelphia Orchestra Association, at the end of the third season of concerts, feel that they have fulfilled their original promise to supply the community with an orchestra of the first class. There are but three other orchestras

of this rank in the country, those of Boston, Chicago and Pittsburgh. . . .

The artistic success of the past season is unquestioned, the work of the orchestra under Mr. Scheel, a leader admittedly second to none in the country, received flattering comment wherever it has been heard, both at home and in other cities, New York especially envying us the possession of an orchestra of the first rank. . . .

Scheel's activities during these years demonstrate that he was, indeed, doing his utmost, to give Philadelphia an orchestra "of the first rank." He recruited players by going to Europe and searching them out, exactly as did the other leading American conductors of the day. In that era, one went to different countries for different specialists—France and Belgium for woodwind players, Germany for brasses, Holland for cellists, the Austrian Empire for fiddlers. Scheel relied heavily on Germans in several areas, and one of his recruits was his brother Julius, a former concertmaster in Hamburg who became leader of the second violins in Philadelphia. Scheel even found a Scottish concertmaster, a Glasgow professor and violinist named Elkan Kosman, who came over for a year in 1901. Kosman's departure from Scotland produced an interesting comment in the Glasgow *Evening Times,* which had its own ideas of American symphonic rivalries, and also of the wealth which was supposedly being poured into the new orchestra. "This is a new combination," the paper commented, "originated by a few American millionaires. . . . The success of the Hub concerts in Boston resulted in the Philadelphia enterprise. The syndicate responsible for its origination sent an agent to Europe with instructions to spare no expense in getting together the best possible band, and thus to prepare for 'licking Boston.'"

From 1900 to 1907, Scheel covered much of the standard symphonic repertoire in his programming, including a week-long cycle of Beethoven symphonies. Despite his aversion to waltzes he approved a special series of "pops" concerts, at which tea was served, to help raise money. He ran several series of young people's and "workingmen's" concerts, ten cents admission being charged for the latter. The audiences for these "people's concerts," as they were called, were

composed mostly of men, in sharp contrast to the Friday ladies' gather-
ings. Scheel also learned of some peculiarly American customs, as
when a Friday concert on the Thanksgiving week end of 1905 had to
be canceled because it conflicted with the Army-Navy football game.
He did his best to counteract any feeling of provincialism by taking
the orchestra on visits to most of the important cities of Pennsylvania
and to Baltimore, Boston, New York and Washington. He invited
such guest conductors as Richard Strauss and Felix Weingartner to
direct the orchestra.

The appearance of Strauss in Philadelphia in 1904 was one of the
most exciting musical events the city had known since the Centennial
of 1876. The German composer-conductor was then forty years old;
he had already written the great tone-poems *Don Juan, Don Quixote*
and *Till Eulenspiegel,* though his operas still lay ahead of him. He
was at the height of his powers, and his wife Pauline, an accomplished
soprano, was still pretty, so his American tour was one round of brilliant concerts, glittering parties and gala receptions. Philadelphia certainly did its part, and Strauss reciprocated by heaping praises on the
orchestra. After leading the musicians at the first rehearsal he threw
his arms around Scheel exclaiming *"Famos! Wunderschön! Ausge-
zeichnet!"* almost in ecstasy.

Strauss conducted the Philadelphia Orchestra not only in its home
city, but in Boston as well. He had wanted to conduct the Boston
Symphony, then commonly regarded as America's best, but had been
turned down, ostensibly because the Boston had a rule against guest
conductors, but more probably because Wilhelm Gericke, its musical
director, simply didn't want to turn his podium over to Strauss. So
the Philadelphians traveled to Boston to repeat two programs given
at the Academy. Strauss and Scheel shared the conducting duties,
Frau Strauss sang several songs, and the concerts were warmly received. The Boston critics were enchanted both with the orchestra and
with Scheel. The *Daily Advertiser* characterized Scheel as an "orchestral genius" for his playing of Brahms' Second Symphony and said the
Philadelphians were the best ensemble to have visited Boston since the
days of Theodore Thomas. Philip Hale, the celebrated critic of the

Herald, said of Scheel at a convivial party after the concert: "He has the right arm of Thomas and the left arm of Nikisch."

Scheel's list of solo guest artists at the Academy was as impressive as almost any in the country, including such names as Josef Hofmann, Ernest Hutcheson, Fritz Kreisler, Edward MacDowell, Moriz Rosenthal, Camille Saint-Saëns and Jacques Thibaud. It was Scheel and his orchestra who early in 1906 introduced not only to Philadelphia but New York as well, a twenty-year-old Russian pianistic phenomenon named Artur Rubinstein who played the Saint-Saëns G minor Concerto. The *New York Times* was unimpressed, Aldrich writing on January 9 that the concert had "served to introduce to New York a young pianist with the somewhat onerous name of Rubinstein." After thus invoking the shade of Anton, he continued acidulously: "His coming had been preceded by circumstantial stories of his past and present prowess. . . . This young Rubinstein is undoubtedly a talented youth, but his talent at present seems to reside chiefly in his fingers . . . (with) no thought of any deeper significance that lay behind the notes."

Perhaps Scheel's proudest moment came on January 29, 1906, when he was invited to the White House in Washington to provide a musical evening for President and Mrs. Theodore Roosevelt and 400 guests. It was to be more or less of a chamber music affair, so only a portion of the orchestra participated. This is how a contemporary account described the performance:

> The orchestra men drove to the White House at 9:30 p.m. and at 10:15 they entered the East Room, where all the guests were assembled. President Roosevelt and Mrs. Roosevelt sat in the front row and listened with the gravest attention.
>
> Then Mr. Scheel played his rat-a-tat-tat baton solo on his stand, and the thirty-two men broke into harmony as easily and gracefully as a flock of seagulls lights upon the ocean.
>
> The concert was to last one hour—no more and no less—and during that hour the audience was treated to Volkmann, Mozart, Svendsen, Beethoven and Strauss in solos, quintets, octets, sextets and altogethers. Alfred Saal was the soloist—he with the long

blond hair and the marvelous cello. He played as only Saal can play and his Serenade in D minor by Volkmann was one of the most delightful numbers of the evening.

Immediately after the closing number, President Roosevelt expressed a wish to meet the musicians, so one by one the men marched up and shook hands with the greatest American of the day.

The next night the entire orchestra played a full-fledged concert in the Columbia Theater in Washington; the Roosevelts did not attend, but they sent a huge box of roses and carnations.

Thus, in a short time, Scheel had established himself as the most important man in Philadelphia's music, and his orchestra as an eminently respectable one. But his end was in sight, and for him it was a tragedy. Scheel was approaching his mid-fifties when he began to display signs of mental breakdown. Miss Frances Anne Wister, one of the first women to take a commanding role in the orchestra's affairs, recalled in later years: "He became irascible with his players, erratic in conduct, and his good judgment in matters musical seemed to forsake him. During the first months of 1907 his programs had to be constantly supervised to guard against excessive severity; and on one occasion he had to be restrained from playing five symphonies at one concert."

The public realized that all was not well with Scheel at a concert on February 6, 1907 of the Eurydice Chorus, which he had been conducting since 1905 in addition to his duties with the orchestra. A violinist in the orchestra had recently drowned, and Scheel had scheduled a number in his memory. Not content with this tribute, however, he began to address the singers and the audience in a rambling and incoherent manner. Medical consultations were held, and Scheel was taken to Atlantic City for a rest. The newspapers wrote sympathetically of his taxing schedule and unrelenting labors, with a Philadelphia *Public Ledger* correspondent reporting that he had long had the habit of propping symphonic scores against a sugar bowl while eating his meals. The *Ledger* followed him to Atlantic City, as indicated in this graphic dispatch of February 10, 1907:

Mr. Scheel was seen by the *Public Ledger* correspondent as he returned to his hotel after a swift stroll down the boardwalk with his physician. He looked haggard and spoke in an excited, almost hysterical tone.

"Please tell my friends in Philadelphia that I am not a sick man," and greeted the newspaperman effusively. "All this talk about my mental condition is absurd. I needed a rest, that was all, and the directors very kindly allowed me to come to the seashore. I will be all right in a few days, won't I, doctor?"

The concluding sentence was directed to Dr. Goodman in a tone of pitiful appeal. Dr. Goodman nodded good-naturedly, as he does to all the proposals and plans that the sick musician unfolds in his illusions, when he talks about purchasing several beach playhouses for great musical festivals.

Scheel, in fact, was able to conduct the Philadelphia Orchestra in a last concert in Reading, Pa., but he was undergoing a complete breakdown and had to enter a sanitarium. There he wrote letters to famous musicians in Europe, offering them large sums of money to come to Philadelphia to teach at a conservatory he proposed to found. He also organized the hospital help into choruses, making nurses and orderlies stand around his bed singing part songs. Weakened by illness and exhaustion, he fell prey to pneumonia and died on March 13, 1907, aged fifty-four.

Funeral services were held at the Lutheran Church of the Holy Communion on Chestnut Street. The orchestra's season had ended, but enough of the musicians remained in town to play the Funeral March from Beethoven's *Eroica* Symphony at the ceremonies. Resolutions of grief were adopted by civic and musical organizations throughout the city, and condolences poured in from musicians in America and Europe. A subscription of $6000 was raised for a bronze memorial plaque with Scheel's likeness in bas relief, which remains to this day in the Academy of Music.* It was unveiled at a memorial ceremony at the Academy on the first anniversary of his death, before an audi-

* Until the Academy's great renovation of 1957, the plaque remained affixed to a wall in the lobby. Ever since, it has been left to languish unhappily amid a pile of debris in the basement.

ence which filled the house and overflowed into Broad Street. Underneath the plaque was a wreath of white roses sent by Mrs. Theodore Roosevelt, who had not forgotten her East Room musicale of two short years before.

♩ ENTER—AND EXIT—POHLIG

Even while Scheel lay dying, the orchestra association began a search for a successor. Its first choice, at least to finish out the current season, fell upon an Italian named Leandro Campanari. He was an experienced maestro who had begun his career as a violinist and done considerable conducting at La Scala in Milan. But when Campanari attempted to take over the orchestra at a concert on February 22 at the Academy a near riot ensued. Prior to Campanari's arrival, the orchestra had been conducted by its first flutist, August Rodemann, who had been Scheel's deputy in such matters and who now filled in for him during his illness. Rodemann evidently intended to go right on conducting in Scheel's place, and did not take kindly to the appointment of an outside successor. The soloist on February 22 was the famous Ernestine Schumann-Heink, who was to sing the Waltraute scene from Wagner's *Die Götterdämmerung*. But Rodemann and many other of the musicians somehow found great difficulty in playing the notes correctly, and the distinguished soloist, seeing that the orchestra wasn't following Campanari's gestures, tried to give them signals of her own. At the end of the number, Rodemann mounted a trunk backstage and, speaking in German, denounced Campanari to the assembled orchestra. Somehow, the concert was completed, but it was apparent to the directors that Campanari wouldn't do as Scheel's permanent successor.

In fact, the more they thought about it the more they seemed to incline in the direction of finding a successor in Scheel's own image. Their eventual choice was Karl Pohlig, director of the Court Orchestra of the King of Württemberg in Stuttgart. Born in Teplitz, Bohemia, he was thoroughly German in background and upbringing.

He was forty-nine, practically the same age as his predecessor had been, and even sported a similar military-type moustache.

Pohlig had studied with Liszt, worked with Mahler, and keenly admired Wagner; he had toured throughout Europe and conducted at Covent Garden in London. The orchestra association sent its business representative, Charles A. Davis, to Europe to check up, and he was advised to hire Pohlig by Felix Mottl in Munich and Fritz Steinbach in Cologne. Every indication was that Philadelphia had the right man.

Yet it didn't quite work out that way. Pohlig's initial concert on October 18, 1907 was favorably received by the local press and public, but there were some complaints about the length of the program. (It included two Beethoven overtures, *Fidelio* and the *Leonore* No. 3, and the Symphony No. 5 in C minor, followed by three Wagnerian works, the *Meistersinger* Prelude, the *Siegfried Idyll*, and the *Tannhäuser* Overture—quite an opening salvo!)

At first Pohlig seems to have done his best to ingratiate himself with local music lovers, paying due attention to Philadelphia pride. "Musically speaking, Germany is the land of the setting sun; America is the land of the rising sun," he told an interviewer. "Philadelphia should get the best!"

The first indications of critical disaffection came not from Philadelphia but from New York, where the critics jumped all over Pohlig on his first appearance at Carnegie Hall on November 5. Typical was the *Sun's* remark that Pohlig "is employed in the pleasant city of Philadelphia where he conducts the local orchestra. Its work was so rough as to cause wonder that the organization should have been brought all the way across the State of New Jersey." The *Times* and *Tribune* were somewhat more temperate in their criticism, but the *World* applied that most infuriating of adjectives "provincial" to the orchestra. Quite understandably, there were heated replies in several Philadelphia papers, including denunciations of New York as unpatriotic, insular, arrogant, commercial, and "the least American of our cities."

New York's disapproval might in itself have been enough to guarantee that Philadelphia would defiantly renew Pohlig's contract for a second three-year term. But his adherents could point to a number of positive reasons for keeping him. He had a phenomenal musical memory, being a pioneer in the now common musical practice of conducting without a score. His devotion to his task was unquestioned, and during his tenure the season was extended from twenty weeks to twenty-five (there then were two concerts weekly, the same program being given on Friday afternoon and Saturday night). Touring was extended, so that the orchestra played a total of eighty-six concerts each year rather than sixty-two, as under Scheel.

Pohlig expanded the orchestra's musical horizons somewhat, introducing a number of modern works including a massive choral symphony of his own entitled *Per Aspera ad Astra*. He also managed to program works of several Philadelphia composers, among them Frank G. Cauffman, Philip H. Goepp, William W. Gilchrist (whose Symphony in C had been introduced by Scheel several years before), Louis von Gaertner and Celeste D. Heckscher—none of them names to conjure with today, but recognizable, at least, to their fellow citizens. Perhaps Pohlig's most lasting contribution was his invitation, in 1909, to Sergei Rachmaninoff to guest-conduct the orchestra in his Symphony No. 2 in E minor and Moussorgsky's *Night on Bald Mountain*. This was the great Russian pianist-composer-conductor's first appearance on an American podium, and also the beginning of his long and warm association with what he was to call "my very favorite orchestra."

It was during Pohlig's regime that the orchestra made its first attempt to perform Sunday concerts. Charles Davis, the business manager, interested the directors in the idea, and Mayor John E. Reyburn came out for it. But the outcry in the city's churches was immediate and emphatic, with Methodists, Baptists and Presbyterians displaying a unity that seldom manifested itself in matters of ritual. Sunday concerts in Philadelphia had to wait until 1916.

As solid a musician as Pohlig was, he never won quite the respect or affection that Scheel had commanded. Miss Wister went on record as criticizing his "difficult disposition, which made dealings between him and the musicians, and the board of directors, trying and difficult." A veteran of Friday matinees, Miss Mary C. Smith, who began going to Philadelphia concerts in 1906 and was still at it in 1968, remembered him as a "hidebound Teutonic." Pohlig must have sensed that he wasn't getting through to the ladies; one account pictures him despairingly appealing to the directors in his heavy German accent: "It says in der program book, will der ladies please take off der hats pecause it hides der view? Von't you please have it in der program book, will der ladies also please take off der gloves so dey can clap?"

Pohlig didn't evoke much enthusiasm from his players, either. After he left, a reporter in the Philadelphia *North American* wrote that he "held himself aloof, and assumed that he was of a higher caste than his players. He ignored them on the street and acted generally as a dictator." On one occasion when the orchestra was holding a rehearsal in the foyer of the Academy building, Pohlig found a boiler temporarily set up for repairs on a stairway, momentarily blocking his entrance; infuriated, he called off the rehearsal, although the orchestra was ready and waiting. If the orchestra began to sound somewhat stiff toward the end of his tenure, there were reasons.

On June 10, 1912, Pohlig's resignation was announced and, after being paid off with a full year's salary ($12,000) for the 1912–1913 season, he returned to Germany, where the musical sun no longer seemed to be setting. In fact, for Pohlig it flared quite brilliantly, for he was given a life appointment as general music director of the Court Opera in Brunswick, Saxony, where he died in 1928.

With Pohlig gone, for the second time in five years the board of directors faced the problem of obtaining a new conductor. This time they pulled off a master-stroke. They hired a young man named Leopold Stokowski.

CHAPTER III

The Stokowski Era

"Perhaps Dr. Stokowski's aversion to publicity and the lack of a great mass of details concerning his life have gone far toward surrounding him with an aura of romance."

—Philadelphia *Public Ledger,* March 10, 1922

⸱ WHO STOKOWSKI WAS

To many musicians and music listeners, Leopold Stokowski has always been a mystery. His name, his age, his accent all are wrapped up in a miasma of romance and reality. When the British conductor Albert Coates was active in America in the 1920s, there was a kind of musical parlor game which went: "Two conductors, Albert Coates and Leopold Stokowski: which was born in England and which in Russia?" The answer, of course, was that Coates had been born in Russia and Stokowski in England.

The birth date usually given for Stokowski is April 18, 1882. That doesn't mean it's the date usually given by Stokowski; for reasons best known to himself he expended a good deal of time and energy trying to prove he was born in 1887. "Birthdays are for children," he once said. In 1955 he actually disrupted a broadcast of the University of Miami Symphony Orchestra by breaking in on an announcer who was giving the 1882 date: "No, no, no, no, no! That is not true. I was born in 1887. . . ." When the announcer ignored the interruption and continued reading from the biographical data which had been supplied to him: "He was born of a Polish father and an Irish mother . . ." the startled radio audience heard Stokowski scream: "My mother was not Irish. This is terrible! Where did you get that stuff?" The concert was finally given, with the critics finding the conducting "electrifying."

According to his birth certificate, Stokowski was born with the name Leopold Anthony Stokowski in the Marylebone district of London on April 18, 1882; his father, a cabinetmaker from Lublin in Poland, was named Kopernik Stokowski, and his mother, of Irish descent, was named Annie Moore Stokowski. However, Stokowski's full name is listed in most reference books as Leopold Boleslawowicz Stanislaw Antoni Stokowski. At various point in Stokowski's long career he was accused of having changed his name from (or sometimes to) Lionel Stokes; however, if he was ever known by that name (and it seems extremely doubtful) it was only for a brief period, possibly as a convenience during his student days.*

Stokowski became a musical eclectic early in life; he studied first the violin, then the piano, finally the organ, all as a youngster, and apparently developed ambitions to become a conductor while still in his teens. After all, there was plenty of opportunity in London for a young music student to expose himself to good orchestral concerts. Stokowski attended Queen's College, Oxford, and the Royal College of Music; he was talented and he had good teachers, among them Sir Charles Villiers Stanford and Sir Hubert Parry. He studied additionally in Paris and Munich and, at the age of eighteen, already a Fellow of the Royal College of Organists, he was appointed organist at St. James, Piccadilly. Five years later he journeyed to America to take a similar post at St. Bartholomew's Church in New York City.

---

* According to one story, the Stokes legend cropped up as late as the 1940s, when Stokowski found himself listed under that name on a program of the All-American Youth Orchestra in Montevideo, Uruguay. He refused to appear until the listing was changed, saying, according to one member of the orchestra: "Let Stokes conduct; Stokowski is going home."

At St. Bartholomew's Stokowski's duties required him to serve as choirmaster as well as organist, and it was in the organ loft there that he obtained his first experience as a musical organizer and conductor. In three years at St. Bartholomew's Stokowski achieved something of a reputation in musical circles as a young man who could get things done.

One of the organizations whose attention he drew was the Cincinnati Symphony Orchestra, then in the process of reorganization after a labor dispute, and in the market for a conductor. It seems to have been Herman Thumann, music critic of the Cincinnati *Enquirer*, who tipped off the board of directors to the twenty-seven-year-old conductor, and Stokowski was invited out for an interview. He captivated the women's committee, an accomplishment at which he remained adept throughout his life, and they strongly recommended that he be engaged. Nevertheless, one important figure remained unconvinced. He was Lucien Wulsin, founder of the Baldwin Piano Company, who happened to be traveling in Europe when Stokowski was approached, and he had doubts whether the orchestra should be turned over to so young and untried a conductor. Fortunately, Wulsin was still in Europe when Stokowski arrived there for a vacation visit. Still eager to gain conductorial experience, Stokowski managed to give a concert with the Colonne Orchestra in Paris. Wulsin went to hear it and was convinced. When the Cincinnati Symphony Orchestra began operations in the fall of 1909, its new conductor, with a five-year contract in his pocket, was Leopold Stokowski.

Stokowski energetically set about rebuilding the orchestra. He raised its membership to seventy-seven; he beguiled the ladies and gentlemen who paid the bills into finding additional monies; he led the orchestra to Pittsburgh, Chicago and Cleveland; he played more stirring and exciting concerts than the Midwest had ever known. But it's doubtful that he ever really intended to remain long in Cincinnati. The musical heartland of the country, then as now, lay in the East. Besides, by now Stokowski had a bride, and she, too, wanted to come East.

Stokowski's wife, the first of his three, was Olga Samaroff, who was almost as dynamic and ambitious a musician as himself. Samaroff was a pianist or—to use the feminine form preferred in the journals of the time—*pianiste*. She had been born Lucie Hickenlooper in San Antonio, Texas, but had adopted the name Samaroff as more suitable to a concert career. She was a brilliant performer, and after giving up the concert stage in 1927 became first a music critic, then a teacher and proselytizer for music appreciation. She married Stokowski in 1911, divorced him in 1923, and died in New York in 1948.

Some people think that Samaroff played an important part in Stokowski's move to Philadelphia, even acting as a go-between in the negotiations. She certainly was in Philadelphia often enough, appearing as guest soloist under both Scheel and Pohlig, starting in 1905. In any event, after three years in Cincinnati, in April, 1912 Stokowski suddenly demanded a release from his contract, which still had two years to run. When the shocked Cincinnatians asked to know why, the conductor enumerated his complaints: he had not been given full authority over the orchestra, the audiences were unresponsive, one of the city's music critics was conducting a vendetta against him. When the board, headed by Charles P. Taft, brother of the President of the United States, offered to make "adjustments," including a substantial salary increase, Stokowski magisterially replied. "What cannot be adjusted is my loss of enthusiasm, which enthusiasm is absolutely necessary in the constructive work of building up an orchestra." The board finally gave Stokowski his release in a not very polite letter: "The undersigned notify you that your recent behavior and repeated aspersions on members of the Board of Directors and your unfounded reflections upon the musical public of Cincinnati have destroyed your usefulness to the C.S.O. and we now notify you that you are released from your contract. Enclosed you will find check for $875.00, which makes, with what you have received heretofore, your $7,000.00 salary for the year."

Stokowski cashed the check, left Cincinnati, and headed for Europe, where he had several guest-conducting dates, including two with the London Symphony Orchestra. However, before taking ship in New York he had a meeting with representatives of the Philadelphia Orchestra. Reportedly, negotiations with Philadelphia had been going on since January with an eye toward his succeeding Karl

Pohlig when the latter's contract expired in 1913. However, Pohlig's retirement from Philadelphia was suddenly moved up a year to 1912, just when—by coincidence or not—Stokowski was getting his release from Cincinnati. Before Stokowski and his wife sailed he signed a preliminary agreement to become the conductor of the Philadelphia Orchestra that fall; and it was subsequently made final by cablegram to Europe. His salary was $12,000, nearly double his pay in Cincinnati.

¿ A SOCIAL AND MUSICAL LION

Never had Philadelphia looked to the advent of a musical personality with more anticipation and curiosity. In fact, the excitement stirred up by Stokowski's arrival in October, 1912, was surpassed only by that caused by his departure twenty-three years later. When he came to Philadelphia he was just thirty years old, stood six feet tall, had a lithe, slender figure, a Grecian nose, blue eyes, and a halo of blond hair. Whatever they were to hear, Philadelphians had never *seen* a conductor like him. Musically, too, he was a revelation. Philadelphia's symphonic traditions, like those throughout America at the beginning of the twentieth century, were thoroughly German. And while a Furtwängler or a Klemperer can provide a transcendent experience, there is nothing in music quite as dull or as plodding as a second-rate Germanic conductor—which is pretty much what Pohlig had been. Stokowski in effect introduced a new kind of personalized, broad, sweeping, boldly romantic conducting to the United States, setting a style that prevailed for many years, and Philadelphians responded to it with delight.

Even before he began to conduct, Stokowski was busy giving interviews and making statements. He said that he had spent much of his summer in Munich looking over old Philadelphia programs and that he'd noticed there hadn't been much Brahms. So he scheduled the Brahms First for his opening program. He also announced that there would be at least five contemporary composers, Strauss, Rachmaninoff, Debussy, Sibelius and Elgar (all of whom were alive and flourishing at that time) on his programs, and also dropped hints of such even more unfamiliar names as Glière and Enesco. To a reporter who commented on his youthful appearance he said gallantly: "Anybody looks young when he is happily married." Another reporter informed his readers: "Mr. Stokowski, because of his early years spent in London, speaks perfect English," an interesting remark in view of the ineluctable accent which subsequently appeared. By his third concert Stokowski was overflowing with admiration for his new city which, he proclaimed, "combines the best features of Europe, such as tradition and solid informative conservatism, with the salient best qualities of American life, progress, alert enterprise, and clean, clear thinking."

Stokowski's opening program at the Academy on Friday afternoon, October 11, 1912, included Beethoven's *Leonore* Overture No. 3, Brahms' Symphony No. 1 in C minor, Ippolitov-Ivanov's *Caucasian Sketches,* and Wagner's *Tannhäuser* Overture. This is how the *Public Ledger* described the event the next day:

NEW CONDUCTOR OF PHILADELPHIA ORCHESTRA TENDERED OVATION IN ACADEMY

Leopold Stokowski made his début yesterday afternoon at the Academy as conductor of the Philadelphia Orchestra, in the opening concert of its thirteenth season. Every seat was taken and the extra chairs had been placed within the orchestra rail. There was much enthusiasm, manifesting itself at the beginning in prolonged applause as Stokowski came forward with bowed head, evidently pondering the content of his musical message. Those who went forth to see a hirsute eccentricity were disappointed. They beheld a surprisingly boyish and thoroughly business-like figure, who was sure of himself, yet free from conceit, who dispensed with the score by virtue of an infallible memory, and held his men and his audience from first note to last firmly in his grasp.

Mr. Stokowski has known the players, and they have known him, for only four days of actual rehearsal, and it was not to be expected that the organization at the outset would manifest the homogeneity to be expected later. Yet in this brief time the new leader has been surprisingly successful in welding the several choirs into a single coherent entity. They played yesterday with a unity of purpose—particularly among the first violins—not usually attained until mid-winter. They brought out the full value of the lights and shadows. The climaxes were duly accentuated, the pianissimos with the utmost delicacy and refinement were contrasted with the full-throated polyphony.

Mr. Stokowski's conducting is after the order of Nikisch, whom he frankly admires. He does not tear a passion to tatters. He holds his thunders and the winds of Aeolus in a leash. His gestures are graphic, the arcs and parabolas he describes tell of a kind of geometrical translation going on in his mind, whereby he visualizes the confluent rhythms in outward action. At impassioned moments his movements have the freedom of a violinist's bow arm; at other instants he brings his fists against his shoulders with vehement concentration, or his uplifted eloquent left hand pleads with some suppressed choir to come forward and assert itself in power. There is, from first to last, no languor or slackened moment; he directs with a fine vigor and intensity that mounts to ecstasy yet does not lose its balance or forget its sane and ordered method.

At the close of the symphony a laurel wreath was laid on the dais ere Mr. Stokowski found his way to the footlights in response to the tumultuous applause. The wreath was so large that he stood in it while he called upon his musicians to rise, himself applauding their efforts and modestly disavowing his leonine share of the credit.

In view of Stokowski's later reputation as an innovator and individualist, it is striking that his "sane and ordered method" should have impressed so many of those initial listeners. The *North American* remarked: "It is comforting to observe that Mr. Stokowski is likely to inject nothing freakish into his innovations." The *Evening Bulletin* praised the musical interpretations, saw "no excess of temperament," and detected a "deportment" denoting "refinement, seriousness, studious love of his work, and sane, sensible ideas." Philadelphia showed every sign of contentment with its new conductor, and season subscriptions that first year reached an all-time high.

Stokowski and his attractive, artistic wife were equal successes socially. The young couple took a house at 2117 Locust Street which quickly became one of the social centers of the city. At that time the custom of paying "calls" and leaving visiting cards still prevailed, and Mme. Samaroff later estimated that in her first years she received and returned some 700 calls. On one occasion, she remembered, she even was kept waiting downstairs by a maid while the lady of the house, in an upstairs bedroom, was busy giving birth to a child. The Stokowskis were wined, dined and feted. The young conductor was painted in oil by Leopold G. Seyffert, a local art luminary; the resulting portrait, which made him look like a youth wise beyond his years, was hung at the Pennsylvania Academy of Fine Arts and was proudly reproduced in local newspapers and magazines. Stokowski had been engaged with a four-year contract, but he hadn't gone very far into his first season before Alexander Van Rensselaer, the princely and generous banker who headed the orchestra association, proposed publicly that the new conductor "think not of his four-year contract, but of staying eight years, and many more." Which is exactly what he did.

♪ BUILDING AN ORCHESTRA

Although Stokowski, as befits a young man trying to get along in a new job, publicly expressed his satisfaction with the organization he had been given to work with, he really didn't have a high opinion of the Philadelphia Orchestra as he found it. Gradually he set about making changes both in its personnel and its procedures. He found that the customary language of rehearsals was German, and though he spoke that language, began to employ more and more English with the men. Stokowski, notwithstanding his "eloquent left hand," used a baton at the time, as did virtually all conductors. He did, however, conduct without a score, but Pohlig had done the same. Actually there were occasions both then and in later years when Stokowski did use a score, notably when he was conducting certain new works and also when he was playing accompaniments for a soloist in a concerto.

Naturally, the men of the orchestra looked on the newcomer with a certain wariness. He was not yet, of course, the world-famous conductor who could intimidate many an orchestra merely by showing up; in fact, he was younger than most of the players, and had been conducting only a little more than three years. Nevertheless, he quickly displayed a firmness of manner much as Pohlig had shown. But he tempered it with a greater feeling of considerateness than his predecessor had ever displayed. One of his earliest innovations during rehearsals was what the Italians then called a *pausa* and the Americans now call a coffee-break—an interlude during which the musicians were invited to take a fifteen-minute break in which they might smoke, chat or otherwise relax.

But almost at the very start, Stokowski began a weeding-out of musicians whose tone, flexibility or expertise didn't meet his standards. Many years later, when he was conducting the American Symphony Orchestra, an organization of young musicians with a rather high turnover rate, Stokowski explained his ideas about personnel replacement. "An orchestra is not a machine," he said. "It is a collection of human beings. If a conductor is sensitive and can master the ensemble, it shouldn't matter if there is a large turnover. In some cases, in fact, it's preferable. Dead wood accumulates easily in any orchestra. Some players, like wine, become better with time. Others become careless if they stay too long in the same place."

Several of the musicians Stokowski found in the Philadelphia Orchestra remained with him for many years. Thaddeus Rich, who had joined it as concertmaster in 1906 at the age of twenty-one, held his post until 1926, serving at times as assistant conductor and achieving a warm personal following. Anton Horner was a stalwart of the horn section, not only for his own solo work, but for the help and guidance he gave others who came into the section through the years. Oscar Schwar, the timpanist, was a great popular favorite. Schwar, who was born in Saxony and joined the orchestra in 1903, was one of the most remarkable kettledrummers in the country, with a far more musical and mellow tone than timpanists customarily achieve. Soon after joining the orchestra he gave such a spectacular performance in Tchaikovsky's *Romeo and Juliet* Overture that the rest of the orchestra stood up and applauded him. Stokowski was glad to have him.

Other musicians, though, began to find that their contracts were not renewed with the passing seasons. Auditions for newcomers were held regularly, with Stokowski inviting the first-desk men to sit in while applicants for their sections were tested. Some years the changes were fairly extensive—in 1921 there were twenty-one new faces— but for the most part they proceeded gradually. Stokowski, who deliberately spent part of each summer studying the technique of the various instruments, wound up with some splendid players, as instrumentalists destined to become famous began to flock into the orchestra —contrabassist Anton Torello in 1914, oboist Marcel Tabuteau in 1915, cellist Hans Kindler and clarinetist Daniel Bonade in 1917.

In 1918 a seventeen-year-old New York trumpeter named Saul Caston, previously rejected by several other conductors including Ossip Gabrilowitsch of Detroit, applied to Stokowski for an opening he had heard was available. The orchestra was playing in New York, and Stokowski agreed to hear the boy in a vacant, dimly lit Carnegie Hall before the concert. He hired him, but with the proviso that he study musical theory under a teacher of Stokowski's choice.

After playing five years with the orchestra, Caston was asked by Stokowski to become first trumpet. "Do you think I can do it?" he asked. "Have you any doubts?" countered Stokowski. "There are a few parts that would frighten me," admitted Caston, citing particularly the tricky A natural for solo trumpet which opens Wagner's *Rienzi* Overture. Stokowski went ahead with the appointment. He also opened the 1923–'24 season with the *Rienzi* Overture. Caston played his A perfectly. He remained with the orchestra for twenty-seven years, becoming associate conductor in 1936, and in 1945 he became conductor of the Denver Symphony.

In much the same way other players either came to the orchestra as masters of their instruments or developed their skills within its ranks to undreamed-of heights. By 1921 only five players still re-

mained from the original orchestra of 1900. From then on, to be a
member of the Philadelphia Orchestra became a hallmark of the
highest musical professionalism.

♀ THE GREAT MAHLER EXPLOSION

Somebody once called Stokowski "a nineteenth century man with
a twenty-first century mind," and there is no reason to doubt that
right from the outset he planned to immerse Philadelphia in the music
of the day—if not of the morrow. But for the first few years, at least,
the extremes were avoided. The breakaway from a traditionally Germanic repertory was gradual, novelties and first performances began
to spice the programs only occasionally.

It was not until 1916, his fourth season, that Stokowski really put
both himself and Philadelphia on the musical map with the most
sensational American premiere of a musical work the country had ever
witnessed. This was Gustav Mahler's Symphony No. 8 in E-flat, the
Symphony of a Thousand, so called because it requires eight soloists
and 950 choral performers to go along with an orchestra of 110.
Mahler had conducted in New York from 1908 to 1911 (the year of
his death at the age of fifty), but as a composer he still represented a
fairly exotic figure. In fact, it wasn't until the 1950s that his music
found a really broad public in the United States; in 1916 his music
was definitely far-out and forbidding.

The work Stokowski selected was particularly extravagant.
Mahler himself had conducted the *Symphony of a Thousand* for the
first time in Munich in 1910, so it was only six years old when
Stokowski proposed to play it in Philadelphia. Stokowski had attended the premiere in Munich, and had been wildly excited by the
massive, eighty-minute work, a mystical setting of the hymn *Veni,
Creator Spiritus* (in Latin) and the closing scene from Goethe's
Faust (in German). Four years later, Stokowski was again in Munich,
and now he made up his mind to give the Mahler Eighth its American premiere with his new orchestra. He obtained the performance
rights, stuffed the score in a handbag and, in August, 1914, with

World War I about to break out, he managed to escape from Munich, leaving most of his personal luggage behind in his haste. At the time, he was still a British subject, having only taken out his first papers (he became an American citizen in 1915). It is interesting to speculate how his own history, and that of Philadelphia, might have changed had he been interned by the Germans.

Stokowski, of course, wanted to prepare immediately to put on the symphony, but there were formidable difficulties. The sum of $14,000 would have to be forthcoming from the board to pay for the additional performers and the extra rehearsal time required. The stage of the Academy would have to be practically rebuilt to accommodate the horde of singers and instrumentalists. Besides, no one was sure how the gigantic work would be received; Mahler's music was almost totally unfamiliar to the city, and there was only the word of the new young conductor to go on as to its worth. For a year the perplexed and worried directors temporized. Finally it was decided to present the gigantic work on March 2, 3 and 4 as the climax of the 1915–'16 season.

Lest anyone think the Mahler Eighth totally absorbed Stokowski's energies, it should be noted in passing that in the same season he also gave premieres to such works as Schoenberg's *Kammersymphonie,* Scriabin's *Divine Poem,* and Richard Strauss' *Alpine Symphony.** But all these seemed insignificant when the workmen began to expand the stage apron of the Academy and the work of recruiting and training choristers got under way. The orchestra until then had no chorus of its own, relying on the co-operation of the city's choral societies in putting on such works as Beethoven's Ninth Symphony or an occasional oratorio. Now, however, the name "Philadelphia Orchestra Chorus" was applied to a special group of 400 trained by Stokowski himself. A second group of 400 was rehearsed by Henry Gordon Thunder, who had remained active in Philadelphia musical affairs after his own orchestra had been absorbed by Fritz Scheel's in 1900. There also was a children's chorus of 150, and the eight soloists

---

* Actually, the *Alpine Symphony* was performed almost simultaneously by the Cincinnati Symphony Orchestra in its May Festival in 1916, so that both cities claimed the distinction of the premiere.

were sopranos Florence Hinkle, Inez Barbour and Adelaide Fischer; contraltos Susanna Dercum and Margaret Keyes; tenor Lambert Murphy; baritone Reinald Werrenrath, and bass Clarence Whitehill. The grand total of participants was 1068, and some of the more timid among the directors were worried lest the performers outnumber the audience.

But Stokowski took charge not only of the musical aspects but of seeing to it that the public was kept well informed of the preparations for the great enterprise. Columns of preliminary articles filled the papers, telling in great detail all about Mahler and his symphony, and Stokowski and his orchestra. Rehearsals began in October, 1915, and it was sternly announced that choristers who were inattentive or who missed a session would be dismissed. Stokowski informed all comers that the Mahler *Symphony of a Thousand* was a "divine" work, a masterpiece, one of the landmarks of symphonic literature, and that Philadelphia was privileged above all other American cities to be able to introduce it. The performance became a matter of civic pride as well as of musical import. As the date drew near, excitement and anticipation approached a feverish level usually produced in Philadelphia in those days only by Connie Mack's pennant-winning baseball teams. When the low-price tickets (35 to 50 cents) went on sale the day of the first concert, a queue formed on Locust Street at 5 a.m. in 12-below-zero weather. By mid-morning of the premiere scalpers were getting $100 a seat. Stokowski had seen to it that invitations were sent to luminaries throughout the country, and the trains from New York disgorged such personages as Harold Bauer, Artur Bodanzky, Ossip Gabrilowitsch, Josef Hofmann, Ernest Hutcheson, David Mannes, Ernest Schelling, and many others. Never had the orchestra —and its conductor—played before such a musically distinguished gathering.

The performance was a stupendous success, and so far as the press was concerned, little else of significance took place that day in Philadelphia or, for that matter, the rest of the world. All the papers carried the story on Page 1, and most featured eight-column photographs of the massed forces poised at the ready on the Academy stage. The *North American* actually gave its account precedence over the Battle of Verdun, then raging in Eastern France. The *Public Ledger's* account was ecstatic:

MAHLER'S WORK AND STOKOWSKI SCORE TRIUMPH

Thousands at Academy of Music Aroused to High Pitch of Enthusiasm. Noted Musicians Give Praise to Production. Prominent Persons From All Over Country Attend Rendition Here.

Every one of the thousands in the great building was standing, whistling, cheering and applauding when Leopold Stokowski, his collar wilted, and his right arm weary, but smiling his boyish smile, finally turned to the audience in the Academy of Music last night.

He had scored, so famous musicians agreed, the greatest triumph of his career, the greatest triumph the Philadelphia Orchestra has known in its sixteen years of life, and he had done it on a stupendous scale with the American première of Gustav Mahler's Eighth Symphony. He had carried along with him to triumph an orchestra numbering 110 pieces and a chorus of 958 singers, to say nothing of the city's music lovers and scores of musical pilgrims from other cities.

For every one who is any one in musical America was here for the Mahler American première last night or will be here when the tremendous work is repeated this afternoon and tomorrow night. The boxes were filled with famous musicians and musical authorities. One and all stood, applauding Mr. Stokowski and the symphony, while the orchestra members blared a 'touche' in honor of their leader.

The scenes at the Academy set nerves tingling. Two weeks before the performance every seat had been sold. Fifteen minutes before Mr. Stokowski swung his baton upon his augmented orchestra and upon the great chorus, banked 24 tiers high, horns blew a fanfare in the foyer of the Academy of Music, following an ancient custom at Bayreuth. The curtain rose and the audience gasped.

The 958 singers filled the great stage from footlights to roof and the orchestra was upon an apron that has been built out into the house.

The first twelve rows of singers were women, dressed in white. Above them were twelve rows of men, with a gardenia-like spot of girls, members of the children's chorus, pinned, it seemed in their midst.

Alexander Van Rensselaer presented a wreath for the orchestra. It was inscribed "To Leopold Stokowski in commemoration of the first performance of Mahler's Eighth Symphony in America, March 2nd, 1916."

In presenting the wreath, Mr. Van Rensselaer said:

"The directors of the Philadelphia Orchestra Association feel that the presentation of this Eighth Symphony of Mahler this evening for the first time in America marks an epoch in the musical history of Philadelphia to which no other event is comparable. . . .

"We of Philadelphia are indebted for the production of this great work to you, our brilliant and talented conductor. . . .

"We feel that not only the musical public of Philadelphia, but the entire city, owe you a debt of gratitude that can never be repaid. And as a testimonial from the Board of Directors of the Philadelphia Orchestra Association, and as an expression from them of their thanks, I have pleasure in presenting the victor's crown of laurel, made in perpetual bronze."

Mr. Stokowski was given two great demonstrations; the first during the intermission, the second at the conclusion of the performance. Both lasted for more than five minutes. The noise was so great that the Academy doormen said it could be heard across Broad Street in the foyer of the Walton.

Such was the response that Arthur Judson, a young former critic and advertising manager from *Musical America* who had switched to the business side of music and become the Philadelphia Orchestra's manager in 1915, immediately began to schedule extra performances. Before he had finished, the Mahler Eighth had been given nine times in Philadelphia, including a special performance for school children. At the final performance, 1500 were turned away.

On Sunday, April 9, the show hit the road. Stokowski and Judson had no intention of staging such a magnificent production without taking it to New York. The Metropolitan Opera House was engaged for the night and two special trains totalling eighteen cars were hired at a cost of $4500 to convey 1200 participants and staff members, including four chaperones for the children's chorus, to Pennsylvania Station. All were given dinner at the McAlpin Hotel at a cost of $1750. The Met was jammed, with scalpers again in the streets and the audience including some of the prominent musical figures who hadn't got down to the Philadelphia performances—Pablo Casals, the entire Flonzaley Quartet, Percy Grainger, Fritz Kreisler, Ignace Jan Paderewski and Mme. Schumann-Heink. Again the reception was tumultuous, and W. J. Henderson, the critic of the *Sun,* warned Philadelphia in mock seriousness that if it wanted to keep Stokowski, it had better not let him conduct any more concerts in New York. "He has personality, force, authority, temperament, scholarship and imagination," Henderson wrote. "He would be a valuable factor in the musical life in New York." At that time the New York Philharmonic was being directed by the sluggish and plodding Josef Stransky, and the possibility that Stokowski might shift his activities to Manhattan was to cross more than one musical mind in the years ahead—including Stokowski's.

Amid the applause and acclaim that poured in following the Mahler performances in Philadelphia and New York, a few querulous voices were raised. Most were directed more against the work itself than the interpreters. Not everybody was convinced that the *Symphony of a Thousand* was as masterful a work as its Philadelphia protagonists made out, and several journalistic observers evaded the issue by appealing to the last refuge of a music critic, posterity. One journal, *Musical America,* actually seized the occasion to launch an attack on the young conductor himself, and as it was the kind of charge often repeated against Stokowski in ensuing years, it is worth noting. The actual review of the *Symphony of a Thousand* premiere in *Musical America* had been quite enthusiastic, but in the "Mephisto's Musings" column a letter appeared from an "anonymous Philadelphian" saying there were "detractors" who insisted that Stokowski "is a man of limited ability, who is a *poseur,* who has managed to interest a large number of impressionable and emotional ladies wherever he has been, and has, by their aid, been boosted from one position to another, for which he is scarcely adapted by his knowledge or temperament." Subsequently another anonymous correspondent denounced Stokowski for producing a "stupid, uninteresting work," and ascribed the entire excitement surrounding the event not to musical significance but to "Philadelphia patriotism." Needless to say, this kind of carping fell on deaf ears in Philadelphia, although whoever kept the orchestra's press scrapbook in those days did care enough about the complaint to paste it carefully on a back page.

An interesting echo of that unforgettable Mahler premiere was heard years later in Carnegie Hall on April 6, 1950. Once again, Stokowski stood before a New York audience to direct the *Symphony of a Thousand*. This time he was guest-conducting the New York Philharmonic, with a wholly different set of soloists and choristers, and an audience which could hardly have remembered the performances of thirty-four years before. And once again the effect was electrifying. Virgil Thomson, who had never heard the work before, described it in the New York *Herald Tribune* as "a glorious experience" and said "such handsome loudnesses as took place in its perorations one does not encounter often in a lifetime." So much for Mephisto and his musings.

⸮ BIG-TIME ORCHESTRA

The Mahler's Eighth performance can fairly be said to mark the beginning of the Philadelphia Orchestra's days of greatness. The musical public throughout the country began to hear of the slim, handsome, boyish conductor with the eloquent gestures and the peculiar interest in modern music. As for Philadelphia, even people who had never heard a note of classical music in their lives began to be aware that a civic asset had arisen in a thoroughly unexpected quarter. In 1917 the Chamber of Commerce even put out a booklet entitled *The Commercial Value of Music to Philadelphia,* which was another way of spelling Stokowski.

Luck was with both the orchestra and its conductor in that the nearby competition happened to be at a very low ebb. In 1911 the

New York Philharmonic Orchestra fell under the routine leadership of Stransky, from which it was not to be rescued until 1923. The New York Symphony, under the direction of Walter Damrosch, was never a first-rank orchestra. The Boston Symphony, which had reigned unchallenged for years as the American orchestra *par excellence,* had fired Karl Muck in a patriotic frenzy during World War I, and neither Henri Rabaud nor even Pierre Monteux could restore its former eminence. In Chicago, Frederick Stock had a fine orchestra, but he never succeeded in establishing himself as a personality. From about 1917 on, Stokowski just about had the scene to himself as the glamor boy of the baton, America's first conductor to become a matinee idol. And he reached this status, remember, without the aid of television, radio, celebrity magazines, fan clubs or any of the other modern publicity appurtenances by which such heroes are created and magnified. Even when Serge Koussevitzky took over the Boston in 1924, and Arturo Toscanini was appointed principal conductor of the merged Philharmonic-Symphony in 1928, Stokowski took his place as a member in good and equal standing of the Big Three and, incidentally, outlasted and outlived his colleagues.

It's entirely possible that had fate brought Stokowski to some other city than Philadelphia in 1912, he might never have achieved the same results. Although Stokowski, after leaving the city, pursued a distinguished career, conducted unforgettable concerts, and made memorable recordings, he never again achieved the same triumphant identity of conductor and orchestra that was his in the Philadelphia years. He probably never could have created the same kind of virtuoso orchestra elsewhere, either. Boston and New York, each with an audience that regarded itself as thoroughly sophisticated musically, each with plenty of past artistic heroes to worship, might well have proved more resistant to the English wonder boy with the Polish name. At least they might have been less willing to let him exercise a kind of thought-control over their musical tastes, and to give him such ardent support in almost everything he did. "To build that orchestra he needed a cohesive public and a malleable audience," is the way Arthur Judson put it a half-century later.

In Stokowski's early days in Philadelphia, nearly everybody was a believer. His social doings and family occasions (such as the birth in December, 1921 of his daughter Sonia) were eagerly chronicled. His plans for the next season were avidly awaited and debated. When he disembarked each fall after his annual summer vacation in Europe, the Philadelphia newspapers sent their reporters to New York for shipboard interviews, and to learn what contemporary goodies Stokowski had brought back for performance by the orchestra. In later years, Philadelphians, thanks largely to the liberal musical education given them by Stokowski, began to be more certain of their own musical likes and dislikes, and opposition began to arise to some of his programming. But in the period immediately after 1916 he could do no wrong, and into the musical life of the city he introduced a unique, super-charged excitement—a quality that never diminished.

By 1916 the orchestra had also become big business. Since the beginning its deficits had been made up and its continuation assured by a Guarantee Fund which had to be raised at various intervals, sometimes at the end of every season. To assist in this work, a women's committee was established in 1904, among its most energetic directors being Mrs. William W. Arnett and Miss Frances A. Wister, a sister-in-law of the novelist Owen Wister.* Apparently this was the first such women's committee ever associated with a symphony orchestra, bringing upon Philadelphia almost as great a trail-blazing distinction as Betsy Ross won by designing the American flag. Eventually the women's committee subdivided into a number of regional and suburban groups, forming a federation that played a considerable part in the ensuing fortunes of the orchestra. It is not too much to say that save for the work of the various women's committees, the Philadelphia Orchestra might never have survived its early years. Not only did they see to it that the matinees were well filled on Fridays, they sold tickets for other concerts, raised money, ran benefits, signed up subscribers, and in general served as a vital link between the orchestra and the public, a function they have continued to fulfill to the present day.

* Wister, author of *The Virginian*, had married a cousin with the same surname.

But money remained a crucial problem. A series of "pops" concerts with lemonade and sandwiches served at tables was tried in 1915 without appreciably advancing either the orchestra's fiscal or musical prosperity. Even Stokowski's success, and the great upsurge in subscriptions that followed it, were not enough to erase the annual deficits. Ways and means were discussed of raising a permanent endowment fund to give the orchestra financial security and to end the annual ritual of hat-passing by the women's committees and others. Various plans were advanced and discarded when, quite unexpectedly, the following statement was sent to subscribers:

To the Friends of the Philadelphia Orchestra:

A friend of the Philadelphia Orchestra Association, who desires to remain unknown, has offered to meet any deficit of the Orchestra for each of five years, beginning with the season of 1916–1917.

The conditions under which this gift will become available are as follows:

1. That an Endowment Fund of $100,000 yearly for five years shall be created by the Orchestra Association, so that the total Fund may be $500,000 at the end of this period.

2. That the contract of the present conductor, Leopold Stokowski, shall be extended to cover this period of five years.

3. It is earnestly desired that each friend of the Philadelphia Orchestra will pledge a generous amount to create this Endowment Fund. Heretofore, all subscriptions to the Philadelphia Orchestra have been spent year by year, to meet the annual deficit. Under this offer the money now contributed will not be so spent, but will be invested to insure the permanency of the Orchestra as an institution of Philadelphia.

The orchestra is a civic asset. If it is to fulfill its destiny and place Philadelphia in the front rank among the musical cities of the world, it must be endowed. In order to do this, the Orchestra Association must depend upon the generosity of its friends. We ask that the enclosed blank be signed and returned to us at your earliest opportunity. While it is hoped that all gifts may be for a period of five years, yearly contributions will be gratefully accepted. Payment of subscriptions will be on November 1st and March 1st of each year, beginning with November, 1916.

> ALEXANDER VAN RENSSELAER
> FRANCES A. WISTER
> EDWARD W. BOK
> Endowment Committee.

The three signatory names were significant aside from the individual wealth they represented, for each was symbolic of the basic support upon which the orchestra depended. Van Rensselaer, known as "Mr. Van" to all who worked with him, embodied the oldtime financial and insurance leaders who dwelt in Philadelphia's marble halls; Miss Wister represented the women of the old town houses or the Chestnut Hill and Main Line suburbs; Bok, who had made a fortune as editor of the *Ladies' Home Journal* and as a partner in the Curtis Publishing Company, and a profound admirer of Stokowski, stood for the power of the press and the younger business element which realized how the orchestra was helping spread Philadelphia's fame.

Eventually the campaign to raise $500,000 for an endowment fund was extended to seven years, and a total of $788,400 raised— 25 per cent of it by the women's committees. In the meantime, the "Unknown Donor," as the anonymous benefactor was called in the newspapers, kept meeting the annual deficit, at a total personal cost estimated as high as $250,000. In 1920, his identity was finally disclosed. He proved to be none other than Edward Bok himself. Bok went even further in his campaign to make the orchestra financially sound. By 1919 it was evident to him that the endowment fund drive was going to succeed. He promptly persuaded the directors to launch concurrently a campaign for an additional $1,000,000 to be raised during one month, October, in honor of the orchestra's forthcoming twentieth anniversary. Once more the women's committees went into action, and this time the appeal was made to the entire city, with huge "Save the Orchestra" banners raised over the main streets, including one in front of City Hall, from whose tower the colossal statue of William Penn looked down benignly over the "greene countrie towne" he had laid out. Stokowski himself joined in the campaign, speaking on its behalf and writing eloquent appeals which were inserted in the orchestra's programs. It was one of the most extraordinary efforts ever undertaken on behalf of a symphony orchestra, and it was a success. When the Philadelphia Orchestra reached its twentieth anniversary, it was not only the most talked-about orchestra in the United States, it was also one of the most fiscally secure.

? THE AUDIENCES

For success in Philadelphia (and in his further adventures in later life) Stokowski not only needed an orchestra and solid financial backing; he also needed an audience. No actor, no singer, no circus performer ever lived out his life more thoroughly on the public stage than Leopold Stokowski. Like any serious musician he had his hours of contemplation or replenishment studying scores alone, or sitting in solitude at a piano or organ keyboard. But it was as a showman— probably the greatest that orchestral music has ever had—that Stokowski was in his element. Harold C. Schonberg of the *New York Times* aptly compared the three great American conductors of a generation ago: "Toscanini loathed publicity. Koussevitzky enjoyed it. Stokowski could not live without it."

Very early in the game Stokowski established his unique relationship with his audiences. Already in Cincinnati he had begun to make little platform statements when he was about to play an unusual work or when there was some point to which he wished to draw the audience's attention. But in Philadelphia he really flowered as a stage personality. People came not only to hear what he played, but to see what he did, and listen to what he said. Recalled Arthur Judson in later years: "Stokowski on the stage always was a fascinating picture, to men no less than to women." The town's music critics often found that their reports were more in the nature of reporting a happening than of analyzing a concert.

When Stokowski took over the orchestra, and for many years thereafter, two concerts were given weekly, on Friday afternoon and Saturday night. The programs were the same, but the audiences different. Friday matinee was a women's affair from the start; there were some afternoons when practically the only man in the audience was Mr. Van Rensselaer. Certain of the young ladies' colleges, such as Bryn Mawr, had seats reserved for their girls. But mostly it was an audience of Old Philadelphians—and some were very old indeed— who came to the concert after a suitable luncheon at the Acorn Club or a similar institution.

It was not a notably demonstrative assemblage. The Friday audience may have appreciated the music it heard, but its applause ranged from the tepid to the temperate—never beyond. Once Orville H. Bullitt, who became president of the board of directors in 1938, publicly scolded the audience of ladies for their lack of demonstrativeness. "I'd like to see an audience let loose at the end of a performance or shout 'bravo' if they feel like it," he told them. They applauded him—politely.

The bravos usually came on Saturday night, when the audience was far more masculine and generally more youthful. Professional men and their wives sat downstairs, and university and musical students crowded the upper reaches of the hall. When Stokowski was in his element, there was no containing the enthusiasm of these youngsters. Izler Solomon, later to become an important conductor himself, but during the 1920s a violin student in Philadelphia, recalled in after years how he and other young musicians pooled their resources to purchase scores of the works Stokowski was going to play on a Saturday night. Each took one score, studied it, and analyzed it for the benefit of the others while all waited in line for the balcony doors to be opened. Then Solomon, being the fastest, sprinted upstairs and held seats for his friends panting behind him. Solomon even met the girl who would become his wife in the standee line at the Academy, which was the place for any young man or woman with any intellectual pretensions to be on Saturday nights. On several occasions, when a guest conductor was leading the orchestra, Stokowski himself climbed the stairs on Locust Street to sit among his young friends in the amphitheater.

Friday matinees and Saturday evenings shared one element in common: in both audiences there were those who were receiving their introductions to music at the hands of the dashing, Byronic young conductor. On one occasion, when Stokowski had led a particularly stirring performance of the tumultuous march movement of Tchaikovsky's *Pathétique* Symphony, the audience rose cheering to its feet and then, as the ovation began to subside, headed excitedly toward the exits, not realizing that there was still a fourth movement to come. For once Stokowski was at a loss for words, and stared at their backs completely nonplussed by this show of inexperience.

Philadelphia's inherent musical conservatism was demonstrated almost every year, when an annual poll was taken of audiences to determine their favorite works for inclusion on a special "request program." The vote at the end of Stokowski's first season was 454 for Tchaikovsky's *Pathétique* Symphony, 268 for Beethoven's Fifth, 244 for Schubert's *Unfinished,* 138 for César Franck's D minor, and 138 for Tchaikovsky's Fifth. Among shorter works, the list was headed by Carl Goldmark's *Sakuntala* Overture (229) and Sibelius' *Valse Triste* (172). It was not an audience exactly panting to hear *Le Sacre du printemps,* which had been given in Paris in 1913, the year after Stokowski arrived in Philadelphia.

♩ LADIES' DAY

Stokowski was not only determined to remake the Philadelphia Orchestra; he also set out to reform the Philadelphia audience—which was, perhaps, an even more difficult task. His especial target was the Friday afternoon gathering. The ladies for the most part doted upon the blond young man, but they had no intention of letting him alter long-established habits which went back to the days of Scheel and Pohlig. They sat and knitted while the music was being played. They kept their hats fixed firmly on their heads despite requests in the programs to remove them. They talked and coughed and rustled. Most irritating of all to the new conductor, they arrived late and left early, for when there was a conflict between the running time of a Brahms symphony and the Paoli local, the train always won out.

Soon after his triumph in the Mahler *Symphony of a Thousand* had securely established his place as the city's virtual musical dictator, Stokowski, armed with a new contract running through 1921 at an estimated salary of $40,000 a year, began to turn on his feminine audience, subjecting them to a torrent of words, some as acerbic and prickly as the modern music he was now playing in increasing amounts. Of course, they adored being admonished by him for their sins of deportment, and he relished lecturing, scolding, and chiding them. This is a verbatim transcript of a typical Stokowski speech, delivered November 18, 1921 at an all-Wagner program to a matinee audience some of whose members were heading up the aisle just before the final number:

"Try as hard as we can, we cannot make a divine music amid so much untranquility. There is constant walking in and out. You know you cannot live in the material life alone. You must have something else. All the rest of the week you are immersed in worldly affairs. On Friday you come here. Will you not say to yourselves: 'I will give to the other side of life the two hours or less that the music requires'? You will gain enormously and so shall we.

"Even at four o'clock I see old ladies rushing out at the side doors with packages in their hands. (Laughter and applause.) Cannot you make the music the all-important thing? Give me the two hours with no noise and no moving about. I only speak this to those who are the moving ones. For the sake at least of musical good manners to each other let us have that atmosphere of tranquility in which alone the best musical results are obtainable." (Prolonged applause.)

Then, turning back to the orchestra, Stokowski led a performance of the *Liebestod* from *Tristan und Isolde* which the critic of the *Public Ledger* described in these rhapsodic terms:

"Doctor Stokowski led all the music with a passionate surrender to the coursing floodtide of the score that was unusual even to his ardent temperament. His hands described huge arcs or were outflung in appeal, the head and body quivering in sensitive coincidence. The men took fire from his flame."

The battle over arrivals and departures went on for years, and was never really resolved. Although Stokowski did shame some of the worst offenders into quiescence, the afternoon outflux never quite stopped altogether. One famous Stokowski story tells of his being greeted by a female American tourist one summer in Rome. "I recall your face, madame," said Stokowski, "but I can't quite remember who you are." "I'm one of the old ladies with bundles," replied the tourist sweetly. Reminiscing about the old days, veteran concertgoer Mary C. Smith of Haverford, Pa. recalled her grandmother, Mrs. E. Wallace Matthews, stomping up a side-aisle during an early performance of Richard Strauss' *Death and Transfiguration*, calling back over her shoulder: "When *my* time comes, I hope there won't be so much brass."

Stokowski's war on latecomers reached its climax on a Friday afternoon in April, 1926, in an incident that not only had Philadelphia talking for weeks, but was reported widely throughout the United States. The program for that day was highly unusual. It opened with a very obscure work, a Fantasie by the late nineteenth-century Belgian conductor Guillaume Lekeu, and closed with Haydn's *Farewell* Symphony. Somewhere between was Wagner's *Ride of the Valkyries*.

This was, to put it mildly, an odd combination, but its significance became apparent quickly. The Lekeu work is written for small orchestra, with only the first violin and first cello playing at the start. These were the only two players actually on the stage when Stokowski mounted the podium and began to conduct, the others drifting in just before they were due to start playing. In fact, one or two had to start while they were still walking toward their seats, so tardy were they in arriving.

When the time came for the *Ride of the Valkyries* to begin, only the small band required for the Lekeu was on the stage; the rest of the players' seats were still empty. Nevertheless, Stokowski raised his baton preparing to give the downbeat. Before he could start, a group of brass players rushed in to take their seats. Then another breathless group arrived as the conductor again lowered his baton. After several more instrumentalists hastened into their seats the full complement was finally in place and the performance began. By now the audience realized that its own habitual tardiness was being mimicked, and there were some murmurings and a few hisses. The climax of the concert came in the *Farewell* Symphony in which, of course, the score calls for the players to depart individually until only the last two violinists remain to play the concluding measures—almost the reverse of the opening Lekeu work. Stokowski embellished the *Farewell* Symphony a bit, by having the players look at their watches and stir about impatiently just prior to their departure. At the end, as he faced an empty stage, Stokowski signalled to his phantom "orchestra" to take a bow, then turned around himself and bowed solemnly to the buzzing house.

While many in the audience accepted the ribbing in good humor, a considerable number of the matinee regulars were outraged by Stokowski's behavior. The next day management officials tried to explain that the Lekeu and Haydn works had simply been played as written, with no insult to the audience intended. Later on, though, it became known that Stokowski had instructed the players to imitate the actions of the latecomers in the audience. In any case, he felt that he had made his point, and that particular experiment was not repeated.

Stokowski also took to haranguing his audiences whenever he felt they were coughing or sneezing too much during performances. Many women began arming themselves with cough drops on the way in, and one subscriber suggested to the management "that booths be installed at convenient locations in the Academy lobby on concert days for the sale of cough-drops and soothing syrups of divers kinds, after the manner of sale of opera books and librettos."

But cough drops, wherever bought, didn't seem to help much. Stokowski once bid the audience cease its "disagreeable and disgusting noises," and when a sneeze occurred during Gluck's *Alceste* Overture, followed by the arrival of several stragglers, he simply stopped playing and walked out. In the spring of 1927, when it was announced he was taking a six-month furlough to travel to the Far East, he bid farewell to his Friday matinee audience with this parting shot: "Goodby for a long time. I hope when I come back your colds will be all better."

⁇ THE VISIBLE CONDUCTOR

On October 19, 1926, the following notice was inserted into the programs at a Carnegie Hall performance by the Philadelphia Orchestra:

The conviction has been growing in me that orchestra and conductor should be unseen, so that on the part of the listener more attention will go to the ear and less to the eyes. The experiment of an invisible orchestra is for the moment impossible—so I am trying to reach for a similar result by reducing the light to the minimum necessary for the artists of the orchestra to see their music and the conductor.

Music is by its nature remote from the tangible and visible things of life. I am hoping to intensify its mystery and eloquence and beauty.

—LEOPOLD STOKOWSKI.

By now New York audiences, no less than Philadelphia, had fallen under the Stokowski spell. The previous occasional visits became coalesced into a series first of eight, then of ten Tuesday night concerts at Carnegie Hall. By 1920 these were announced as being entirely subscribed for the season.* In bringing his "invisible orchestra" idea to New York, Stokowski was proceeding with an experiment he had inaugurated in Philadelphia. The entire hall was darkened as he began to conduct his own arrangement of Bach's Chorale-Prelude *Wachet auf.* Tiny lamps on the music stands enabled each player to see—just barely—the music in front of him. The only really bright light shone on Stokowski's aureole of golden hair, and on his hands. Stokowski always contended that a conductor got an orchestra to follow his signs much more with his eyes than with his hands, anyhow. The experiment was highly dramatic, even spectacular; one observer thought that Stokowski's head seemed almost disembodied, acting as a kind of a floating medium between the music and the listener. The trouble was that the musicians couldn't really follow him in the dim light and that Stokowski himself felt he was losing "essential rapport" with the orchestra. The experiment was quickly dropped.

But many others were tried. Philadelphians who came to concerts were never quite sure where the musicians would be seated, for Stokowski decided at a fairly early stage that the traditional orchestral

---

* Before the advent of Toscanini to the Philharmonic-Symphony, "Philadelphia Tuesdays" were the major symphonic event of the New York musical week. On that night the Metropolitan Opera then made a weekly trip to Philadelphia.

floor plans no longer suited modern needs. He had the basses play on audience left rather than on audience right so they would face toward, instead of away from, the listeners. He shifted the brasses in relation to one another so their sound would blend as he wanted it to. At times he moved the woodwinds in front of the strings, and then he sent them back. He tried the orchestra playing on a flat stage and banked on risers. This all created extra-musical as well as musical excitement, and it's easy today to look back on some of these shifts as foolish and fleeting. But Stokowski all his life was obsessed with sound (which after all is how music transmits its message) and he worked experimentally with his orchestra just as Haydn had done when he was trying out various compositorial techniques at Esterhazy. And there were positive achievements to come out of the constant moving and shifting. Stokowski broke up the traditional arrangement of first violins to the left of the conductor and second violins to the right in favor of massing all the strings fanned out around him with first and second violins on the left, violas in the middle, and cellos on the right—which in recent years has become the standard deployment of most American orchestras.

Stokowski was similarly fascinated with the instruments themselves. He regarded the slide trombone as a relic of the fifteenth century and tried (unsuccessfully) to persuade a number of players to further the development of supplemental valves. One of the Philadelphia's players recalled in an article for *This Week* magazine how Stokowski altered the instruments and their style of playing to achieve certain effects:

> To get a certain quality in one single high note of a transcribed Chopin mazurka he made his first trumpeter go to the machine shop with a design for a radically different mouthpiece. . . . A certain note, an F sharp at the close of the Tchaikovsky *Pathétique* Symphony, always dissatisfied him because it logically belonged to the violins but was given to the bassoons since G is the lowest note on the violin. Stokowski solved that simply by having his violins continue to play while they slid the G string down to F sharp via the tuning peg. As the thirty-six violins reach for the tuning pegs one might think they had got a sudden crazy

whim to tune up in the middle of the concert. But it's only Stokowski's way of getting around the limitations of the instrument.

Stokowski at one point got the idea into his head that every violinist in the ranks wanted a shot at being concertmaster. Nothing, as it turned out, could have been further from the truth. If anything, his short-lived experiment demonstrated that the great mass of mankind, musical and otherwise, prefers being in a comfortable rut to venturing forth into a prominent but exposed position. A lack of enthusiasm on the part of the violinists, some of whom were scared stiff at the idea of moving up even experimentally to the first chair, caused the experiment to be abandoned. Another innovation of Stokowski's met with more success: he told his violinists to bow their instruments any way which was comfortable for them rather than following the exact arm pattern of the leader in their section. This tended to destroy the pretty stage picture of thirty-two arms moving as one, but it did produce a distinctive legato which became one of the touchstones of the Philadelphia sound and the envy of many another orchestra. Similarly Stokowski permitted his wind players to abandon traditional methods of uniform breathing; he told them, in effect, that he didn't care how they made sounds as long as the sounds were beautiful.

From time to time, Stokowski would announce a plan whereby any player who wished would be permitted to have a turn at conducting the orchestra. This idea, though well publicized in the press, advanced little beyond the talking stage. Eventually the Philadelphia Orchestra did produce a number of instrumentalists who took up the baton, but their success stemmed more from their own talent than from a determined drive to recruit conductors from the ranks.

℘ STRAVINSKY, VARÈSE AND OTHERS

Aside from establishing himself as the most spectacular musical personality in the business, Stokowski turned Philadelphia for a time into the country's most thriving center of new music. Whether the city desired such an honor was always debatable, but Stokowski left it no choice. In 1916, when he was accused of discriminating against a local tenor in his selection of an Evangelist for Bach's *Passion According to St. Matthew,* Stokowski said with arch innocence: "My audiences do not ask me if the music the orchestra plays is made in Philadelphia. They classify it as good or bad." The city, he continued, "must not be provincial but become universal."

But some listeners found that being universal merely meant being uncomfortable. In 1919 Stokowski introduced Philadelphia to Scriabin's *Poem of Ecstasy,* and a goodly portion of the audience promptly walked out on it. The ensuing controversy came to the ears of Alexander Van Rensselaer who, as president of the orchestra association, loyally said: "It's a wonderful tone-poem. I admit it's a little over my head but I am beginning to understand it. It is one of those things that will grow on people."

Each year after World War I, Stokowski would come back from his summer in Europe with an armload of new works which he expected to "grow on people." Schoenberg, Elgar, Ravel, Satie, Delius, Sibelius—all were in his suitcases when he stepped onto the pier in the 1920s. "It is rather difficult to deal with Stravinsky, however," he told an interviewer in 1920, "because he has some strange notions and is inclined to be more than a trifle grasping in financial dealings."

Eventually, though, Stravinsky, also succumbed to Stokowski's requests to be permitted to introduce his new pieces to the New World. By 1923 the conductor was reporting to his dockside interviewers: "I spent a lot of time with Stravinsky in Paris. He is a fascinating man, of enormous vitality and imagination. He is absolutely free from stereotyped thought."

The season before, on March 3, 1922, Stokowski had given the American premiere of *Le Sacre du printemps.* He introduced it to the audience by telling them: "Frankly, I can't imagine your liking it on first hearing," and then describing to them the dances and the stage decor of the Diaghilev production in Paris. *Le Sacre* was comparatively well received, as was Stravinsky's *Song of the Nightingale* the following year. Stokowski continued to expose his audiences to *The Rite of Spring* through the years, a procedure some of them found distressing. Once he sternly lectured an unappreciative house as to its general tastes and standards: "If you can relax yourselves for forty minutes from your narrow, comfortable life, with its ice cream, its steam heat, and its Prohibition, the *Sacre du printemps* can be a magnificent experience. . . . It is not comfortable music, but it is tremendous music, magnificent music and important music—the most important, perhaps, of this generation."

Not only did Stokowski keep on producing the *Sacre* in Philadelphia, he also produced Stravinsky himself. On January 30, 1925 the forty-two year old composer made his first visit to Philadelphia to guest-conduct a concert of his own music—*Fireworks,* the *Scherzo Fantastique,* the *Petrouchka* Suite, the *Firebird* Suite, and the *Song of the Nightingale.* He was warmly received by a packed house of Friday matinee matrons; the concert was a huge success.

But what happened afterwards almost scared Stravinsky out of his wits. His thoughts were only of making the train back to New York. But the women's committees insisted upon a reception in the foyer of the Academy after the performance, and though he quailed at the thought of pumping hundreds of feminine hands in a receiving line, he nevertheless went forth to the multitude. Nervously he lighted a cigarette, only to wonder why everyone was staring at it. Then he realized there was no smoking in the foyer and quickly stamped it out. Tea and coffee were pressed upon him—he chose the latter. Finally, invited to say a few words, he climbed on top of a chair and addressed the fair throng in French, saying: "I am grateful for a chance to conduct for people who understand and know my work. You can well be proud of your organization and your orchestra. Thank you so much." Whereupon he hopped down and quickly began shaking hands as a line of women formed before him. Said one woman who had the advantage of speaking French and therefore of understanding his address: *"Cher Monsieur, je vous dis que c'était ravissant."* Stravinsky bowed, his hand on his watch-chain: *"Merci, Madame."* Others, less gifted linguistically, merely murmured "Thank you, thank you." Finally Stravinsky pulled out his watch and uttered a cry: *"Mon dieu!"* It was train time. Assistant manager Louis A. Mattson hurried in with the *maître's* heavy, astrakhan-collared coat,

and off they rushed to the Broad Street station, followed by cries of
"Merci!" and *"Au revoir!"*

Still more memorable, perhaps, was one more Stravinsky night
in Philadelphia. It took place on April 11, 1930 under the auspices
of the League of Composers. That night Stokowski conducted the orchestra in a fully staged performance of *Le Sacre du printemps,* with
the entire work rechoreographed by Leonide Massine. It was the first
time the *Sacre* had ever been *danced* in this country, and the role
of the Chosen One was taken by a young dancer named Martha
Graham. No one who saw that production ever forgot it.

Unfortunately, not all the new music Stokowski chose to play was
by Stravinsky, nor were all visiting composers so warmly received. The
list of contemporary names on the orchestra's programs during the
1920s includes Braunfels, Ornstein, Schreker, Weprik, Zeckwer and
others similarly forgotten today, whatever their merits may have been.
As early as 1921 some members of the audience, in a show of independence (not to mention unusual manners for Philadelphia) actually
hissed a new piece, the work in question being Malipiero's *Ditirambō
tragicō.* Similar reactions greeted several other pieces in the next few
years, but nothing changed as a result: Stokowski kept playing new
works, and some listeners, a minority to be sure, kept hissing them.

At the outset of the 1924 season Stokowski made a peculiar address to his first matinee audience. "I have reformed," he announced
with a smile. From now on, he continued, he would play only "nice,
old-fashioned music," indulging his taste for the moderns only in the
privacy of his own home. Everyone applauded, but no one believed
him. Sure enough, a week later he announced that he had received a
"deluge of protesting letters begging me to continue playing the music
of today."

"So now," he went on, "I shall be able to play with our orchestra
a number of unusually interesting works by young and individual
composers I have found."

On the spot, he asked the audience to applaud or hiss to show
whether they wished to hear a new composition by Alfredo Casella,
the *Elegia eroica.* Hisses, he said, were "crude and primitive, but as
good as any way" to show how an audience felt. The applause far

outweighed the hisses, and the music went on. That year, needless
to say, there was plenty of contemporary music on the program. That
year, also, the board of directors tore up Stokowski's contract, which
ran through 1927, and gave him a new one extending through 1934
and paying him $70,000 a year. Rumors had been heard once more
that New York was interested in Stokowski (and vice-versa) and his
continuance in Philadelphia was thereby made certain. Said Stokowski when asked to comment on his new ten-year contract: "The
directors are men of unusual mental ability, character and vision."

The heavily modern year of 1924 saw Philadelphia's first experience with the radical music of Edgard Varèse. The work was his
Hyperprisms, written the year before; Stokowski, suspecting approval
might not be universal, put the work last on his program to let those
who wished escape hearing it go out. About fifty did so. When the
orchestra repeated the work on its Tuesday night visit to New York
on December 14, the *Evening World* ran a lengthy verse by Frank H.
Warren which went in part:

> 'Twas the night before Christmas in Carnegie Hall,
> Not a critic was stirring; from every box stall
> Stokowski adherents had lauded the swank
> With which the conductor had led Cesar Franck
> And every one heeding the Stokowski rap
> Had just settled back for a good Philly nap
> When out on the air there arose such a clatter
> We sprang from our seats to learn what was the matter
> And up from the program—were all going crazy?
> Jumped Hyperprism, offspring of Edgar Varèse.

But so far as Stokowski was concerned, neither Philadelphia nor
New York was finished with Varèse. On April 9, 1926 the Philadelphians treated a matinee audience to the world premiere of his
Amériques, a large, complex and subtle work which today is regarded
highly by connoisseurs. *Amériques* began with the sound of a siren,
which was enough to start the audience muttering, and the conclusion
of the work brought forth one of the stormiest sessions of hisses and
catcalls the Academy had ever seen. Varèse was present, and Sto-

kowski insisted on leading him onto the stage to acknowledge such applause as there was. A few nights later the orchestra played *Amériques* in New York, and once more it was hissed, though less violently than in Philadelphia. In 1927 his *Arcana* was also hissed at the Academy. Obviously Varèse was not Philadelphia's favorite composer, but that didn't stop Stokowski from playing him.

♩ THE GLAMOROUS YEARS

The decade from 1916 to 1926 had established the Philadelphia Orchestra as the finest sounding symphonic organization in the nation and probably in the world. Testimonials to its pre-eminence were forthcoming wherever it played. After one particularly brilliant season at Carnegie Hall the orchestra ran full-page newspaper ads in Philadelphia excerpting the views of the New York newspaper critics, beginning with a paean from Lawrence Gilman in the *Herald Tribune*: "Philadelphia sent us last night her chief contribution to civilization, her incomparable orchestra."

The season was gradually extended so that by 1925 the orchestra was playing twenty-nine pairs of Friday and Saturday concerts at the Academy plus occasional concerts on other nights. In addition there were children's and special concerts of various sorts, the ten Tuesdays in New York, five concerts each in Washington and Baltimore, and short tours to cities as distant as Toronto. Total concerts for each season in the mid-twenties reached well over 100.

A special series of Sunday concerts was instituted in 1916. There never had been any kind of Sunday music, outside of church, in Philadelphia previously, and a considerable portion of the clergy (abetted by prudent politicians) resisted the idea fiercely. Stokowski and Judson both wanted to give the concerts; when a reporter asked the conductor whether he planned to play "sacred" music, he loftily replied: "All music is sacred." Eventually an all-Wagner program was played before a packed audience of 4000, admitted without charge, at Philadelphia's Metropolitan Opera House, a huge theater on North Broad Street built in 1908 by Oscar Hammerstein during his war with

New York's Metropolitan Opera Company. Sunday concerts there continued for two seasons, being dropped because they simply were too expensive for the orchestra to maintain on a free basis.

Needless to say, virtually every solo musician of importance appeared as a guest artist with the Philadelphia Orchestra. Sergei Rachmaninoff, whose association with it went back to Pohlig's days, never tired of singing its praises in both the Stokowski and Ormandy eras. The orchestra and its audiences welcomed as guests such pianists as Wilhelm Backhaus, Harold Bauer, Feruccio Busoni, Alfred Cortot, Carl Friedberg, Leopold Godowsky, Myra Hess, Josef Hofmann, Wanda Landowska, Guiomar Novaes, Ignace Jan Paderewski, Artur Rubinstein, Olga Samaroff (Stokowski's wife was one of the most popular—and frequent—guest artists the orchestra had), and Artur Schnabel.

The Belgian organist Charles M. Courboin joined the orchestra in special concerts at John Wanamaker's which drew audiences of 10,000 and more in seats set up in the cathedral-like center portion of the great department store. Among the famous violinists appearing as soloists at concerts in the Academy were Mischa Elman, Jascha Heifetz, Bronislaw Huberman, Fritz Kreisler, Albert Spalding, Jacques Thibaud and Efrem Zimbalist. The cellists were headed by Pablo Casals, and many of the great singers of the era appeared, a particular favorite being David Bispham, the baritone, a Philadelphian who in 1896 became the first native American male to sing at the Metropolitan Opera. He made his last appearance with the orchestra in 1921, the year of his death. Guest conductors were not quite so numerous at that time as with other orchestras, but there was a respectable procession of them none the less, some leading their own works, including Ernest Bloch, Vincent d'Indy, Georges Enesco, Willem Mengelberg, Darius Milhaud, Frederick Stock and Felix Weingartner.

Stokowski by no means neglected standard repertory in these years. There was a full complement of Beethoven, Brahms, Franck, Tchaikovsky and Wagner, to go along with such novelties as de Falla's *El amor brujo*, Hindemith's *Nusch-Nuschi Dances,* and Schoenberg's *Kammersymphonie,* which was roundly hissed in 1923,

seven years after Stokowski had first unveiled it. Such new work as
Mahler's *Das Lied von der Erde,* Rachmaninoff's *The Bells,* and
Sibelius's Symphony No. 5 in E-flat also had their American premieres in Philadelphia, and being less far-out than some of Stokowski's other debut choices, were more calmly received. In the
1922–'23 season Richard Strauss paid the orchestra the compliment
of hiring it intact to play four concerts in New York and one in Philadelphia of his own works.

Stokowski's own transcriptions of Bach's organ pieces appeared
frequently on the programs. Stokowski kept his authorship of these
transcriptions secret for years, and untrue stories spread that they had
been made by Lucien Cailliet, the orchestra's bass clarinetist who indeed made other transcriptions of his own. But these were Stokowski's
own works, and in later years it became fashionable to criticize them
as perversions of the originals, with deep thinkers in particular looking
upon them either with horror or derision. Philadelphia must have
been singularly free from musical intellectualism in those days, for
nearly everybody liked the transcriptions and they were highly popular
with New York audiences, too. Stokowski himself was almost belligerent in their defense. "Bach was just a sleepy old man," he told an
interviewer, "but a wonderful musician, of course. If Bach or somebody else writes a piece of music, that doesn't interest me. It doesn't
matter who has written it. The music appeals to me for what can be
done with it." Later on, in his book *Music for All of Us,* Stokowski
wrote: "If Bach were alive today, he would undoubtedly write glorious
music for the highly evolved modern orchestra—he would find no
limits to his expression, but would use every resource of the orchestra
of today as he used every resource of the organ of his own time."

Whatever the purists may have thought about Stokowski's Bach—
"Bachowski," as a wit called it—it is undeniable that he introduced
thousands of people to the glories of the Toccata and Fugue in D
minor, the Passacaglia and Fugue in C minor, the "little" Fugue in
G minor, a dozen chorale preludes, and many others. True, those
works were theoretically available to visitors to organ lofts, but few
people went to church to hear music, and few church organists played
Bach. In our own times it has become possible to hear resplendent

recordings of Bach's organ works played on the organ by superb musicians, with therefore far less excuse for playing transcriptions than in the 1920s. But even today there are music lovers who, remembering Oscar Wilde's aphorism that "truth is never pure, and rarely simple," retain a certain sneaking nostalgia for Stokowski's richly resonant Bach transcriptions, and the pleasure they brought to an earlier, less sophisticated generation.*

The twenty-fifth anniversary of the orchestra was commemorated November 13 and 14, 1924 with Stokowski conducting a replica of Fritz Scheel's first program with the orchestra on November 16, 1900. In 1926, Philadelphia celebrated the Sesquicentennial of American independence with a gigantic exposition, and the orchestra undertook to play two concerts a week for sixteen weeks at the "Sesqui" Auditorium on the fair grounds. The conductors included Willem Van Hoogstraten, Nikolai Sokoloff, Artur Rodzinski (who at thirty-three became assistant conductor of the orchestra that year) and Stokowski himself. The concerts were not a success, even when the original 50 cents admission charge was dropped. Visitors to "Sesqui," as to most world fairs, had their minds on less ethereal matters.

In the mid-1920s Stokowski briefly took up band music, becoming involved in a new organization called, after its brilliant uniforms, The Band of Gold. Stokowski accepted its conductorship with many solemn asseverations of the importance of band music as a medium of artistic expression. He incorporated many of his Philadelphia brass players into the band, and his programs included not only Sousa marches but his own arrangements of Bach and Wagner.

Many Philadelphians who never got to orchestral concerts took deep pride in The Band of Gold and its golden-haired maestro. Sylvan Levin, the conductor, then a young Curtis Institute student who assisted Stokowski in several projects with the orchestra, re-

---

* Although Stokowski wrote many transcriptions of works by Bach, Wagner, Moussorgsky and others, he composed little original music himself. In 1908 he published a short, simple church piece for vocal quartet and keyboard called "*Benedicite Omnia Opera.*" Another work, a *Dithyrambe for Flute, Cello and Harp,* was performed at a war relief concert of chamber music in Witherspoon Hall, Philadelphia, on November 15, 1917, by two members of the orchestra, flutist Daniel Maquarre and cellist Hans Kindler, joined by harpist Carlos Salzedo. The *Evening Bulletin* praised Stokowski's *Dithyrambe* for its "unusual tonal effects" and "melodious and poetic charm," but it has been little heard of since.

called being stopped by a policeman for a minor traffic infringement. "Where are you rushing to?" the officer demanded. "I'm late for an appointment with Mr. Stokowski at the Academy," explained the young man. "Ah, you mean the bandmaster?" replied the policeman. "Go right ahead."

Even if the Sesquicentennial had provided the orchestra with a glittering international showcase, Stokowski would not have been satisfied. What he really wanted to do was to take the orchestra on tour, not only around the country but around the world. In fact, trips to the West Coast or Europe, possibly both, were tentatively scheduled for 1925, only to be canceled by a crisis over wages in 1924. Thanks to the endowment drive the orchestra itself had achieved economic stability, but the financial status of the musicians was a good deal less enviable. The minimum wage for a Philadelphia Orchestra member was $60 a week, for as many weeks as the season lasted. Five of the players were in the $70 to $90 range, and sixteen—mostly section leaders—were being paid $100 or more. The players wanted a new minimum of around $75, and the dispute raged for two months, with some dark talk from the board of directors that the orchestra might have to be abandoned in the face of such demands. A settlement was finally reached with the new minimum established officially at $65, and with many players receiving larger increases on an individual basis.

Just as the orchestra attained nationwide celebrity in the mid-twenties, so did Leopold Stokowski, now well into his forties, become more of a glamour boy than ever. There was almost no end to the honors that Philadelphia heaped upon him. Shortly after his 1916 triumph in the Mahler Eighth, the University of Pennsylvania conferred a Mus. D. degree upon him, and he henceforth became known as "Doctor Stokowski" to some of the Philadelphia music critics. In 1922 Edward Bok established an award of $10,000 to the citizen in any field who had done most for the city of Philadelphia; its first recipient was Leopold Stokowski. Bronze wreaths, loving cups, sets of plates and silver tankards poured in on him as various notable occasions came and passed; he was lionized at a series of annual "smokers" sponsored by Mr. Van Rensselaer, at which the orchestra performed and Philadelphia's bankers, insurance executives and industrialists turned out to admire—so their wives assured them—the city's most fascinating man.

Naturally, Stokowski's personal life, his tastes in food, clothing and women, his daily routine, his opinions on non-musical no less than musical subjects, his comings and goings, all were scrutinized, gossiped about, written up in the press. People were fascinated to learn, under the headline "Stokowski Trains Like Prize-Fighter," that he had a room at the Academy of Music fitted out with hot and cold needle showers and a rubbing table upon which a masseur worked over him before and after each concert. He even granted interviews lying beneath the sheet. Attempts were made, without success, to identify the mysterious and indescribable accent which colored his inflections—sometimes. Hostesses doted on him, and he on them. Most newspaper readers were shocked in 1923 by his divorce from Olga Samaroff, who received custody of their two-year-old daughter. In 1926 he married Miss Evangeline Brewster Johnson, heiress of the Johnson & Johnson drug fortune; they had two daughters before being divorced in Nevada in 1937. His final marriage, in 1945, was to Gloria Vanderbilt de Cicco. He was sixty-three and she twenty-one, but the union lasted ten years and produced two sons before a divorce broke it up, too. Between times, the most publicized of all Stokowski romances was that with Greta Garbo, which kept newspaper Sunday supplements occupied for years, although it never flowered into the marriage so frequently predicted.

Toward the end of the 1927–'28 season it was announced that Stokowski would only conduct half a season the following year, being on "furlough" the rest of the time, during which he would take a trip to the Far East. Several factors were involved. Stokowski had not had a prolonged vacation from conducting in his fifteen years with the orchestra; he had long had a hankering to sample Far Eastern music at first hand; finally, he was suffering from neuritis in his right shoulder, a condition variously ascribed to the exertions of his baton arm and an injury sustained in an automobile accident. It was while he was favoring his right arm that Stokowski first shifted his baton to his left hand and eventually stopped using it altogether and began molding the musical phrases with his ten fingers; in time the expressive fingers became as much his trademark as the halo of hair.

Naturally the announcement of Stokowski's furlough, coming as it did in the wake of several hissing incidents, started reports that he would never come back to the orchestra. These rumors, like so many others concerning Stokowski over the years, proved to be highly exaggerated. Nevertheless, the Far Eastern excursion did mark something of a change in the relations between Stokowski and the orchestra; it was the first indication that he no longer wished Philadelphia to monopolize his operations, and in the years to come he conducted a proportionately shorter part of each season than he had previously.

⸹ GUEST LIST

For the 1927–'28 season, Arthur Judson lined up an impressive array of guest conductors—Fritz Reiner, Ossip Gabrilowitsch, Willem Mengelberg, Frederick Stock, Thomas Beecham, and Pierre Monteux. Stokowski, for his part, headed first for the West Coast and then across the Pacific, with bulletins on his progress regularly reaching the newspapers—first, a statement from California that he regarded the Hollywood Bowl as a "natural setting" for a great "Temple of Music," later word from the mysterious East that Oriental music was "a highly developed and sophisticated art" which he was "learning to understand."

Meanwhile, back at the Academy, a lively season was under way. Reiner and Beecham were especially popular with their audiences; Reiner brought Béla Bartók down to appear as soloist in his Rhapsody for Piano and Orchestra. Guest-conducting is a special art in itself; it is usually enjoyed by conductors who have permanent orchestras of their own to return to, and who are getting a change of scene and of sound for a week or two. But it can be an agonizing experience for a conductor without a permanent post and trying to impress a new audience and, possibly, a prospective employer. The Philadelphia was a remarkably well-adjusted orchestra; all guest conductors seemed to meet with perfectly amicable treatment. The audiences, too, were more than receptive, and with one exception the guest conductors went home happy.

That exception was Pierre Monteux, and his flare-up at the audience remains one of the strangest incidents in Philadelphia Orchestra annals. Monteux had been conductor of the Boston Symphony from 1919 to 1924, being succeeded by Koussevitzky, and since then had been guest-conducting around the world, his short portly figure and walrus moustache being familiar to audiences in a dozen countries. In Philadelphia, naturally, one of the works he included on his programs was Stravinsky's *Rite of Spring*. After all, whether the audience knew it or not, he had conducted *Le Sacre* at its riotous world premiere in Paris in 1913, when the audiences put up such a fierce din the music couldn't be heard. What Monteux didn't know was that Philadelphians also had their own way of reacting to *Le Sacre*. They didn't brawl in the aisles; they simply walked up them. Just such an incident occurred during Monteux's performance in Philadelphia. Immediately after the walkout, Monteux happened to be interviewed by a writer for *The Jewish Times,* a widely respected Philadelphia publication. Although attempts were subsequently made to soften the import of his words, there is no reason to doubt that he said pretty much what was ascribed to him.

It was an astounding interview both in its frankness and comprehensiveness. To begin with, Monteux charged that "95 per cent" of the Academy audiences "knew nothing about this art of music." He went on: "Philadelphians want a tall, slim conductor who pays a great deal of attention to his tailor. Perhaps that is one reason why my popularity here was sort of half-hearted. I overheard two women coming from the concert discuss me. They uttered not one word about the concert, the music, the composers. I was the sole topic of conversation. They agreed it was shameful the conductor was so short and stout. . . .

"Philadelphians, and in fact all Americans, want to be bluffed. They have watched their conductors gyrate upon the dais before the orchestras here these many years, and unless they can be entertained by the action of the leader they are disappointed."

A tall, slim conductor? Who could it possibly be? Monteux denied he was talking about Stokowski. "We are dear and close friends," he insisted. "I do not mean Stokowski. No. He is the great artist. But the others—bah! Acrobats!"

Philadelphia, quite naturally, was in an uproar, with Monteux being denounced as a bad conductor and, even more of a crime along the Main Line, no gentleman. Reiner, who had been so well received earlier in the year and even was mentioned flatteringly as a possible successor to Stokowski, jumped into the fray, snorting: "Monteux is a fool—talking bunk. People in Philadelphia know more about music than in any other city. They are in touch with everything modern musically, and there is no putting anything over on them."

Gradually the controversy simmered down and the season proceeded. Perhaps the most apt comment of all came from Paris, where Leopold Stokowski had now arrived on his travels. "I'm anxious to get back with my men," he said.

ENTER ELECTRONICS

When Stokowski returned from his travels, he understandably had a bagful of Oriental music with him, items and ideas he had picked up in Java, India, Bali and other exotic ports of call. He also was full of talk about what he called the coming "electrical music era." Electrical methods both of producing tones and of preserving music, he said, were going to shape the future of the American symphony orchestra.

The technology of music always fascinated Stokowski; his book *Music for All of Us* abounds in chapters on sound production, acoustics, the "mathematics of music" and similarly arcane subjects, many illustrated with diagrams. Largely because of his interest in the science of music, the Philadelphia Orchestra became a pioneer in recording, broadcasting and televising as each technological advance came into being.

It is not surprising, then, that Stokowski and the Philadelphia made recordings early and often. On October 22, 1917, the conductor and orchestra crossed the Delaware River to go to the studios of the

Victor Talking Machine Company in Camden, N.J. There they spent a whole day recording Brahms' Hungarian Dances Nos. 5 and 6. A few symphonic recordings had been made in Europe, but they were virtually new to America, and Stokowski relished making them. From that first session the Philadelphia Orchestra maintained an association with Victor that lasted until 1943, and was resumed in 1968 after a twenty-five year lapse.

Recordings then were made by the "acoustic" process, which meant the performers played into a horn and their sound was mechanically recorded. Records, which turned at 78 revolutions per minute, lasted a little more than four minutes, so the early Philadelphia recordings were limited to such works as the Gavotte from Thomas' opera *Mignon*, Weber's *Invitation to the Dance*, and the Largo from Dvorak's *New World* Symphony, some of them cut to fit into the four-minute time limit. In 1924 and 1925, though, Victor had Stokowski and the Philadelphia record Schubert's *Unfinished* Symphony and Stravinsky's *Firebird* Suite. The recording site was an old church at 114 North Fifth Street in Camden, which Victor had purchased for its excellent acoustical qualities and which was the Philadelphia's recording home until 1926, when the Academy was used for the purpose.

In March, 1925 electrical recording put new life into the record business, not to mention into the records themselves. Naturally, it was Stokowski and his orchestra who made the first electrical recordings for Victor by what the company labeled the "Orthophonic" process. Both Saint-Saëns' *Danse Macabre* and Tchaikovsky's *Marche Slav* turned out to be revelations for their time in what rich, full sound could be, and in 1926 came Dvorak's *New World* Symphony, which bore the designation "M-1" and thus became the first in the long line of Victor "M" albums. It consisted of five 78 r.p.m. records, sold for $10, and a critique signed R.D.D. published in the *Phonograph Monthly Review* of Boston said: "It amazes and astonishes. . . . Dr. Stokowski senses to the utmost the opportunity of each climax, of each of the striking orchestral effects, and spurs on his men to realize every possibility as richly and as vividly as their abilities allow. And under Stokowski's baton their abilities are apparently unlimited!"

Stokowski and the Philadelphia could also claim the distinction of making the first long-play record, for when RCA Victor brought out an experimental 33 1/3 r.p.m. experimental disk of Beethoven's Fifth in 1931 they were the performing artists. But the idea did not catch on; the heyday of the LP still lay far in the future.

On October 6, 1929, a Sunday afternoon, the Philadelphia became the first orchestra ever to make a commercially sponsored radio broadcast, which was sponsored by Philco, carried by fifty domestic stations of the National Broadcasting Company, and shortwaved via WGY in Schenectady to Europe, South America and Asia. Mozart's Symphony No. 40 in G minor was the longest work on the one-hour broadcast. Stokowski was all over the place, acting not only as conductor, but also as announcer and continuity writer. For the occasion he was casually attired in plus-fours, and he removed his tie and opened his collar (he always claimed that formal clothes made for stiff performances). Before beginning he addressed the unseen audience: "We are eager to make the programs representative of the best music of all times and countries. If you do not like such music, say so, and we won't play any more radio concerts. For I shall never play popular music." For the second program (there were three on successive weeks), the main work was Stravinsky's *Rite of Spring*. Such was the excitement that in Philadelphia various recreation centers with radios were thrown open at 5:30 p.m. Sunday for those with no sets of their own, and prizes were offered to school children for the best essays on the event.

Broadcasting was no toy for Stokowski; virtually alone among serious musicians he realized its potentialities for spreading musical culture and set out to acquaint himself with its theories and techniques. At times he insisted on manipulating the dials in the control room himself, and there was an apocryphal story describing how the engineers had fitted him out with a special instrument panel that had been secretly disconnected just to get him off their backs. In point of fact, most recording engineers had great respect for his technical knowledge, which he enhanced with studies at the Bell Laboratories. There were times when Stokowski even experimented with electrical "boosting" of certain instruments, and he welcomed with open arms and prompt performances such electronic instruments as the Theremin and the Ondes Martenot. On one occasion in 1931 he startled his audience by preceding the regularly scheduled concert by a demonstration of the noises that could be produced on the stage by several oscillators. "Watch the birdie!" he said just before the oscillators were turned on, "Don't talk, don't rattle your programs, just listen noiselessly." Two years later he put on even a more startling sound show in the Academy by having the audience sit in front of an empty stage. Then, from three concealed loudspeakers came the sound of the orchestra, which was located in the ballroom on another level, playing under the direction of Alexander Smallens, the assistant conductor. Stokowski sat at a panel controlling the outpouring of sound by twirling dials and throwing switches. The purpose was to demonstrate a new method of sound transmission by wire developed by Bell Laboratories. It was about as close as Stokowski ever came to achieving his double ideal of a "Temple of Music" and an "invisible orchestra," which he once outlined to a meeting of women at the Academy: "It has been the dream of my life to have a Temple of Music. This very minute I have the plans for such a temple completed at my house. Each of the audience would sit alone in a stall-like seat. No one would see his neighbor. . . . Just before the music begins the light will be slowly dimmed so that the entire temple will be in darkness and the audience will be literally drenched with beautiful music." At one concert he drenched the hall not only in sound but color, utilizing a "color organ" to accompany a performance of *Scheherazade*.

With Stokowski at its helm, the orchestra participated in three Hollywood motion pictures. *The Big Broadcast of 1937* was a supposed satire on radio with, among others, Jack Benny, Burns and Allen, Martha Raye, and Benny Goodman and his band. Stokowski and *his* band got to play transcriptions of Bach's "little" G minor Fugue and the chorale-prelude *Ein feste Burg*. The next picture, *100 Men and a Girl,* carried Stokowski into the dramatic realm as fifteen-year-old Deanna Durbin's leading man. She played the role of a musician's daughter who successfully contrived to get Stokowski to conduct an unemployed orchestra, thereby preserving it. Among other inanities, the film depicted the orchestra rehearsing the accompaniment to

Mozart's *Exsultate, Jubilate* just as Miss Durbin happened along ready to sing it.

But the most famous Stokowski-Philadelphia film, and one which still undergoes revivals—and controversy—today is his collaboration with Walt Disney, *Fantasia*. Whose idea it originally was is not clear, but Disney and Stokowski had met in Hollywood and it was in discussions between them that the project began to shape up. It was to be an animated film to surpass all previous animated films (as indeed it did), with Stokowski and his Philadelphians supplying the music, and Disney and his staff of artists providing the cartoons. Despite the criticism that showered on him for his excisions and revisions in the scores (Beethoven's *Pastorale* Symphony was cut to run only 22 minutes, 5 seconds, a world's record), Stokowski never lost his fondness for the film or his pride in its making, and when Disney died in 1966 he lamented that there was now no one "who could carry still farther all the elements that were in *Fantasia,* with the imagination and technical knowledge that Disney had." Stokowski always reserved one of his most flowery foreign pronounciations for the film's title, invariably calling it "FantaZEEah" (which would have ruined the jingle "*Fantasia* will amaze ya," created for the revival of 1946).

Certainly he did what he could to assure spectacular tonal treatment, by utilizing eighteen separate sound channels, a 1940 precursor of stereo, which left the theater audiences of the time almost awash in seas of sound. Actual recording was done at the Academy in Philadelphia, with a bevy of engineers working with Stokowski in an effort to achieve results never heard before. The cost of *Fantasia* was variously estimated at from $2,400,000 to $4,000,000; certainly it was an enormously expensive picture and it proved to be a financial flop when first released, although the Disney studio, by the time of the 1963 revival, finally got its investment back.

The '63 revival not only recouped the film's finances, it also managed to restore a certain amount of perspective on a work that had created so much of a furor twenty-three years earlier. The lapses in taste were still there—the transformation of the *Pastorale* Symphony into an embarrassing satire on Greek mythology (Stokowski later contended that he had "disagreed" with Disney's interpretation), and the mushily sentimental treatment of Schubert's *Ave, Maria* at the end. But there also were the exhilaration of the *Sorcerer's Apprentice* starring Mickey Mouse, the intricate if not always logical geometric traceries of Bach's Toccata and Fugue in D minor, the wonderfully ludicrous *Gioconda* ballet and, perhaps most memorable of all, the imaginative depiction of the earth's creation, natural upheavals and saurian battles that accompanied Stravinsky's *Rite of Spring.* Stravinsky wrote bitterly about the Disney-Stokowski *Rite* in later years, but it gave many a youngster at the time an image of the music's primordial strength and savagery which dozens of ballet performances since have not been able to efface.

♩ VIRTUOSO ORCHESTRA

On Stokowski's first appearance with the orchestra at the start of the 1928 season, following his return from Bali, Java and points east, he was received with a tremendous ovation at the Academy. He seemed glad to be back, and the audience to have him. But it quickly became apparent that the old problems were still there. Although the departing conductor had wished publicly for everybody's cold to be cured by the time he got back, it turned out that Philadelphians were still as rheumy as ever. He began scolding them anew for their sniffles and sneezes, and one newspaper even asked in a headline in mock alarm: "Will Stokowski Leave Us Because We Cough?" Latecomers also continued to be a problem, and for a time Stokowski attempted to bar them altogether, a practice which Rudolf Bing later instituted permanently at the Metropolitan Opera in New York. But although it was possible to prevent late arrivals, there was no way to stop early departures, so Stokowski decided to make a virtue of necessity by putting new works last on the programs, enabling those who didn't care for novelty to avoid them without missing anything else. The experiment worked successfully with Villa-Lobos' *Choros No. 8,* when the doors were flung open at the end of the preceding number and a portion of the audience hastened into the more familiar cacophony of the Broad Street Station. At a subsequent complete concert perform-

ance of Moussorgsky's original version of the opera *Boris Godounov*,
which ran until 6 p.m. at the matinee, only one-quarter of the audience was still in its seats at the end.

Stokowski now suddenly decided that he didn't like applause.
In a reversal of his previous pronouncements, he declared that mani-
festations either of approval or disapproval were out of place at concerts of "divine" music: all that was required of an audience was to
listen in spiritual silence and then return home refreshed and strength-
ened. He didn't make this suggestion casually; on November 22, 1929
in the green room of the Academy, he actually held a secret meeting
of 100 women—if there is such a thing—to announce his revolution-
ary idea. Somehow word managed to leak out to the press, which
gleefully described how the handsome conductor, nattily clad in a
matching combination of cream, tan and brown, pleaded with the
women's committee to withhold their applause at all future concerts.

"But how are we to let you know we appreciate your programs?"
one bewildered matron asked.

Stokowski's blue eyes took on a faraway look.

"That is of no importance," he said. "When you see a beautiful
painting you do not applaud. When you stand before a statue,
whether you like it or not, you neither applaud nor hiss."

Eventually it was decided that the applause question was of such
importance that only a full vote of the subscribers could decide it.
Ballots were distributed, with nearly 1000 of them returned. The right
to applaud won out by a vote of 710 to 199. Presumably the right to
hiss went with it.

Whatever divisions existed within the audience, the musicians of
the orchestra, with some exceptions, liked Stokowski as much as any
orchestral player likes any conductor. Even those who didn't like him
respected him. As members of the great Philadelphia Orchestra they
shared his glory; although their pay was not high (a nationwide condition at that time for orchestral players) they had status and respect
within their home communities and within the musical world. He
could be rough on them when it came to applying his high standards
of execution; playing in the Philadelphia Orchestra was anything but
a sinecure. At rehearsals he liked to sit in the rear of a darkened hall

and listen while an assistant conductor "read through" a work with the men. When he took over himself at the podium he had a head full of new ideas and approaches, and for a time he would do more talking than conducting. Sometimes he went beyond words to create a mood, as when he brought a pagan icon to rehearsals of Henry Eichheim's *Bali* and burned incense in it.

Recalled Sol Ruden, one of the orchestra's veteran violinists, in later years: "Stokowski always tried to evoke for the men the picture he had in his mind and tried to bring out the corresponding tone quality. Once when we were rehearsing Handel's *Faithful Shepherd* he painted a word picture of a shepherd boy tending his flock on a hill against the night sky, and a different sound came out. That was his big contribution to orchestral playing. You had the technique and you could use it your own way. He would tell the wind players: 'It's your problem to play it but here is the picture I want.' He hated literalism. 'That's a piece of paper with some marking on it,' he would say, 'We have to infuse life into it.' And when you produced what he wanted, he said: 'That's it.' We didn't have to repeat it. So the rehearsals were short and concentrated."

As a result of Stokowski's rehearsal methods, the orchestra usually reached performance time at its peak and ready to go, unstaled by repetition and with a finely-honed edge. But although he never threw tantrums, ripped up scores, splintered his baton or stomped off the podium, rehearsing wtih Stokowski could be a trying experience. In those days conductors had almost instant life and death power over a musician's career; men could be virtually fired on the spot, and they knew it. Stokowski could be sarcastic and cutting and, a born actor, he reserved some of his most pointed dramatic effects for rehearsals. One of his tricks was to pretend not to know who a player was.

"You," he would say. "What's your name?" Upon being told, he would continue: "You didn't play that passage right. Your stand partner played it—why didn't you?" On one occasion he turned to Herman Weinberg, one of the best-known and most popular violinists in the orchestra, as if he had never seen him before. "You, you," he said, jabbing his finger. "What is your name?" Weinberg stood up. "Murphy," he responded in a loud voice. Even Stokowski joined in the ensuing roar of laughter and on this occasion, at least, the tension was broken.

In the fall of 1928 a rehearsal incident led to a falling out between Stokowski and two of his star violin players. One of the works scheduled was Mozart's Symphony No. 40 in G minor, and the conductor hadn't liked the way the violin section played a particular passage. So he made each fiddler play it solo while the rest of the orchestra sat and listened. No orchestral musician likes this kind of procedure, and it is, as a matter of fact, forbidden by many of today's union contracts. In this instance Mischa Mischakoff, who had come from the New York Symphony Orchestra the year before to become the Philadelphia's concertmaster, was infuriated, sensing that Stokowski was implying he hadn't drilled his section properly. Mischakoff announced he was leaving the orchestra, and he was joined by David Dubinsky, leader of the second violins, who had been an original member of the orchestra, although his service had not been continuous.

Another loss that year, though unconnected with the Mischakoff incident, was the departure of assistant conductor Artur Rodzinski, who went to Los Angeles as permanent conductor, another step upwards on a distinguished career that was to lead him eventually to the New York Philharmonic. His function in Philadelphia was filled by Alexander Smallens. Stokowski also hired his first woman player, harpist Edna Phillips, twenty-two, who joined the orchestra in 1930 and remained eleven years.

Through all the comings and goings of musicians the orchestra always retained, and even heightened, the rich and polished patina of sound that was its hallmark. It even managed to develop within its ranks players who shone as individual stars while maintaining unbroken the unique tone of the ensemble. Marcel Tabuteau, the oboist, who played from 1915 to 1954, and William Kincaid, first flute from 1921 to 1960, achieved fame as two of the finest practitioners of their instruments the country had ever known. Tabuteau, who had played for Arturo Toscanini in the Metropolitan Opera Orchestra prior to World War I, imparted a uniquely suave and supple tone to his difficult instrument. An admirer of the pleasures of life as well as of music, he once told an associate: "Three things I've never completely figured out: women, roulette, and how to get a good reed." Tabuteau eventually retired to live in his native France, where he died in 1966 at the age of seventy-eight.

Kincaid was one of the greatest virtuosos the flute had ever known. He played a specially made platinum instrument, which he insured for $6000. It matched his platinum hair, but it also held its tone better, so he insisted, than either silver or gold, the usual flute metals. Kincaid, who died in 1967 at seventy-one, was reared in Hawaii, where he was a swimming protégé of Duke Kahamamoku, the Olympic champion. The flute, he said, was "the easiest instrument to play badly and the hardest to play well." Kincaid and Tabuteau were both active as teachers as well as performers, and between them educated an entire generation of American woodwind players. Their pupils occupy chairs in symphony orchestras throughout the United States today, including the Philadelphia. The same can be said for such other players of the Stokowski era as Anton Torello, the Spanish double-bass player, Anton Horner the hornist, and a number of others. Even today, there are masters and pupils playing side by side in the Philadelphia Orchestra: two generations of a continuing tradition.

⨍ STOKOWSKI AND TOSCANINI

In the spring of 1930 came an intriguing announcement: Leopold Stokowski and Arturo Toscanini would exchange podiums for two weeks. The news was exciting not only because they were two of the three supreme *maestri* in the land (Koussevitzky was just rounding out his seventh season in Boston), but because they represented such exact musical antitheses. Toscanini's characteristic sound was lean, crisp, and some thought, a little dry; Stokowski was the acknowledged master of amplitude, color and sonority. Toscanini's musical credo was to play the work *come è scritto*—as it's written—in literal adherence to the printed score; Stokowski had no scruples about embellishing scores, even to putting a tam-tam in Dvorak's *New World* Symphony where none was indicated. At forty-eight Stokowski was vitally interested in the modern approach to radio, records and matters of orchestral stage rearrangements; at sixty-three, Toscanini couldn't have cared less. And naturally, their two symphonic organizations reflected their philosophies. Toscanini with the Philadelphia Orchestra, Stokowski with the New York Philharmonic—it even *sounded* strange.

Typically, Toscanini approached the exchange, scheduled for the last week of November and the first of December, 1930, without comment, while Stokowski issued a lengthy and flowery "analysis" of his colleague's qualities as a conductor. During the spring, the New York Philharmonic had made a tour of Europe, and Stokowski had sat in the audience during two concerts in Berlin. He had found, he said, that Toscanini was imbued with "divine fire," that his rhythm was "subtle and flexible and vibrant," that "his beat breaks every rule, yet is always clear and eloquent," that "the melodic line he molds just as a sculptor molds in soft clay," and, finally, that "his originality of conception comes from his expressing the essence and soul of the score, instead of merely the literal notes."

Thus heralded, Toscanini came to Philadelphia for the first time and scored a smashing success, although some players were a bit taken aback by the contrast between his style of music-making and Stokowski's. Nevertheless the orchestra as a whole proved amenable and amiable, and Toscanini got what he wanted. He even switched the violins back to their then traditional positions of the firsts to the conductor's left and the seconds to his right, rather than keeping them on one side in the Stokowski manner. His Philadelphia programs included Mozart's *Haffner* Symphony, Strauss' *Ein Heldenleben*, the Beethoven and Brahms First Symphonies, three Bach chorale-preludes arranged by Respighi, and several Wagner excerpts. The orchestra played beautifully, the critics were enchanted, the audiences went home happy.

No such cordiality prevailed in New York, where Stokowski was leading the Philharmonic through such works as Brahms' Fourth Symphony and Double Concerto in A minor for Violin and Cello, Sibelius' First Symphony, Stravinsky's *Sacre du printemps,* and several of his own Bach transcriptions. Quarrels between the guest conductor and the men broke out during rehearsals. According to one account,

Stokowski found himself unable to get on with a Philharmonic brass player who had previously lasted only a few seasons with him in Philadelphia. Another story told how Stokowski tried to get the Philharmonic double-bass players to play certain high notes in his arrangement of Bach's "little" Fugue in G minor. "That passage can't be played on the bass," one of the players told him. "I've got nine in Philadelphia who can play it on the bass," he replied.

Whatever actually happened at the rehearsals, two of the orchestra's members found themselves banished from the ensemble for the duration of Stokowski's visit. Howard Taubman remarks in his biography of Toscanini that "It was not the first or last time that a conductor who followed Toscanini found himself bedeviled. Part of the explanation, one would guess, was that Toscanini had been so insistent on unlimited output of energy and concentration from the men that they were weary and tended to let up when another man took the podium. . . . Stokowski left little doubt that he knew just what he wanted in the way of sound and pacing and shading. The chances are that since he was a man of temperament himself and since this was his first appearance at the head of the New York orchestra, he would brook no obstacles." In any event, whatever the comparative merits of the two guests, the Philadelphians had proved themselves beyond doubt the more gracious hosts.

As a result of his experience in New York, Stokowski and the Philharmonic remained on the outs for years. It was not until 1941 that the wounds were healed. That year the Philharmonic, celebrating its centennial, invited both Stokowski and Toscanini to appear as guests. In the interim, Toscanini had retired from the Philharmonic and presumably from New York musical life as well, but he had been brought back to the city as head of the newly created National Broadcasting Company Symphony Orchestra, not without some ill-feeling on the part of the Philharmonic directors. So 1941 marked a reconciliation of the Philharmonic both with Stokowski *and* Toscanini. In subsequent years Stokowski made many other Philharmonic appearances.

It was also in 1941 that Toscanini returned to the Philadelphia Orchestra once again. This time he made two visits in one season to guest conduct at the Academy, in November, 1941 and January-

February, 1942, for a total of eight concerts. Once again the Philadelphia critics and audiences were ecstatic, and once again, the
orchestra proved a responsive instrument. Wrote Charles O'Connell,
then RCA Victor's director of classical music: "The conductor was
amazed and delighted with the orchestra. Its quickness, agility, musicianship, glorious tone and unique sonority were a revelation to him, as
well they might be, for neither in Europe nor in America had he ever
conducted an orchestra the equal of this one. . . . At the first rehearsal
he went completely through the program without once interrupting
the orchestra. At the end he bowed, smiled, told the men there was
nothing he could suggest to improve the performance, and walked off
the stage in high good humor."

O'Connell's contention, made in his book *The Other Side of the
Record,* is that Toscanini's visits to Philadelphia were made for the
explicit purpose of subsequently recording the music played on his
programs. Whether this is so or not, it remains a fact that an imposing
list of recordings were made at extensive—and expensive—sessions
held at the Academy early in 1942, with results unforeseen by the
participants, and unheard by the public at large.

For, through an astonishing and still somewhat inexplicable series
of circumstances, the recordings, with one exception, were never released by Victor. With the Philadelphia, Toscanini recorded Schubert's Symphony No. 9 in C Major, Tchaikovsky's *Pathétique,*
Debussy's *La Mer* and *Iberia,* Mendelssohn's *Midsummer Night's
Dream* incidental music, Respighi's *Feste Romane,* Strauss' *Death
and Transfiguration,* and Berlioz' Queen Mab Scherzo from *Romeo
and Juliet.* As months and then years went by, musicians and those
members of the public who were aware of the sessions wondered
increasingly why the recordings were never released. In time, they
began to take on an almost legendary quality, like the ancient El
Dorado, which no one ever saw, though everyone was sure it existed.

Various reasons were given for the failure to bring out the
Toscanini-Philadelphia recordings. It was said that the recording
sound level was too low, that there were occasional flaws (such as an
oboe that couldn't be heard in *La Mer*), that in some instances no
duplicate masters were cut. Apparently one important factor was the

labor shortages and material deficiencies attendant upon World War II: in some manner, the wax and acetate master records were mishandled so that they emerged scratched, pitted and with an intolerable level of surface noise. Toscanini, who had the right to reject any recording he made, refused to pass them. According to O'Connell, who disliked Toscanini personally and said so in his book, the Maestro also vetoed the records out of petulance because "in certain respects, they did not compare with the best of Stokowski's recordings or . . . with the best of Ormandy's."

Whatever the reason, the master records reposed in RCA Victor's vaults for nearly twenty years. Then, in 1961, with the help of new electronic transfer techniques, it was found possible to release a long-playing record of one of the Toscanini-Philadelphia products, the Schubert Symphony in C Major. The critics welcomed it warmly, even though the recorded sound was, of necessity, that of a distant era. But none of the other recordings made in the Academy was ever released, and to this day, there remains some fine Philadelphia music, 1942 vintage, in RCA's vaults.

♭ NEW TITLE, OLD FEUDS

On March 10, 1931, a new position was announced for Stokowski. Henceforth, the orchestra association said, he would be not merely conductor but musical director of the Philadelphia Orchestra, with complete control over all programs, guest conductors and policies. He himself would conduct sixteen weeks—about half the season— and it was noted by some observers that Ossip Gabrilowitsch, the Detroit Symphony director, who had been the principal guest conductor in Philadelphia since 1928, would not be returning this year.

Stokowski's ascension to the title of music director marked the summit of his career in Philadelphia, but also the start of its decline. He took over complete control of the orchestra just as the Depression was tightening its hold on the country. With money needed for the essentials of life, ticket sales to concerts declined, subscribers failed to renew, the board of directors looked more anxiously than ever to the orchestra's precarious finances. Yet Stokowski continued to schedule new works as if financial matters were none of his concern (as indeed they technically were not); not only did they fail to swell the subscription lists, but many of them were in themselves expensive to stage.

A disgruntled American composer once complained that when it came to contemporary music Stokowski gave more first performances than any other conductor—and fewer seconds. The argument was that he sought novelty for novelty's sake rather than really trying to familiarize audiences with specific new pieces. Whatever the merits of the complaint, there is no doubt that whatever Stokowski did in new music, he did in style. Somehow, he let Toscanini beat him to Ravel's *Bolero,* introducing it in Philadelphia on December 20, 1929 only after it had been played in New York. But he followed up his staged production of Stravinsky's *Sacre du printemps* by doing the same with Schoenberg's *Die glückliche Hand,* in which Doris Humphrey and Charles Weidman were the featured dancers. Both the Stravinsky and Schoenberg works were repeated, after their Philadelphia premieres, on the stage of the Metropolitan Opera in New York under the auspices of the League of Composers. As a result of these productions, Stokowski's visage decorated the cover of *Time* Magazine on April 28, 1930, the first conductor to receive this lofty honor.

As spectacular as these stage works had been, they were far overshadowed by the famous Stokowski performances of Alban Berg's opera *Wozzeck.* Berg's masterpiece was only six years old at the time; it had never been given in America. When Stokowski put it on, March 21, 1931, in co-operation with the Philadelphia Grand Opera Company and with a young baritone named Nelson Eddy in the cast, the excitement recalled that which had surrounded the Mahler Eighth of 1916. Again musical luminaries converged on Philadelphia; again there were the lengthy expository articles in the press; again the subsequent trip was made to New York for a performance at the Metropolitan Opera House, which was rented for the occasion. Most of the Philadelphia critics were cautious, if not equivocal, in appraising Berg's modernistic score, but Olin Downes of the *New York Times,* who was among those journeying to Philadelphia, wrote two

A Philadelphia Orchestra concert inside the Academy of Music. Orchestra, auditorium and audience have been in perfect equilibrium with each other since 1900.

Fritz Scheel, the first conductor. He performed in New York, Chicago and San Francisco before he came to Philadelphia, where the musicians he gathered for a pair of charity concerts eventually became one of the world's great orchestras.

Karl Pohlig, Scheel's successor, resembled him in physical appearance and in his solid Germanic musical background. But his interpretations seldom rose above the routine and he departed abruptly a year before his contract expired.

Leopold Stokowski, thirty years old, was tall, handsome and commanding when he arrived from Cincinnati to take over the orchestra in the fall of 1912.

Heroes of the Mahler's Eighth. Left to right, Margaret Keyes, contralto; Susanna Dercum, contralto; Inez Barbour, soprano; Clarence Whitehill, bass; Leopold Stokowski; Alexander Van Rensselaer, president of the orchestra association; Florence Hinkle, soprano; Reinald Werrenrath, baritone; Adelaide Fischer, soprano; Lambert Murphy, tenor.

Philadelphia (and most other cities) had never before witnessed such a stage array as Stokowski assembled to give Mahler's *Symphony of a Thousand* its U.S. premiere on March 2, 1916. Observe the extended stage in front, and also the "gardenia-like spot of girls" that one reporter noted in the midst of the male choristers. Stokowski had not yet given up use of baton.

In 1919, $1,000,000 was raised for the orchestra in one month, with the help of street banners like this, flying over Broad Street in front of City Hall.

Studio portraits of Stokowski usually
also included his celebrated hands.

A Grecian-looking Stokowski as a
Time Magazine cover boy in 1930.

The conductor's aversion to audience noises inspired this 1929 cartoon in *The
Saturday Evening Post.*

Someone Drops a Handkerchief During a Performance
of the Philadelphia Orchestra.

When painting of Stokowski by Leopold G. Seyffert was hung at the Pennsylvania Academy of Fine Arts in 1913 it became known familiarly as "Whistler's Father." In later years it decorated Stokowski's own mantel.

Fantasia brought together talents of commentator Deems Taylor (left), Stokowski, and movie cartoonist Walt Disney in 1940. Here they examine sketches of lady centaurs in Beethoven's *Pastoral* Symphony, one of film's most criticized segments.

Unusual overhead shot of the Philadelphia Orchestra in action was taken
from the ceiling of Philharmonic Hall, Lincoln Center, New York.

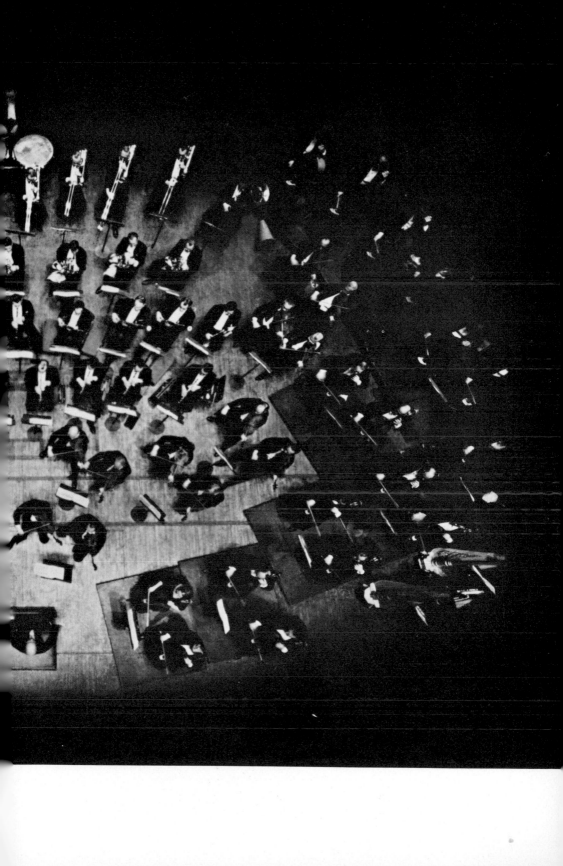

The budding Budapest violin virtuoso is Eugene Ormandy, aged three.

Ormandy in his early days in Philadelphia with Sergei Rachmaninoff.

Robin Hood Dell has been a summer home for the musicians since 1930. Modern shell and facilities were erected in 1956. Admission is free, audiences large.

When the Philadelphia Orchestra made its first television broadcast on March 21, 1958, crowd gathered in front of a store to watch the program, which beat a rival telecast by Toscanini and the NBC Symphony by ninety minutes.

Ormandy led the orchestra to Britain on its first trans-Atlantic venture in 1949 aboard the *Parthia*.

Last train from Broad Street. Demolition of the old station found Ormandy conducting crowd in *Auld Lang Syne* as "Orchestra Special" pulled out.

Jan Sibelius (left) stands with
Ormandy on porch of his villa in rare
photo taken during the orchestra's
visit to Finland in 1955.

Tour of Japan in 1967 found
orchestra's presence well advertised,
as sign along the Ginza in
Tokyo attests.

One of the few pictures ever taken of
Eugene Ormandy and Leopold Stokowski
together. It was made in Philadelphia
on November 19, 1965, just after
Stokowski guest-conducted a matinee
concert. Together, the two men represent
fifty-six years of conducting with the
Philadelphia Orchestra.

Ormandy, a former violinist, is a specialist in eliciting a rich string tone from orchestral musicians. Here he seems to be playing a violin himself as he demonstrates what he wants.

Playback. Ormandy and RCA recording
director John Pfeiffer listen to tape
during interval in session.

In traditional manner, Ormandy's left hand
indicates expression and intensity while
right hand gives tempo and rhythm.

Stokowski's hands were his hallmark in
late years when he returned as a guest
conductor with the orchestra, just as
in years when he directed it regularly.

and a half columns calling the score "beautiful" and reporting that the work had scored "an astonishing success" with the audience.

Hardly had the hubbub over *Wozzeck* died down than Stokowski announced he was presenting two more "shockers," Stravinsky's *Oedipus Rex* and Prokofiev's *Le Pas d'acier,* again with the co-operation of the League of Composers. He also put on a cantata called *Lindbergh's Flight* by Kurt Weill, which was a failure, and Aaron Copland's *Dance Symphony,* which was better received. He wound up by promising a performance of Schoenberg's *Gurrelieder* for the following year. When the books were closed for the season, it was found that expenses had hit the $750,000 mark, that ticket sales were off, and that the first deficit had been registered since the establishment of the endowment fund.

The feast of modernity continued with the start of the 1931–'32 season, with segments of the audience becoming increasingly restive and some of the directors increasingly angered. Anton Webern's *Symphony for Small Orchestra* was hissed so roundly on October 23 that Stokowski abruptly stopped conducting, though the work was nearly finished, left the stage, and then after a few minutes returned and played it through again. The Webern composition was part of a contemporary music festival which Stokowski was putting on prior to leaving the orchestra for a brief vacation during which Arturo Toscanini was scheduled to make a return engagement as guest conductor. Other works he presented included Mossolov's *Soviet Iron Foundry,* a Toccata by Alexander Tansman, two Etudes by a Russian named Vladimir Vogel, and Robert Russell Bennett's *Abraham Lincoln: A Likeness in Symphonic Form.* Audiences and critics alike could hardly wait for Toscanini to arrive with more standard, and palatable, fare.

But Toscanini never came; he was suffering from neuritis in his baton arm, and regretfully sent word from Italy that he would have to cancel. A young conductor named Eugene Ormandy who had previously led a few summer concerts at Robin Hood Dell but who did most of his current work on the CBS radio network in New York, was presented as a last-minute substitute, not without trepidation on everybody's part, except his own. Ormandy's program included

Brahms' Symphony No. 4, Richard Strauss' *Till Eulenspiegel* and *Rosenkavalier* Waltzes, and the Polka and Fugue from Jaromir Weinberger's *Schwanda the Bagpiper*. Reported the Philadelphia *Record* ecstatically: "An audience that was genuinely pleased to hear a program of beautiful music, instead of foundry imitations and noises from the nethermost depths accorded Eugene Ormandy, guest conductor of the Philadelphia Orchestra, an enthusiastic welcome yesterday afternoon at the Academy of Music.

"If Mr. Ormandy had cunningly chosen a program which would contrast with the cacophonous effusions sponsored by Mr. Stokowski last week, he could not have shown to better advantage the ineffable charm of the tonal art which needs no intellectual diploma for enjoyment." What the *Record's* critic didn't know was that the program had actually been selected for Ormandy by Stokowski. Several of the works were brand new to the young conductor, and he had had to learn them in the few days available to him before the concert.

But he learned them well, for his success was unquestionable, and as a direct result of his triumph on October 25, 1931 Eugene Ormandy was launched on a path that was to lead him first to Minneapolis and later back to Philadelphia—a remarkable journey which we will later follow in detail.

Stokowski made good on his promise to perform *Gurrelieder* on April 8, 1932. Schoenberg's massive work was presented on the stage of the Metropolitan Opera House in Philadelphia with an augmented orchestra of 123, three male choruses, a mixed chorus, five soloists including Jeannette Vreeland, Paul Althouse and Rose Bampton, and a speaker—a grand total of 532 participants. Again there was a trip to New York for a performance, and this time it was recorded by RCA Victor—its only recorded version for twenty years to come.

Although all these activities added up to a huge *succès d'estime* for the orchestra, they also represented something of a *débacle du fisc*; the combinations of heavy outlays, dwindling receipts, and lowered subscription lists oppressed the board of directors. Its president, Alexander Van Rensselaer, who had been in office since the orchestra's start, was still a Stokowski partisan, as was Frances Wister, longtime head of the women's committees. But there were mutterings among the other officers, and before the next season began—Stokowski was out of town at the moment—came an astonishing announcement of future plans. The board declared that despite the Depression, the full personnel of the orchestra would be retained, that ticket prices would remain unchanged, that four guest conductors—Eugene Ormandy, Issay Dobrowen, Alexander Smallens and Artur Rodzinski—would alternate with Stokowski through the season, and that everybody associated with the orchestra had accepted a 10 per cent pay cut. Although some of this was unwelcome news, none of it was entirely unexpected. But now came the bombshell. The announcement continued: "The programs will be almost entirely devoted to acknowledged masterpieces. The directors feel that in times such as the present, audiences prefer music which they know and love, and that performances of debatable music should be postponed until a more suitable time. With these opinions the conductors fully concur."

Why that last sentence was included has always been one of the profound mysteries of the Philadelphia Orchestra's history. Stokowski made it clear at once that he had never been consulted, that he was away when the statement was prepared and issued, and that he didn't intend to pay the slightest attention to it. In fact, he immediately announced that far from conforming to the injunction against "debatable music," he was scheduling for his opening concert a new contemporary work, Werner Josten's *Jungle*, a tone poem inspired by the paintings of the French primitivist artist, Henri Rousseau. Previously played by the Boston Symphony, it featured voodoo rhythms and leonine roars—in other words, about as "debatable" as music could be. Furthermore, said the defiant conductor, he was scheduling *Jungle* as the last work on the program, and he proposed to play it *twice*, thereby giving the board and any other dubious listeners a better chance to appreciate it. In case that wasn't sufficient, he further indicated that he had a new Shostakovich symphony, the Third, in the offing, and although he didn't mention it at the time, he also had scheduled for the season a work by a Negro composer, the Symphony No. 1 of William Levi Dawson, director of the Tuskegee Choir.

Stokowski made good on every one of his threats or, rather, promises. The women's committees, that devoted band of Stokowskians, sprang to his support. Society girls circulated through the Academy with petitions in favor of modern music—and Stokowski. A few days later the board, staggered by the reaction, lamely explained that they had meant only to put a "reasonable limit" on debatable music; that their entire motivation was economic, since subscriptions were down by $100,000, and that they retained "full confidence" in Stokowski who, as before, remained in complete charge of the musical side of the Philadelphia Orchestra. Everything went pretty much as Stokowski had planned except, perhaps, that Josten's *Jungle,* after its few hearings, dropped out of sight and has seldom been heard of since.

Stokowski himself was in a position to escape the rigors of the Depression. A few years previously his annual income had been estimated at $200,000* and in November, 1932, he took legal steps to incorporate himself as a means of co-ordinating his various musical business enterprises. He had never been one to undersell himself. Samuel R. Rosenbaum recalled that when he joined the board of directors in 1928 he had a conversation in which money was the main subject. As Rosenbaum remembered it, he told Stokowski that many on the board felt the conductor set his pay demands too high. Replied Stokowski: "I know what compensation Jack Dempsey and Charlie Chaplin receive. Mine doesn't compare to theirs. Yet we are all entertainers of the great American public. I'm underpaid." Rosenbaum tried to argue it wasn't the same public, but Stokowski answered: "It's up to you to make it possible to have a mass audience for music. You don't know how to run your business."

With the arrival of hard times, Stokowski lent his services freely to the needy, conducting benefit concerts by and for unemployed musicians both in New York and Philadelphia. In 1934 he led an orchestra of 1000 at Yankee Stadium, New York, in a benefit for Jewish refugees from Nazi Germany.

In the 1933–'34 season, the Depression closed in even further over the Philadelphia Orchestra, for on top of their previous 10 per cent cut the musicians accepted, though only after bitter protest, a

---

* Eventually it went even higher. One estimate broke down his earnings this way: $2000 a concert for fifty-five concerts a year, totaling $110,000 annually. $70,000 for radio appearances. $60,000 in record royalties. Grand total for one year: $240,000.

further 9 per cent reduction. This brought their minimum pay to $73.71 a week, and since the season lasted only twenty-five weeks, the year-round remuneration figured out to $35.43 weekly. In these difficult times the orchestra suffered a further blow on July 18, 1933 when Mr. Van Rensselaer, who had done as much as any other individual to keep it afloat since its inception, died at the age of eighty-two. His successor as president of the board of directors was Curtis Bok, son of Edward Bok.

℘ YOUTH MOVEMENT

Leopold Stokowski was never much troubled by the generation gap. The older he grew, the more he became interested in young people—and vice versa. In common with most other orchestras, the Philadelphia ran a series of children's concerts from its earliest days, but Stokowski instituted his own series in 1921, often conducting himself, sometimes leaving them to assistant conductors like Saul Caston.

They were children's concerts like none other, for they enabled Stokowski to give full play to his showmanship. When the orchestra played the *Carnival of the Animals* of Saint-Saëns, nothing would do but to present a live menagerie on the stage, including several young elephants. For Prokofiev's *Peter and the Wolf*, Stokowski undertook to have an actual wolf present, and when none was available, settled instead for a huge dog.

One year Stokowski stirred up tremendous anticipation by telling the children he planned to present Charlie Chaplin as a performer at a concert; apparently an invitation was actually extended, but Chaplin could never make it. Still, the children kept expecting him from week to week, so Stokowski did the next best thing: he persuaded Adrian Siegel, one of the orchestra members who resembled Chaplin somewhat in build, to impersonate him.

Siegel was a cellist, and Chaplin's instrument was the violin, but it was figured, quite correctly, that this was a detail no one was likely to notice. When the concert came, Siegel, in baggy Chaplin clothes, shuffled onto the stage carrying a cello. He stumbled over a bulky instrument case which had been purposely left in his path, bringing a roar of laughter; in feigned anger he picked it up and flung it into the wings, where it landed with a tremendous crash into a specially-prepared handtruck full of loose metal and broken glass. More laughter. Then he played the song *Trees* and several other numbers to such Chaplinesque effect that the audience remained delighted. So successful was Siegel's impersonation that most of the children actually thought he was Chaplin, and a crowd of several hundred gathered outside the stage door on Locust Street to await his departure. Siegel asked Stokowski what he should do and was advised to remain inside until the crowd disbanded. It took two and a half hours before the last youngster reluctantly departed and Siegel could go home.

On another occasion, Stokowski somehow discovered that the Philadelphia police force had a motorcycle officer who was an expert xylophonist. So he invited him to a children's concert and made him the centerpiece of a surprise charade. Stokowski himself opened the program with Mozart's *Marriage of Figaro* Overture. But he played it at a mile-a-minute clip—so rapidly that the orchestra could hardly keep up with him. Just as it was ending, the motorcycle cop, in full uniform including helmet, goggles and black gloves, strode out on the stage and sternly seized Stokowski's elbow. "You're going too fast," he told him while the children gaped. "I'm giving you a ticket for speeding." Stokowski, in the manner of most citizens in similar situations, attempted to talk his way out of it. The policeman finally offered to let him go in return for a chance to play with the orchestra. "What do you play?" asked Stokowski in pretended astonishment. "The xylophone," said the cop. One was promptly wheeled out, off came the gloves and goggles, and *The Flight of the Bumblebee* resounded through the Academy—one of the most tumultuously acclaimed performances it ever had there. With events like these taking place, it was small wonder that adult Philadelphians tried to crowd into the children's concerts—so much so, that a rule was adopted that grown-ups were not allowed unless they were chaperoning no fewer than ten children. Even at that, all sorts of ruses were attempted to gain entrance. One prominent Philadelphia couple attempted to get in by having the wife dress up in pumps and a short skirt, while the husband put on a false beard and passed himself off as her father. Some Philadelphians remember Stokowski's children's concerts more vividly than those they attended in later years.

In 1933 Stokowski decided to supplement the children's performances, which had an audience age ceiling of twelve, with a novel set of youth concerts for the thirteen to twenty-five age group. This probably became Stokowski's favorite, as well as most loyal audience in Philadelphia, and it was established on a basis like none other in the country. Stokowski, in effect, turned over the management of the youth concerts to the audiences. The young people ran publicity and advertising, sold the tickets, printed the programs, wrote the program notes, staffed the hall, and consulted with Stokowski on the music to be played. Soloists for the most part included young artists, some selected by competition. The young people congregated around Stokowski almost like a personal guard, and his apartment on Rittenhouse Street often became a hubbub of their activities. Later on, when Stokowski's dispute with the board reached its peak, it was his "youth corps" which rallied most vociferously to him.

The youth concerts became the center of a rather ludicrous controversy during the 1933–'34 season. Stokowski, who had been on a summer trip to Soviet Russia in 1931 and had several times expressed the desire to lead the orchestra there for a tour, suddenly announced his intention to play the Communist anthem the *Internationale* at a youth concert, along with the *Star-Spangled Banner*. The outcry from the American Legion was immediate: not only would the young people be forced to listen to the Red anthem, they would actually be made to *sing* it! For days the controversy went on in press and pulpit until a compromise was reached: the *Internationale* would be played by the orchestra and sung by the audience, but *in French*. The atmosphere was tense when concert time came, with police alert to the possibility of trouble, and a full corps of newspaper reporters on hand. But the singing went off without incident, the Republic stood, and Philadelphia went back about its normal business.

⨒ THE GREAT OPERA FIASCO

At the last concert of the season on April 28, 1934, Stokowski turned to his surprised audience and said: "You know, my contract runs out tonight. And I have not signed a new one. I am not going to sign a new one—unless I am sure that my audiences want me."

There was a vigorous outburst of applause and, obviously pleased, the conductor went on.

"I have asked for a year's sabbatical leave," he said. "But the orchestra association wants me to take only a half year. What I want to do is study and conduct researches to find new things to make our orchestra better. My new contract will provide that I have the last half of next year's season off. Then I will go away to study."

There is no reason to doubt the absolute sincerity of everything Stokowski said. He was sorely tempted to leave the orchestra, with its increasing bickering with the board of directors over programs and policies, and investigate elsewhere—Hollywood, for instance—those technological and musical matters which so intrigued him. He certainly had the means to do so, and yet it was not easy to end so long and fruitful an association so abruptly. For its part, the board, though tempted to let go of the man who had been such a builder but also such a nuisance, was afraid of what might happen to the orchestra if he did depart. The Stokowski-Philadelphia affair was one of the great love-hate relationships in the history of music, and when it finally began to break up in the fall of 1934 it set off waves that shook staid Philadelphia to its roots, threw the musical world into an uproar, and caused personal wounds and hurts that have not healed until this day.

The 1934–'35 season began on a peculiar note, when the orchestra announced plans to go into the opera business. The Metropolitan Opera, which had been coming down to Philadelphia on Tuesday nights for years past to give performances, had canceled such outings as part of its Depression cutback. Rather than co-operating with a local opera company, the orchestra decided to do opera at the Academy itself, hiring outside singers and utilizing its own men in the pit.

In view of the disaster that ensued, it became somewhat difficult afterward to apportion exact responsibility both for the decision to perform opera and the way it was carried out. But there was no doubt that Curtis Bok, who had taken over as president of the board and was an avid opera-lover, advocated such a season. Arthur Judson, now in his twentieth year as manager, was also regarded as behind the operatic venture, and certainly had a great deal to do with its preparation. Stokowski's position was considerably more equivocal; while the season could not have been presented without his acquiescence, he showed little enthusiasm for it, and conducted none of the operas himself.

One thing was certain: this was to be no ordinary season of opera. Both standard and uncommon works were to be given, some in English, some in their original language. The list of ten presentations included Wagner's *Tristan und Isolde* and *Die Meistersinger,* Bizet's *Carmen,* Strauss's *Der Rosenkavalier* (with Lotte Lehmann, Elisabeth Schumann and Emanuel List), a double bill of Humperdinck's *Hansel and Gretel* and Stravinsky's *Mavra* (receiving its American premiere), Moussorgsky's *Boris Godounov,* Shostakovich's *Lady Macbeth of Mtsensk,* Gluck's *Iphigenia in Aulis* (also an American premiere), Verdi's *Falstaff* and Debussy's *Pelléas et Mélisande.* The conductors were Alexander Smallens and Fritz Reiner and, as stage director for the series, Judson brought over from Europe Herbert Graf, a young Viennese making his first appearance in America. Several singers were also imported from Europe, and a large complement of young American singers engaged.

All this cost money, of course, and additional expenses quickly began to pile up. Stage rehearsals had to be held on Sundays, since that was the only time the Academy building was available, necessitating double pay for stagehands. The scenic design for *Tristan* had to be discarded because it proved impractical. A revolving turntable, built in New York and trucked to Philadelphia in forty segments, was installed for *Carmen.* For all the operas, sets, costumes and even curtains were made to order. Nothing was borrowed or improvised.

Once again, Philadelphia's musical enterprise attracted attention throughout the country. The New York critics, headed by Olin

Downes of the *Times* and Lawrence Gilman of the *Tribune*, came down to review the performances. The President's wife, Mrs. Franklin D. Roosevelt, journeyed from Washington for the opening *Tristan*, conducted by Reiner. It was given uncut and its length appalled some listeners, with Graf later reporting that he heard one gentleman ask as he left the theater: "Is Roosevelt still President?" But artistically, as well as socially, the season was a brilliant success, and attendance was high. The orchestra's playing came in for particular praise.

But the financial loss was staggering. So expensive had the undertaking proved, that within a few months the orchestra's entire surplus of $250,000, carefully built up and husbanded over a twenty-year period, was gone. The original idea had been for the operas to be repeated over a three-year period, thus amortizing their costs, but it quickly became apparent that further opera seasons might put the orchestra out of business altogether. So the project was abandoned, the elaborate scenery and costumes permitted to decay into dust, and the orchestra never again undertook such a venture.

♎ EXITS, FALSE AND REAL

Hardly had the opera experiment got under way, when Arthur Judson announced his resignation as manager of the orchestra, effective the following May. The causes undoubtedly ran deeper than the opera season. After two decades, Judson, too, had had his share of tension and turmoil in Philadelphia. Although he had originally been hired at Stokowski's instigation, he and the conductor were no longer getting along; besides, he had flourishing musical interests to look after elsewhere, including the management of the New York Philharmonic and the Columbia Concerts Corporation, which he headed.

If Judson's announcement made a stir, the news that came on December 6, 1934, created consternation. For on that date, Leopold Stokowski announced that he, too, was resigning from the Philadelphia Orchestra. He gave two reasons: "deep-lying differences" with the board of directors, and the fact that no successor had yet been appointed to Judson, whose resignation plans had been announced on October 8. Such a delay, he insisted, made it impossible for him to plan ahead for the following season.

It seemed evident to most observers that what Stokowski was really seeking was the power to hand-pick a successor to Judson, and that the board was resisting this. For a time speculation centered about Miss Esther Everett Lape, a New Yorker whom Bok had brought to Philadelphia as an assistant in his philanthropic and administrative work. The general feeling was that if Miss Lape was chief administrator, real control of the orchestra would be exercised by Stokowski and Bok. This the rest of the board was unwilling to tolerate, and Miss Lape dropped out of the picture.

Stokowski also seized the opportunity to unfold his grievances against the board in an eight-page letter. He wanted, he made it clear, to extend the orchestra's broadcasting and recording, both to bring in more money and expand its audiences. He proposed widespread touring, including a trip to the Soviet Union. He insisted on full control himself of any future operatic activities, though he indicated these should be reduced. He himself would continue conducting only half a season, he said, but he wanted to engage guest conductors like Bruno Walter and Wilhelm Furtwängler, rather than the men "of less experience and less established fame" (unnamed) who had been chosen by the board. While he favored lower ticket prices and the throwing open of empty seats in the Academy to students and others, the board, he charged, was interested only in running the concerts as social functions for the wealthy. In fact, he concluded, the only solution was to oust the present directors as too elderly and too conservative and "to elect in the near future a new board which can carry on this season and begin to plan for next season."

The reaction was immediate and overwhelming. When Stokowski made his first appearance at the Academy after his resignation announcement, bedlam broke loose. The men of the orchestra rose in tribute and remained standing. The audience of Main Line ladies cast its usual Friday decorum aside and applauded until their "bonnets conductor had to signal three times before the program could start, shook with enthusiasm," to quote one newspaper report. The smiling and the ovation was repeated at the end. Said Stokowski in a curtain speech: "I'm hoping that some day we'll find a way to continue. But it looks impossible to me now."

But the tumult had hardly begun. A mass meeting of 200 orchestra subscribers in the Bellevue Stratford Hotel, down Broad Street from the Academy, demanded that Stokowski be kept. The women's committees adopted a resolution that backed the board of directors, but also strongly urged that Stokowski remain. Mrs. Mary Louise Curtis Bok, widow of Edward Bok and mother of board president Curtis Bok, and herself a member of the board, declared: "For Philadelphia to lose Stokowski is unthinkable." Perhaps the most fervent expression of all came at a youth concert on December 15, when Stokowski's most ardent supporters packed the hall 3500 strong. Eugene List, a sixteen-year-old Philadelphia boy, was soloist, playing the Shostakovich Piano Concerto No. 1. But the big excitement, of course, was Stokowski. The crowd of boys and girls unanimously adopted a resolution demanding that the board resign and the conductor remain. As they entered, each was handed a mimeographed song sheet. Then, while Saul Caston conducted, they sang, to the tune of the Pilgrim's Chorus from *Tannhäuser,* a poem ending:

> "Too long we've followed customs old,
> Youth shall be free from the shackles' mold.
> To music's call the earth shall rise,
> And youth shall lead 'neath peaceful skies."

While all this was going on, Stokowski, with admirable detachment, was busy preparing his scheduled Christmas time performances of nothing less than Bach's B minor Mass. The board of directors, for its part, continued in a state of turmoil. Curtis Bok demanded that it resign, leaving him, as president, free to select a new board which would be sympathetic to Stokowski. "By sympathetic," he explained pointedly, "I mean more than acquiescent. I mean an inner understanding and awareness of what he is trying to do." The board refused, whereupon Bok and his mother resigned from it. Defensively, the board put out a statement saying that it had felt "for some time past" the necessity for "a thorough reorganization in the operating methods of the orchestra, and the scope, functions and personnel of the board itself." Toward this end, the statement went on, a committee had been appointed to meet with Stokowski in order to settle their differences.

Once the meetings got underway, it became quickly obvious that the board was now ready to give Stokowski virtually everything he wanted. The board itself, which had consisted of twenty-four members, was reduced to fifteen, with only seven of the previous group remaining. The new president was Dr. Thomas S. Gates, president of the University of Pennsylvania, with Samuel R. Rosenbaum, an attorney, as vice-president. Mrs. Bok was included in the new board, as was Harl McDonald, head of Penn's music department, and a warm admirer of Stokowski. The new board's membership was also to include an elected delegate of the musicians themselves, and a representative of the youth concert audiences. Stokowski, who sat in on the first meeting of the new board, promised to give it "everything I have." It was also announced that the problem of Judson's successor had been settled by the designation of Reginald Allen as manager. Allen, a member of a prominent Philadelphia family who later became an administrator at the Metropolitan Opera, was a thirty-year-old protégé of Stokowski, who had made the conductor's acquaintance while working as an advertising executive for Victor Records in Camden.

When the orchestra's subscribers, numbering 3500, approved these arrangements at a meeting, it was like the ratification of a peace treaty, with Stokowski the victor. And yet there were ominous aspects to be noted. Stokowski's appearances in the coming 1935–'36 season would be limited to three months in the fall and a brief return in the spring. A long list of guest conductors was named, including Sir Thomas Beecham, Bernardino Molinari, José Iturbi, Eugene Ormandy, Hans Kindler, Fritz Reiner, Alexander Smallens, Vladimir Golschmann and Werner Janssen. In a procession like this, Stokowski himself would be hardly more than another guest conductor, leaving the question of his permanent status with the orchestra up in the air. It seemed symbolic that he ended his final concert of the season with selections from Wagner's *Götterdämmerung*.

§ COAST-TO-COAST FAREWELL

On January 2, 1936 Stokowski announced his final and, as it turned out, irrevocable decision: he would no longer be musical director of the Philadelphia Orchestra. It was ironical that he made the move after the board had yielded to his demands, but after twenty-three years he had had enough. He could have retained his title; indeed, the board offered him a three-year contract as director, which he declined. He had interests in Hollywood (among them Greta Garbo), he had researches to pursue, he had a headful of travel plans. Besides, departures were in the air; Toscanini, his great rival in New York, was about to leave the Philharmonic. Stokowski didn't want to give up conducting in Philadelphia altogether, and in fact the arrangement he made with the directors enabled him pretty much to have his orchestra and leave it, too. Henceforth he would be officially designated co-conductor of the orchestra, directing it for twenty concerts (only six fewer than in the season just past). The new conductor in Philadelphia, on the podium for approximately two-thirds of the season, was to be Eugene Ormandy of Minneapolis, with a three-year-contract.

This time there was no great public outcry, as in 1934. The musical public was emotionally spent. Besides, it was clear to everybody that Stokowski himself, rather than the board, had determined on the change; it was also self-evident that the break was not to be complete. Moreover, after such a long and tumultuous epoch, perhaps a change would have its benefits. Twenty-three years, after all, is a long time for one job, one home, even one love; and in point of fact, both Stokowski and the orchestra were to go their separate ways to further triumphs. All was graciousness as the era drew to an end. Said Stokowski in his valedictory at his last seasonal concert at the Academy: "I feel so warmly to this audience because so many of you are my personal friends. I thank you for your kindness to me, and hope you will forgive every one of my shortcomings, just as I forgive you for every time you coughed."

Before leaving the orchestra he had practically created, Stokowski realized one of his fondest dreams by taking it on its first transcontinental tour. For years he had been trying to arrange such an expedition, and now RCA Victor decided to sponsor it. Over a thirty-five-day period the orchestra gave thirty-three concerts in twenty-seven cities from Boston to San Francisco, Minneapolis to Atlanta. Stokowski, who traveled with his own masseur and valet, did most of the conducting, being spelled occasionally by Saul Caston and Charles O'Connell, who went along as assistant conductors. A crowd of 1000 led by Mayor S. Davis Wilson gathered at the Broad Street Station to see the special ten-car train off. By secret ballot of the musicians it had been decided to leave wives at home, so the only women on the trip were three members of the orchestra, harpists Edna Phillips and Marjorie Tyre, and cellist Elsa Hilger. Miss Phillips had married Samuel Rosenbaum of the board of directors, and to cheer up the orchestra "widows" who had been left behind, he threw a gala party for them.

The tour was triumphant from start (Hartford, Conn.) to finish (New York City). Tremendous crowds poured out to see and hear the celebrated orchestra and its controversial, blond-maned conductor. Programs had been selected from newspaper polls conducted in the various tour cities, with the composers most frequently played being Bach, Wagner, Sibelius and Brahms. More than 12,000 attended a concert at Madison Square Garden in New York. In Holdredge, Neb., the smallest town on the tour, a packed house sat through the program even though the auditorium roof sprang a leak and rain poured in on the audience. In Toronto, when Stokowski leaped to the podium the crowd leaped to its feet with him, expecting *God Save the King*. Instead they got Brahms' First; Stokowski was saving the anthem for the end. New Orleans was favored with one of the conductor's stern lectures on the need for audiences to remain in their seats quietly. In Hollywood, Stokowski was greeted effusively by many old friends including Bing Crosby, and the movie colony turned the orchestra's concerts into a noisy celebrity parade that tied up traffic. In Ann Arbor, Mich., Stokowski repaired to a collegiate tavern after the concert and led 150 beer-happy University of Michigan students in an impromptu campus songfest.

When the orchestra pulled into Broad Street, they found a large delegation, led by their wives, out to meet them. A great civic dinner was held in their honor, with speeches by all. When it came Stokowski's turn he stood up and recounted some of the triumphs tasted by the orchestra on its expedition. Then he said: "We must make more tours. Philadelphia must share its orchestra with the whole world." Certainly he had devoted his musical life to doing just that.

♭ THE STOKOWSKI STAMP

Leopold Stokowski's conductorial career, far from ending with his tenure at the Philadelphia Orchestra, had not even reached its halfway point. Outliving all of his great contemporaries, including Toscanini, Koussevitzky, Beecham, Walter, Monteux and Furtwängler, he went on to conduct the All-American Youth Orchestra, the NBC Symphony, the Hollywood Bowl Symphony, the New York Philharmonic, the New York City Center Symphony, the Houston Symphony, and the American Symphony Orchestra, a group of young people organized for him in 1962. His association with the Philadelphia Orchestra never died completely; although it underwent one nineteen-year period of suspended animation, Stokowski outlasted even that and returned in triumph. As the last survivor of the greatest generation of conductors the musical world had so far known, he could say, like Job's servant: "And I only am escaped alone to tell thee." If anyone in those hectic Philadelphia years had foretold that some day Leopold Stokowski would become an elder statesman of music he would have been set down as a fool or a visionary; yet that is what happened. But he became a statesman strictly in the Stokowski mold, for though he lived to see most of his predictions about broadcasting, recording and the application of electronics to music come true, he never lost his zest for experimentation or exploration. Even in old age he remained an apostle of young performers and new composers, and to see him conduct a concert in 1969, his posture erect, his gestures firm, his beat precise and his head encircled by white, was every bit as magnetic an experience as it had been forty years earlier, when the halo of hair was golden.

And yet so indelible was the Stokowski stamp that he and the Philadelphia Orchestra were inextricably linked together in the public mind for years to come. That there were hard feelings afterwards is undeniable; according to one persistent story, Stokowski for many years had the habit of drawing the blinds in his railway compartment whenever he was on a train passing through Philadelphia. Moreover, for all his later exploits, he never really achieved the triumphant identity of man and organization, the sense of being musically at home, that had been his in Philadelphia, and his return there in later years was always an exciting experience for him and an emotional one for his audience.

Perhaps the highest accolade that can be given to Stokowski during his Philadelphia years is that no one really liked him, except the public. The musicians respected him, the board of directors feared him, the critics were intimidated by him. But the audience really adored him, and it was this ability to communicate with and stimulate his listeners that gave him his unique place. Singlehandedly, he turned Philadelphia into a place of cultural ferment and adventure, especially for the young. Wrote Samuel Grafton, the newspaper columnist who had been raised in Philadelphia, years later: "The stone steps [at the Academy] were our Boulevard Raspail and Café Dome for one night a week." Few symphonic conductors anywhere have ever made concert-going the exciting, exhilarating experience that Stokowski did for twenty years in Philadelphia.

Some critics argued that Stokowski achieved his effects by tampering with music. Even back in his Cincinnati days he had been castigated in the Cleveland *Leader* as a conductor "who made Beethoven dance on his ear; who made Brahms a puling, sickly sentimentalist; who calcined Strauss in more clashing and fighting colors than Strauss ever knew; and who Stokowski-ized each composer whom he took into his dictatorial hands." Stokowski's Bach transcriptions were particularly irksome to some of the critics; he was accused of blowing the music up out of all proportion, of exaggerating its contours and over-emphasizing its cadences, of coloring it Stokowski rather than Bach. Oscar Thompson, the critic of the New York *Sun*, once said that Stokowski achieved his excitement by tinkering with the score, while

Arturo Toscanini achieved equal impact by playing the music straight. Yet not everybody agreed. Said a veteran violinist of the orchestra in 1968, recalling his years under Stokowski and Toscanini's guest appearances: "Orchestral men are always very conscious of how music sounds as they play it. Stokowski always used the utmost freedom in his phrasing of Bach and Wagner, and yet we could always follow him, and what he did worked. It took the kind of imagination Stokie had, to picture the mood and intensity of a thing and then make the orchestra sound the way it was in his mind. When we played Siegfried's Funeral March from *Götterdämmerung* with him it was like nothing else in this world. But I remember when Toscanini came down and did Wagner, he wanted everything exact, just as it was written down. There was almost a feeling of revolt in the orchestra: how could we play music in that schoolboy way, note by note, one at a time, instead of in an imaginative, creative way?"

Perhaps the best argument in favor of Stokowski's style of conducting is that it has never gone out of fashion. He was the greatest exponent of the sound spectacular who had ever conducted a symphony orchestra up to then; if anything, he was somewhat ahead of his time, because the era of stereo recording and artificial sound enhancement did not arrive until after his Philadelphia days. But the public was ready and waiting for his thundering Tchaikovsky, his rolling Rachmaninoff, his vivid Stravinsky, his ecstatic Wagner, his full-bodied Beethoven and Brahms, and Stokowski delivered them all in rich measure. True, his Haydn and Mozart were no models of eighteenth-century authenticity, but who is to say that even those two composers might not have reveled in the sheer sound of the Philadelphia Orchestra playing the *Surprise* and *Jupiter* Symphonies?

No one in his right mind would deny that Stokowski was guilty of excesses, that many of his experiments were failures, and that he emphasized one side of music, the purely sonic, at the expense of others. Just as there were musicians in the orchestra who admired the broad sweep of his conceptions and the unrivalled brilliance of his tone-painting, there were others who felt a sense of incompleteness. To quote another old-time violinist who played under him for years: "He always had a tremendous sensuous feeling for sound. He knew how to exaggerate this and be effective. But it was at a terrible musical sacrifice. Because not all music is sex."

Sex may be too strong a word for the quality which Stokowski sought for in music, but romanticism certainly is not. And he found it in Bach no less than in Tchaikovsky and Stravinsky. He approached orchestral music much as Franz Liszt must have approached piano music: as a virtuoso who knew how to draw the utmost expressivity from his instrument, and to make the greatest possible effect upon his hearers. He was a supreme showman, yes, but a charlatan, never; he never gave an unprepared concert or a dull one; he was absolutely devoted to music as a living, changing art throughout his long life. And in the Philadelphia Orchestra, so we must believe, he created his enduring monument.

♩ A TALK WITH STOKOWSKI

(Transcript of a conversation between Leopold Stokowski and the author in New York City, June, 1968).

H.K. Do you remember what the Philadelphia Orchestra was like when you took it over in 1912?

L.S. Yes, I remember. When I went and started to rehearse in Philadelphia I noticed that all the men were talking German. I was told: "Our first conductor, Scheel, was a German, then we had Pohlig, another German, so we always rehearse in the German language." I speak German, so at first we rehearsed in German. It was ridiculous to be doing that in Philadelphia, but that was the custom there at that time.

H.K. How about the quality of the playing?

L.S. I began to notice that the orchestra was extremely stiff in rhythm. The tone was very hard. The manner of playing was very mechanical. But I noticed there were three great players. One was the first horn, Anton Horner. Another was the third horn, Otto Henneberg. The other was the extraordinary timpanist, Oscar Schwar. These were the three good players, the rest not. Another difficulty was we were not permitted to rehearse in the Academy of Music where we gave the concerts. We had to rehearse in a comparatively small room with a low ceiling, so that the sound of the orchestra was like thunder. It really hurt my ears. But those were the conditions under which we had to work.

H.K. And you changed that as you—

L.S. No, we did not. We had great difficulty. This went on a long time, and I was complaining all the time and trying to explain to everyone we could not make the balance of the instruments in good proportion to each other unless we rehearsed exactly where we gave the concerts. One evening a gentleman came to me behind the scenes and said: "I have been told you are having great difficulties here. I've read about it in the press. What is the trouble?" I explained to him what it was. He said: "You are quite right; you should rehearse under good conditions in the same hall, and I will help you." His name was Edward Bok, and he managed to persuade them to let us use the hall for rehearsals. From that time on the performances were a little better, but still we had too many poor players in the orchestra. I began to look around immediately to find a good flute, a good oboe, a good clarinet, a good trumpet, and so forth, to have leaders of sections. Gradually we found great players as leaders, and then we filled in back of them with good players. It was difficult because we could not put out the previous players because they would be without employ-ment; they would starve. It was a very difficult situation; it took a long time.

H.K. Did you conduct with a baton at that time or had you stopped using it already?

L.S. No, I conducted with a baton, with a baguette, as most con-ductors do, until in the middle of one concert I made a strong motion to the brass players and the stick broke in half. I suddenly felt freer. Instead of one stick I had ten fingers and two hands to conduct with. From that time I never conducted again with a piece of wood. But most conductors still use the baton, and it is their right to do what is best for them. They prefer the baguette. I prefer not the baguette.

H.K. Would you remember when that happened?

L.S. Oh, I don't remember, no. Time is very valuable in our lives, extremely valuable. We cannot replace time if we lose it. I'm very narrow-minded: I live entirely in the present and the future, not in the past.

H.K. I'm wondering if you have any recollections of the city of Philadelphia as you found it?

L.S. I do. When I first came to Philadelphia I was amazed to see how dirty it was. The streets were dirty, the houses had not been painted for half a century, and it was unbelievably careless. Today, it's hard to believe it's that same city, because in the last few years particularly the improvement in Philadelphia is extraordinary. I don't know who it was, but somebody had wonderful ideas. They planted more trees. All the houses are painted now. The streets are being made wider. And many beautiful eighteenth century houses in various parts of the city have been renovated—renovated, not changed. The outside is just as it was in the eighteenth century. The insides are probably modernized, but the outsides are just as beautiful as when they were first designed.

H.K. What kind of an audience did you find in Philadelphia, and how did it change over the years? Or did it change?

L.S. Oh, it changed very much—enormously. At first it was nosiy, and came late to the concerts. If there was at the end of the concert a crescendo leading up to the final chords the audience seemed to feel that crescendo, and they all stood up and rushed out before the orchestra had finished. This was particularly true at the Friday afternoon concerts because, it was explained to me, there was a certain train the ladies wanted to make on the Main Line. In those days the Main Line was almost a sacred part of the universe. Not only that, but the ladies would come to the concerts with big bundles of shopping which they would put on the edge of the stage where the footlights are. All along the stage were those packages. And when it became time to catch that sacred train on the Main Line they came up and took their packages. Sometimes they dropped them a little bit, which added to the sound of the orchestra, of course. I used to talk to them about leaving early and making noise, and soon we had two groups in the audience, those who liked what I said and those who didn't, and there were discussions between them on the subject. But very gradually the audience began to be more concentrated in listening and finally it became, and still is, an extraordinary audience, truly loving music, never making any sounds to disturb anyone else, and concentrating on their reaction to the message that is in all great music.

H.K. How did the audience respond to the repertory you presented?

L.S. They didn't like it at all. They hissed and I used to say to them: "Thank you for hissing. I am happy that you are reacting to the music. As we are in a free country I think it is wonderful that you express yourself either in favor or disfavor of the music." The reason they hissed was that we played very much twentieth century music and they only wanted to hear the great masters. Well, we all love Bach, Mozart, Beethoven, Brahms, of course, but not only them. We like to hear the music of our day, and our country. Of course, some things they did like. I remember when we played Ravel's *Bolero* for the first time on a Friday afternoon. The audience was very enthusiastic and after the concert I was walking home along Locust Street. I saw a very old lady whom I knew slightly being helped into her limousine. She had a stick in each hand, and on one side of her was the chauffeur and the other the butler. She had been to the concert and when she saw me she said: "Oh, Maestro, please do play again that divine *Bordello!*" Now the question is, how did she know a word like "bordello"? I didn't even know it myself at that time.

H.K. What reaction did your repertory have on the board of directors?

L.S. They especially did not like it. Some of the gentlemen were very frank in their discussions with me, and that was why I finally left Philadelphia—because I saw that certain persons had the power to try to stop progress—or not so much progress as the evolution of music. Everything in the universe is evolving all the time, and that includes music. These gentlemen did not wish that. There was a wonderful man who was the president of the orchestra association. His name was Van Rensselaer, a wonderful person. He and I were great friends. One day he came to me and said: "We had a board of directors meeting yesterday, and they have asked me to say that they *instruct* you not to play this modern music." I didn't like that word "instruct." I had at that time a long contract with the Philadelphia Orchestra. I completed it, but when they asked me to renew it I was not willing, because I did not wish to be "instructed" not to play the music of our time and our nation.

H.K. What is your opinion of symphonic boards of directors in general? Would you describe your experience in Philadelphia as unusual or is this the customary attitude of boards of directors?

L.S. No, it is not unusual. It is part of the quality of life today all over the United States, which is that there is a certain percentage of persons in every city, even in every little town and village, which is interested in music and in everything that is of the mind and the spirit—and there are also those who are not interested. Some of the great cities like Philadelphia, New York, Boston, Cleveland, Chicago, Los Angeles, Minneapolis, Detroit, San Francisco, etc., have developed symphonic orchestras—orchestras of the first class which compare with any orchestra in Europe or anywhere else in the world. Every concert that is given by a great orchestra costs more than do receipts for tickets, so that for every orchestra in the United States, every concert is performed at a loss. The result is at the end of the season a deficit, and the question is who will pay it, so there can be a next season. That problem exists everywhere, all over the United States. And it is met by rich men, usually bankers, and men at the head of great—how to say?—productive firms. . . .

H.K. Industrialists?

L.S. Industrialists. Rich men. They make up the deficit and then —it's perfectly natural—they say: "We pay the deficit, we pay the money, and we like to make the decisions." So they make the decisions. But they make the decisions about something—orchestral music —concerning which they do not know very much. They know very little. So sometimes they do not make very good decisions, in my opinion. But perhaps I am wrong and they are right. Perhaps they know more about orchestral music than I do. I hope they do.

H.K. Could you recall for me your experiences with Rachmaninoff, who was so closely associated with the Philadelphia Orchestra?

L.S. We engaged all the great players, all the great soloists of that time—violinists, cellists, pianists, singers. Among these as you rightly say was one of the greatest, Rachmaninoff. Whenever he had finished composing a score he would send it to me and I would study it and begin to rehearse it. When we had rehearsed it enough we would invite him to come to Philadelphia from New York, where he lived, to listen, and, if it was a piano concerto, to play it with us. He was a very great composer and pianist, and a very great person, too. But unfortunately when he finished composing he would give it to the printer and then send us the printed parts. When he came to the rehearsal he would wish to change many things because it didn't sound the way he wanted it to sound, and we would make those changes. He did this with the *Rhapsody on a Theme of Paganini*, for example. Those changes were written down in my score, and penciled into the parts. But what saddens me is that anyone now who receives a printed score of Rachmaninoff's music receives it as it was first conceived and not with all the important changes he later made.

H.K. If I can go further back to the early days, how did you change over from the organ to the podium?

L.S. Now, the organ was only a part of my life. As a child, when I was seven years old, my grandfather—his name was Leopold Stokowski, I'm named after him—my grandfather, who was very kind to me, took me to a club—I don't remember the wording of that time—but it was a place where there were many men. And they were speaking Polish and Russian and German . . .

H.K. In London, this was?

L.S. Yes, because I was born in London. My grandfather had to bring the family from a place near Lublin, right on the border between Poland and Russia. Outside of Lublin is an agricultural center called Stokki, and that's where my family lived. But the Czarist secret police would bring in Russian farmers during the night, drive out the Polish farmers, and tell the Russians: "That's your farm." My grandfather lost one farm after another, so he left. He brought the family first to Vienna, then to Paris, and then to London. And I was born there. But to come back to that club. We used to go to the club and they used to sing. They sang the folksongs of their country, and they sang them fortissimo, with tremendous energy and enthusiasm, remembering the country they came from. But sometimes they would sing soft songs and I would see tears coming down in their beards. One night a man walked in with a little something in his hand and began to make wonderful music from the little something, which I learned afterwards was a violin. So I said to my grandfather, "I want a violin." And he finally bought me a quarter-sized one, and I began to play it. We found a teacher and I began to play better, until gradually my hands grew larger and I had a larger violin. After a time I taught myself to play the piano because I wanted to play the music of Bach on the piano, which I did. I used to play soccer and football with another boy whose father was a priest, and I used to go to the church and hear the organ being played in there. I asked his father to let me play the organ and he did, though my legs were too short to reach the low C and the high F of the pedals. But gradually I grew taller and then I could play the organ more. That's how I began to play the organ. I love the organ, of course, it's a glorious instrument, but my favorite instrument was then, and always will be, the violin.

H.K. What made you decide to try your hand at conducting?

L.S. I always wanted to conduct, because with the symphonies of Beethoven and Mozart and all the other great music for orchestra—such extraordinary music—I just always wanted to conduct it. I played it first on the violin, then the piano, then the organ, and finally I had the opportunity to go to Cincinnati to conduct, with the orchestra there, and then to Philadelphia.

H.K. There is a saying of the English music critic Ernest Newman that there are no such things as great orchestras, only great conductors. Do you have any comment on that?

L.S. It's utterly ridiculous. The real truth is that a great orchestra conducted by a poor conductor will give a poor performance. The players will be irritated by a conductor who is obviously not good and after a time they will begin to do bad things. I have heard them purposely play wrong notes just to see whether he would notice. But in the reverse case, a great conductor with a poor orchestra, the performance will again be bad because the conductor will ask for things which the players are not capable of doing. They will become irritated with him, he will become irritated with them, and the performance will be very bad. There is only one way: good conductor, and good players.

CHAPTER IV

The Ormandy Era

"Gene, there's a vacancy in Philadelphia, but it could be suicide for you."

—Arthur Judson to Eugene Ormandy, October, 1931

♪ MOVIE MAESTRO

Eugene Ormandy once told an interviewer that he "was born in New York City at the age of twenty-two." It was his way of indicating that his life had a slightly unreal, almost fantasy-like quality about it —the kind of life that could lead a near-starving young fiddler from Hungary to the directorship of one of the world's great orchestras. Vernon (Lefty) Gomez, master practitioner of another art, sagely observed on the eve of a World Series game that he would "rather be lucky than good," and Ormandy, by nature a modest man, always was the first to acknowledge that fortune, as well as talent, had played a considerable role in his musical advancement.

However, far from smiling on him from the start, it played him a couple of nasty tricks in his early years. Ormandy was born in Budapest on November 18, 1899, almost one year to the day before his orchestra-to-be was born in Philadelphia. His father, Benjamin Blau, was a dentist by profession and a violinist by inclination, and he wanted his first-born son to be a violinist, too. He even named him Jenö in honor of Jenö Hubay, the greatest Hungarian violinist of the day. Little Jenö, or Eugene, to use the English equivalent he later adopted along with the name Ormandy after he came to America, proved to be a fantastically apt pupil. He had perfect pitch, an acute sense of timing, a general musical precocity, and he handled his instrument with ease. He was playing a tiny fiddle at the age of four, and at five-and-a-half he was accepted in the Royal State Academy of Music as an authentic *Wunderkind* in the making. Hubay himself taught there, and accepted his namesake at the age of nine-and-a-half as his own pupil. Ormandy became the youngest graduate in the history of the Royal Academy, receiving his diploma before he was fourteen. At seventeen he was teaching at the Academy as well as taking courses at the University of Budapest from which he ultimately received a degree in philosophy. In 1917 he made a short tour of Germany and Hungary with the Blüthner Orchestra, both as concertmaster and soloist, and in 1920 he toured Austria and France. A promising violin career seemed in the making.

But America was the place a star violinist could really earn money, as such European youngsters as Jascha Heifetz and Toscha Seidl were then demonstrating. So Ormandy listened attentively to a deal proposed to him by two budding concert agents, one a liquor salesman, the other a dentist, who came backstage after he had given a successful recital in Vienna in 1920. They "offered" him a tour of 300 concerts in the United States at a total fee of $30,000. The promoters proved to be as inexperienced as their star; the closest Ormandy came to giving a recital in the United States was to play two concerts aboard ship for the benefit of widows of lost seamen, accompanied by another passenger, a French pianist. Even this took some arranging, as she was traveling first class and he second. Lacking Heifetz' European reputation, Ormandy discovered when he arrived in the United States that no one wanted to hear an unknown lad from Hungary no matter *how* good he was. The best offer he and his associates received was three Carnegie Hall concerts provided they put up $4500 to cover the costs.

None of them had the money, so that particular dream died, and performer and promoters went their separate ways.

So in December, 1921 Eugene Ormandy found himself in cold, bleak New York City with a Balestrieri fiddle, several suits of clothes, and no means of support. He heard of a vacancy in the violin section in the pit orchestra of the Capitol Theater, a movie palace at Broadway and 51st Street then run by the celebrated "Roxy," S. L. Rothafel. The Capitol, which was torn down in 1969, maintained an eighty-five piece orchestra which played light classics and occasional symphonic pieces as well as accompanying silent films. Its conductors were Erno Rapee and David Mendoza, both excellent musicians. Playing at the last desk of the second violins in a movie house orchestra—even though it possibly was the best of its kind in the country—was a long way from occupying the center stage at Carnegie Hall, but it possessed one incontestable advantage: it paid a salary. Ormandy's starting pay at the Capitol was $60 a week, and he figured that in a year or two he might have enough money saved up to launch a solo career after all. It became rapidly apparent that Ormandy was a violinist of superior quality, for within a week he was advanced to the position of concertmaster, with an increase in pay. He held the job for two and a half years, playing four shows a day and seven days a week, with only an occasional day off. Traditionally, the concertmaster should have the capacity of replacing the conductor in an emergency, but Ormandy says he had no thought of making a career on the podium. With an almost instinctive musical memory, however, he soon learned by heart not only his parts but a good many of his colleagues'.

One day in September, 1924 Ormandy arrived at the theater at 1:45 p.m. for the 2 o'clock show and was told that the scheduled conductor for the afternoon had fallen ill. The doorman delivered the message: "Roxy says you have to conduct." Ormandy was shaken at first, but he had had conductorial work at the Academy in Budapest, and he knew by memory the music for the day, three movements of a capsule version of Tchaikovsky's Fourth Symphony. Besides, with only fifteen minutes he had little time to be frightened; he got into a cutaway coat, walked the unfamiliar path to the podium, and directed the performance without missing a cue or an entrance. In

1926 Rapee left to go to Rothafel's new theater, the Roxy, and Ormandy was made full-time associate director of the orchestra. For his own edification, he also began sitting in on rehearsals of the New York Philharmonic, where Toscanini was just coming in, first as guest, then as regular conductor, beginning a career-long admiration for the Italian maestro's style and musical approach.

By now word was beginning to spread in musical circles about the diminutive young movie maestro with the reddish-blond hair who could conduct almost anything in an efficient, musicianly way. He was engaged to direct a group of musicians from the Philharmonic at Carnegie Hall for a dance recital by Isadora Duncan's adopted daughter, Anna. Arthur Judson, who was in the audience, said later: "I came to see a dancer and instead I heard a conductor." He offered to take Ormandy under his managerial wing, and the conductor promptly resigned from the Capitol.

Judson at that time was developing a substantial musical empire in radio broadcasting, which was then coming into full flower as the prime home entertainment medium. With his movie background, his sharp sense of timing, his musical adaptability and his willingness to provide what was wanted, Ormandy, then in his late twenties, quickly became the conductorial stalwart of what was called the Judson Radio Corporation. The future music director of the Philadelphia Orchestra was kept busy conducting the Dutch Masters Hour, the Jack Frost Melody Moments, the McKesson-Robbins and Endicott Johnson programs, and similar broadcast specialties. Then as now there was money in broadcasting, and after a time Ormandy was earning $500 a week for his radio stints, more than he got when he made his first moves into symphonic conducting.

Judson also put Ormandy out on the summer concert circuit. In 1929 he conducted the Philharmonic-Symphony at Lewisohn Stadium in New York, and in 1930 he traveled to Robin Hood Dell in Fairmount Park, there to conduct the Philadelphia Orchestra for the first time. He was engaged for three concerts at the Dell and received so favorably that the following summer he was invited back for a set of seven.

As already noted, Ormandy's summer successes at the Dell led to his being asked to substitute during the regular fall season for Arturo Toscanini when neuritis prevented the latter from filling a two-week guest conducting engagement at the Academy of Music. It was Judson who selected Ormandy, but he was anything but a first choice.

What gave Ormandy the job, simply, was that no one else would take it. Few established conductors wanted to undergo the comparisons that would inevitably befall anyone who was simultaneously replacing Toscanini and following Stokowski. "I couldn't find another conductor," recalled Judson years afterwards. "All of a sudden, everybody was busy that week." Finally, according to Judson, because there was no one left he offered it to Ormandy with the warning it might mean "suicide." "He told me," says Ormandy, "that frankly he wouldn't blame me for turning it down, too. But I took it. I had everything to gain and nothing to lose."

In later years Ormandy remembered that when he walked out onto the stage of the Academy there was a murmur of surprise from the Friday afternoon audience, many of whom hadn't seen the newspapers or consulted their programs and were looking for Toscanini to emerge when the young stranger walked out from the wings. Ormandy was then thirty-one years old, but he looked younger, with his slight stature and his shock of reddish blond hair. The concert went well—so well that at the intermission Judson came backstage and invited Ormandy to substitute again for Toscanini in the second week of the guest-conducting engagement—a matter which had deliberately been left open pending the outcome of Ormandy's first concert. The programs for the second week included Beethoven's Symphony No. 7 in A, the Nocturne and Scherzo from Mendelssohn's *Midsummer Night's Dream,* Debussy's *Afternoon of a Faun,* and Stravinsky's *Firebird* Suite. Furthermore, Ormandy was forthwith invited to conduct the orchestra at a "Philadelphia Forum" program, part of a special series run by the Philadelphia *Inquirer.* Here he played Tchaikovsky's Symphony No. 4 in F minor, Rimsky-Korsakov's *Capriccio Espagnole,* and again the *Firebird.*

The response of the local newspaper critics to Ormandy was overwhelming. The *Inquirer* found "vigor, incisiveness and dramatic quality" in his work and praised his "verve and exuberance." The

Bulletin noted approvingly that he dispatched his task in an "unhurried, self-effacing manner." The *Record* sported a headline that raised the interesting question: "Will Phila. Jilt Stokowski for Ormandy?" and noted that the Ormandy concerts had been the first sell-outs of the year.

Even more important to Ormandy's immediate future than the critics was the presence in the audience during his second week of concerts of a Minneapolis lawyer named Willis I. Norton, who happened to be in Philadelphia on business. The conductor of the Minneapolis Symphony Orchestra, Henri Verbrugghen, had suffered a stroke which incapacitated him; the orchestra needed a new conductor desperately. Ormandy's success in Philadelphia had made national news, and the Minneapolis manager, Mrs. Carlyle Scott, asked Norton to attend one of the concerts. He phoned her while the concluding ovation was still in progress and told her: "You couldn't do better." Arrangements were quickly made with Ormandy (and Judson) and after his final Philadelphia concert, the conductor, still wearing his full-dress suit and white tie, boarded a train headed for Minneapolis.

⸮ MIDWESTERN INTERLUDE

When he went west, Ormandy was a far different figure from the forlorn young man who had knocked on Roxy's door barely ten years earlier. He was, for one thing, an American citizen, for he had taken out his first papers almost instantly upon arrival in this country and, in fact, attained naturalization in the minimum time possible, five years plus ninety days. He was, furthermore, married, for in 1922 he had wed a harpist he had met in the Capitol Theater Orchestra, Stephanie Goldner, who later played in the New York Philharmonic. They had two children, a girl and a boy born twelve years apart, both of whom died in infancy because of Rh factor complications. In 1947 the marriage was ended by divorce, and in 1950 Ormandy married Margaret Frances (Gretel) Hitsch, a Viennese who had emigrated to the United States, become a citizen, and during World War II, served with the U.S. Navy. A gracious and charming woman with a good knowledge of music, she became a popular and widely admired personality in Philadelphia.

As a conductor Ormandy at that time wasn't yet world renowned, but he knew his business. And he presented what was then a rather unusual combination of abilities—a musician of European background, tradition and training who had the outlook, flexibility and adaptability of an American organization man. He hadn't learned his trade, as so many of his contemporaries did, in European provincial opera houses; he learned it in American movie theaters and radio studios. He found no difficulty in being a traditionalist and a twentieth century man at the same time.

No long-term commitment had been made over the phone by the Minneapolis authorities; Ormandy traveled west strictly on a look-see basis. But if he felt intimidated by the challenge he didn't show it, and everybody, including the orchestra, was impressed by the direct, businesslike approach of his first two rehearsals. Ormandy arrived and went to work in Minneapolis on a Monday morning; by Wednesday he had a five-year contract in his pocket. The Minneapolis was then, and still is, an excellent orchestra, but Verbrugghen's last years had seen a certain decline, with one program of familiar pieces following another repetitively, so that a certain slackness had crept into rehearsals. According to one story which Ormandy heard in later years, about an hour and a quarter after he had begun work with the orchestra, a Welshman named Cunningham who played bassoon told his fellow musicians during a break: "Well, boys, you can send your armchairs home; you won't need them any more."

The critics asserted that they heard an almost instantaneous improvement in the orchestra's quality. Wrote John K. Sherman of the Minneapolis *Star-Tribune* of Ormandy's first concert: "The tone had come alive, the phrases had grown sharp and purposeful, the climaxes made the blood pound. Overnight the ensemble had acquired a youthful vigor, flexibility and unanimity, with compelling rhythmic impulse." Ormandy also did his best to bring improvements in the orchestra's relations with the community. He appeared at rallies and social functions to help raise money for the orchestra, ridden, as most American cultural institutions were, by Depression deficits. He began a series of "Viennese afternoons," at which Strauss waltzes were featured, to win a wider audience. He took the orchestra on tours of the hinterlands to keep the musicians playing and also to seek new listeners in places that had never heard a symphony orchestra before. He became an important civic, as well as musical figure in the Midwest.

His most important contribution, both to the orchestra's finances and his own reputation, came in the form of recordings. Through a contractual quirk, the Minneapolis Symphony, under Ormandy, became for a few years the most frequently recorded major symphony orchestra in the United States. This state of affairs resulted from an extraordinary contract between the orchestra management and the musicians' union which provided the players with no extra compensation for recording sessions. Instead the men were required, for their stated salaries, to give a certain number of hours per week, which might be spent in rehearsals, concerts, broadcasts, or making records, whichever the management elected. No other orchestra of like stature had such a contract; in fact, the Minneapolis didn't have it very long, for once the union awoke to what was going on, it insisted on negotiating a change.

But RCA Victor, which was beginning to expand its record catalogue after some years of low productivity, took full advantage of its opportunity once it learned of it after Ormandy's arrival. It was Arthur Judson who called the contract loophole to the attention of Victor's recording director, Charles O'Connell. Ormandy, though he, along with the orchestra, was unpaid for his labors, was more than willing to record, with the result that in 1934 Victor's engineers came out to Minneapolis for a solid two weeks, during which the orchestra recorded daily, including Sundays, for six hours a day. This was repeated in the following year, and in those four weeks, more than 100 separate works were recorded. One release, a set of Strauss waltzes, became one of the first 78-r.p.m. classical album best-sellers. O'Connell later calculated that the royalties accruing to the orchestra over the next ten years amounted to $163,362. He also reported that for the second two-week session in Minneapolis the men were given a special compensation of $5000 to share, half of this coming from RCA Victor, and half being contributed by Ormandy from his own pocket.

Although Ormandy received no royalties from the recordings, the returns to him in the form of nationwide exposure and publicity were enormous. To the record executives and orchestral managements he became known as a conductor who could work quickly and co-operatively in the studio; to the public at large "Eugene Ormandy and the Minneapolis Symphony" became a hallmark of high-quality music making. There also was an element of musical adventurousness, for although much of what they recorded was, of course, standard repertory, the Ormandy-Minneapolis-Victor collaboration also produced such phonographic "firsts" as Kodály's *Háry János Suite*, Bruckner's Symphony No. 7 in E, and Schoenberg's *Verklärte Nacht*.

When Radio City Music Hall opened in New York City, Ormandy was offered its musical directorship at a salary considerably higher than he was getting in Minneapolis, but he turned it down; he was determined to remain in symphonic music. During his five years in Minneapolis, he retained a strong lifeline to Philadelphia. Or perhaps it was the other way around, for with the orchestra's relations with Stokowski as strained as they were, the question of a possible successor was on everybody's mind, and Ormandy had come out of nowhere to add his name to the lists. Shortly after his departure for his new job in Minneapolis, it was announced that Ormandy would be one of four guest conductors of the Philadelphia Orchestra the following season, the others being Smallens, Rodzinski and Issay Dobrowen. Ormandy's guest-conducting appearances included one performance in New York, and after his Carnegie Hall concert of December 6, 1932, Olin Downes wrote in the *Times*: "He has a very healthy musical sense, much temperament, and a conductor's flair for effect." Ormandy returned during the 1933–'34 season, this time sharing the guest conductorships with Otto Klemperer and José Iturbi, and in '35–'36 he was one of the parade of conductors who occupied the podium most of the season while

Stokowski's feud with the directors approached its climax. Each time he conducted in Philadelphia he was enthusiastically received both by the critics and the subscription audiences.

Curiously, relations between Ormandy and Stokowski appear to have been unusually amicable during this period. Conductors are a jealous breed, and it's doubtful that any really ever likes to see another succeed. Stokowski may have regarded Ormandy as strictly a junior member of the club, or he may have admired his proficiency with an orchestra—most likely, a combination of both. In any event, he spoke of him in complimentary terms and appeared glad to have him as a guest conductor. According to Sam Rosenbaum, who as vice-president of the board of directors was in a position to know, when the board asked Stokowski, who was finally determined to resign, to propose a successor, he suggested three names: Carlos Chávez, José Iturbi, and Ormandy.

♩ THE PARTITIONED PODIUM

Not only Stokowski recommended Ormandy; he was the choice also of the great majority of the directors and of a number of outsiders who were asked for advice. Among the latter were Sergei Rachmaninoff, Fritz Kreisler, and Stokowski's former wife, Olga Samaroff. All were strongly for Ormandy, with Samaroff especially insistent. Ormandy's success in Minneapolis, his popularity with Philadelphia audiences, the recordings that had made his name familiar across the country—all these convinced the directors that they were getting a man on the way up, just as Stokowski had been more than twenty years ago, though without any of Stokowski's imperious, intractable ways.

For Ormandy himself, the job was a paradox. On the one hand, at the age of thirty-seven he was becoming head man of one of the country's greatest orchestras, having been selected over many other musicians more experienced and renowned. On the other, he was following one of the most spectacular and successful conductors the musical world had ever known, and inheriting an orchestra whose

instrumental technique and sound were generally considered to be
the ultimate. Any diminution in quality was certain to be observed
and criticized, and most authorities awaited it as inevitable. Only
one other conductor faced a comparable undertaking: John Barbirolli,
an Englishman of exactly the same age, who was selected to succeed
Toscanini at the New York Philharmonic in 1937. Barbirolli, though
he later became a major figure, was not yet ready, as it turned out,
to face such a challenge. Ormandy was.

His task was complicated, and the likelihood of comparisons
increased, by the fact that the public announcement of his appointment said he would share the Philadelphia podium as co-conductor
with Stokowski. Ormandy says that this was the way he wanted it;
that he had too high a regard for Stokowski and his achievement
with the orchestra to see the connection severed completely. Besides,
Ormandy was conducting twenty-two weeks of the season, Stokowski
only six. For five years the two conductors alternated on the podium,
although on September 28, 1938 the title of music director was
officially conferred on Ormandy, thus formalizing a status which he
had really, to all intents and purposes, held all along.

In the years of their joint tenure, Stokowski and Ormandy worked
out the question of repertory between them without serious difference—a state of amicability which was achieved largely by
Ormandy's willingness to defer to the wishes of his eminent partner.
On one occasion they even conducted simultaneously, when the
forces of the Philadelphia Orchestra and the Curtis Institute Orchestra
were combined into a 163-piece aggregation in a 1940 benefit for
Chinese war relief.

Some differences did arise between them in the matter of
orchestral seating. Stokowski, who never tired of rearranging the
instrumental choirs, in 1939 came up with a brand-new arrangement for his concerts: brass, woodwinds and percussion in front,
and strings behind. The reason, he explained, was to put the strings
closest of all to the acoustical shell built at the back of the Academy
stage; in this way, he said, the string sound would be reflected
most strongly to the audience out front. Ormandy was not impressed;

when he took his turn a few weeks later he promptly moved the players back where they had been before.

To mark the twenty-fifth anniversary of Stokowski's association with the orchestra, at the concert of November 5, 1937, Dr. Gates, as president of the orchestra association, presented him with a set of eulogistic resolutions adopted by the board. Said Stokowski, to a roar of laughter: "I am happy the board of directors have made some resolutions." Then he felt it fitting to defend himself against allegations that he had been leading a gay life in Hollywood, where he had been reported in the press to have been spending considerable time with Greta Garbo. He told the fascinated audience in the Academy that people in Hollywood were really very industrious and dedicated. "Sometimes," he said, "we work all night—the sun is coming up as we finish. Do you do that in Philadelphia?" Finally, he paid a warm tribute to his co-conductor: "I thank Mr. Ormandy for keeping the orchestra as it is. The delightful friendship between Mr. Ormandy and myself is unusual between conductors."

Keeping the orchestra as it was turned out to be a more difficult job than anticipated. In New York, a new orchestra was being formed by the National Broadcasting Company for the benefit of Arturo Toscanini, who had been induced to end his retirement from conducting. The proposal had been advanced by Reginald Allen, the manager, that the Philadelphia be engaged to act as the NBC symphony, but the broadcasting company had decided on creating a new orchestra. To get players for it, orchestras across the country were raided, with their top men being offered salaries considerably higher than they were getting. The Detroit Symphony was hardest hit, and both Chicago and Cleveland lost important players. Boston at that time was a non-union orchestra, so its personnel was not touched. The New York Philharmonic was also unscathed, presumably because it was Toscanini's old orchestra, and NBC wished to avoid additional bitterness. But Philadelphia, which paid its first-chair men comparatively well, was considered fair game by the NBC head-hunters, and three men were actually signed early in 1938, first horn Arthur Berv, first trombone Charles Gusikoff, and first bass Anton Torello. But the orchestra management reacted swiftly: contracts were produced showing in the fine print that no one could leave the orchestra without filing six months' notice of intent to resign. In the end, only Berv was lost; both Gusikoff and Torello remained in Philadelphia.

But the incident had an unsettling effect for a time, and a year later another Gusikoff (there were four of the family in the orchestra) was discharged. This was first cellist Isadore Gusikoff, and the reason given was a "clash of temperaments" with Ormandy, who charged the cellist had gone on a "silence strike" by merely going through the motions of playing his instrument. Gusikoff had the unusual distinction of being fired during the intermission of a concert on February 7, 1939. He promptly signed up with the NBC Symphony, but the musicians' union insisted that he also be paid his Philadelphia salary of $125 a week to the end of the season. Shortly afterwards two other players resigned, issuing statements comparing Ormandy unfavorably with Stokowski.

Not unnaturally, reports began to circulate of dissension and low morale in the orchestra. It so happened that Stokowski was conducting the orchestra just then, and he promptly leaped into the breach with a stage speech in which he praised Ormandy's work and the condition of the orchestra. Further, he denounced "certain disturbing and destroying influences" which were attempting to impair the orchestra. Even more important, the men of the orchestra rallied around Ormandy, unanimously adopting a resolution "wholeheartedly" supporting him as "a fine musician and conductor." Among the signatories were the last two original players remaining from 1900, trombonists Paul P. Lotz and C. E. Gerhard. Gusikoff, incidentally, was replaced not by one but by two first cellists, for it was announced that first-chair responsibilities would be shared by Benar Heifetz and Samuel Mayes. At twenty-one, Mayes became the youngest first-desk man in the United States. A remarkable musician who was one-quarter Cherokee Indian in descent, he had joined the orchestra's cello section at the age of eighteen. He was to leave the orchestra after a twelve-year stay to become first cellist of the Boston Symphony, and then to return again to the first chair in Philadelphia in 1964. The rest of the 1938–'39 season was relatively placid, its most unusual event being the appearance on the podium March 10 and 11 of Nadia Boulanger, the first woman ever to conduct the Philadelphia Orchestra.

A really major personnel crisis struck the orchestra in 1940. On March 14, it was announced that eight players had been fired jointly by Ormandy and Stokowski "to maintain the high artistic standards of the orchestra." Simultaneously, it was disclosed that ten other players had been given raises for "exceptional ability."

What had happened, obviously, was that the conductors were weeding out players who they felt were no longer as good as they should be. At the time, orchestral musicians were afforded virtually no protection against summary dismissal, severance pay was virtually unknown, and pensions were pitifully small. All these were situations which the American Federation of Musicians subsequently succeeded in rectifying (indeed, conductors now complain that it's impossible to fire *anybody*). But at the time the management insisted that it had the contractual right to proceed as it did.

Most of the eight were players of many years' service who had literally grown old in the orchestra. One of them was none other than Anton Horner, the celebrated and popular horn player who had been in the orchestra practically since its inception. Another was a sixty-seven year old flutist who had thirty years' service. A third was a violinist who had been with the Philadelphia for seventeen years. A fourth was a versatile young musician, Allen Farnham, who played violin, piano and celesta, and who expressed bafflement over his discharge, pointing out that since he played three instruments, the orchestra had been saving money on his one salary.

The purge brought a considerable outcry, especially when it became known that some of the discharged musicians were to get an annual pension of only $400. Even that portion of the press which upheld the orchestra's right to hire and fire was uncomfortable over the way the deed had been done. Ormandy said nothing publicly, but Stokowski, as usual, was ready with a stage speech. "With certain others," he told the Academy audience, "I am responsible for the solution of certain problems for which no ideal solution has ever been found. I hope this situation can be straightened out, and I shall be glad to do what I can about it."

After much deliberation among the directors, a compromise was announced. The ousters of four of the eight would stand, but they would receive "severance allowances" amounting to nine weeks' pay. The other four were reinstated, including Horner the hornist, Farnham the triple-threat violinist, Napoleon Cerminara, a clarinetist, and Matthew J. Mueller, a violinist. All went back to work forthwith, Mueller, for one, playing for another thirteen years until 1953, when he was killed by an automobile at the age of sixty-four in Worcester, Mass., where the orchestra was participating in the annual Worcester Festival.

Each of the four players who did not return was replaced by a younger instrumentalist with the start of the 1940 season. It was also announced that Ormandy had been given a five-year contract as music director and that Stokowski's connection with the orchestra would continue as before. However, in March, 1941, Stokowski took the final step. He disclosed that he would no longer conduct in Philadelphia. World War II was under way in Europe, although the United States was not yet a participant, and Stokowski vaguely ascribed his departure to the war. "I would like to conduct the concerts you have suggested for next season," he wrote to the management, "but in view of the national emergency, which daily is becoming more serious, I feel I should for a period keep myself free and available to serve our country and government."

Actually, the reasons for Stokowski's termination of his joint-conducting arrangement with Ormandy and his complete departure from Philadelphia were a mixture of ancient grudges and new irritations. He had never really forgiven the board for past differences and for spreading what he called "false rumors" about himself. Even his short season of conducting at the Academy represented a responsibility he no longer wanted. More immediately, bitterness arose over recording questions. Since 1940 Stokowski had been conducting and touring with the All-American Youth Orchestra, which he had organized, and now he was recording with it, too. But he recorded for Columbia, and the board of directors felt that this activity was directly competitive with the Philadelphia Orchestra's recording for RCA Victor—especially when the same repertory began to appear on both labels. A good deal of unpleasantness ensued in the discussions of these matters, and Stokowski's termination of his ties to Philadelphia followed. In March of 1941, at the age of fifty-nine, he once again made a farewell appearance with the orchestra at the Academy of Music, conducting a full-scale performance of Bach's *Passion According to St. Matthew*. In view of the devotional nature of the work, the audience was requested not to applaud at the end. So Stokowski took his leave of the orchestra and the audience in a highly uncharacteristic way—total silence. At that, most of the listeners in the hall as well as the musicians on the stage, remembering previous rifts that were healed and departures that were revoked, expected that this time, too, Stokowski would be back before too long. In point of fact, nearly twenty years were to pass before he would once again stand before the Philadelphia Orchestra.

♎ THE SUCCESSOR SUCCEEDS

When Ormandy was formally invested with the title of music director in 1938, the board of directors announced that it was "in recognition of his splendid musical achievements that have made the last three years a succession of triumphs for conductor and orchestra alike." The essential triumph, so far as the board was concerned, had undoubtedly been scored at the box office. Ormandy was an instant success with the audience. His first program, on October 9, 1936, included two Bach transcriptions by bass-clarinetist Lucien Cailliet, Mozart's Violin Concerto No. 4, K. 218, with Fritz Kreisler as soloist, and the great Schubert C Major Symphony. According to the *Public Ledger,* a journal not given to exaggeration, the result was "a wild ovation." "This is the happiest day of my life," Ormandy said when it was over, and no one doubted him.

A week later, about 200 women walked out on William Walton's Symphony No. 1, a totally unfamiliar work which Ormandy had programmed, but this was regarded simply as an upholding of the tradition against new music rather than a reflection on the new conductor. Actually, crowds queued up on Broad and Locust Streets in Ormandy's early days just as they had in Stokowski's; everybody wanted to see the young man who was to follow the old master. Even the all-important New York reviews were favorable; when Ormandy arrived for his first regular Carnegie Hall appearance, playing the Walton symphony, Lawrence Gilman called him "an inseparable part of the American musical scene" in the *Herald Tribune,* and Winthrop Sargeant in the *American* praised him for his "youthful and energetic" music-making.

With Ormandy and Stokowski both leading the orchestra, no great need for guest conductors was felt that first year; however, Paul Whiteman and his band were invited to join the Philadelphians for several jazz-flavored joint concerts. At the end of the season, the orchestra embarked on a repetition of the previous year's coast-to-coast tour, though this time without Stokowski. Ormandy and José Iturbi did the conducting, and once again the trip was a succession of triumphs.

Almost simultaneously with Ormandy's accession to the musical directorship, changes were made in the orchestra's administrative side. Orville H. Bullitt succeeded Dr. Gates as president of the association, and Reginald Allen resigned as manager after a four-year tenure. His successor was Harl McDonald, an astonishingly versatile musician who was one of the most frequently performed American composers of the 1930s and '40s.

McDonald's early career had included episodes as a cowboy and a prizefighter; eventually he followed music as a profession until it led him to the University of Pennsylvania. It was as a composer that he first came to the attention of Stokowski, who frequently programmed his works, including *The Santa Fé Trail* and the *Rhumba Symphony*—McDonald always had a way of concocting catchy titles. He also guest-conducted the orchestra and in 1934 became a member of the board of directors. His appointment as manager made him one of the few musicians who has ever actively run the administrative side of an orchestra while maintaining careers as a composer and conductor, but he proved a shrewd and able business man. "He was a very efficient man at watching a dollar," Orville Bullitt remembered years afterwards. Once Rachmaninoff demanded extra rehearsal time to present a new work of his properly, and McDonald, aware of the cost of orchestral overtime, refused it. "But you are an artist, Mr. McDonald," expostulated Rachmaninoff. "You understand these things." "You, too, are an artist," replied McDonald gravely. "Let us split the amount of your fee to assure a perfect performance." Rachmaninoff quickly settled for the regular rehearsal time.

McDonald remained manager of the Philadelphia Orchestra from 1939 until his sudden death in 1955—the longest that anybody besides Judson has lasted in that demanding job. Ormandy also played his works, though fewer of them than Stokowski, and he was well-represented on the programs of such important groups as the Boston, Detroit and National Symphony Orchestras. But today his music is seldom heard, and his name is not even listed among the hundreds of composers in the Schwann Long-Playing Record Catalogue.

With Stokowski's final severance of all ties to the orchestra in 1941, Ormandy at last was in full command. He could have publicly asserted his authority, made it clear that changes were going to be made, set the orchestra off on a new course. But he did no such thing. Ormandy never was given to uttering bold pronouncements and he had no intention of making drastic changes in a going concern; if Stokowski knew enough to transform a second-rate orchestra into a first-rate one, Ormandy knew enough not to tinker with the first-rate one he found. In the five years he co-conducted with Stokowski he had established himself in Philadelphia and opened up channels of communication with the orchestra; whereas a more assertive and self-centered conductor might have chafed at sharing the podium with one of the great personalities of the time, Ormandy had made a virtue of necessity by patiently preparing for the day when the orchestra would be his alone. He knew how to wait.

When he did make changes, he made them gradually, almost deferentially. Gabriel Braverman, violist and assistant librarian who came into the orchestra in 1938, recalls the transition between

Stokowski and Ormandy as "almost imperceptible." The new conductor carefully considered the question of bowing—the manner in which string players draw their bow across their instrument, which vitally affects both the sound and phrasing of the music. Stokowski had been an advocate of free bowing, leaving the method up to the individual player, while the usual method is uniform bowing, in which up- and down-strokes are carefully marked by the conductor or section leaders and all players comply. Stokowski, who put sound above everything, liked the cascading, unbroken tones that free bowing produced.

Braverman recalls that Ormandy tried both free and uniform bowing for a time, before settling on the latter; sometimes he had the section leaders indicate the strokes, sometimes he did it himself. As a former violinist himself, he knew exactly how to get what he wanted from his string sections. Today the Philadelphia's strings bow in unison but still manage to preserve their seamless legato string tone.

Ormandy also gradually relaxed Stokowski's somewhat aloof rehearsal methods. He built up more of a personal relationship with the players. Ormandy never was a back-slapper, his men always called him "Maestro" and not "Gene," but informality and fraternization backstage and at rehearsals became far more characteristic of his regime than of his predecessor's. "Ormandy wanted us to save ourselves for the actual concerts," says another violist, Leonard Mogill. "At rehearsals sometimes he would tell us not to use a *tremolo*, but to save it for the performance. Then, of course, we give everything." First cellist Samuel Mayes describes Ormandy as a conductor who "gives you an idea of what he wants and then lets you, with your basic individuality, produce it." Says Mayes: "He never made the mistake some conductors do of trying to conduct every note, of hamstringing you by beating a stick in your face."

Ormandy also succeeded in keeping the support of the audience. After the constant surprises and turmoil of the Stokowski years, the city was ready for a period of less hectic programming. Ormandy didn't exactly administer a dose of musical soothing syrup, there were still novelties and premieres (such as that Walton symphony the first week), but essentially the Three Bs began to assert their traditional prerogatives more firmly than before. Ormandy also restored Haydn and Mozart to what he considered their rightful place in the repertory, to such an extent that one of the Friday matinee ladies complained to him: "Mr. Ormandy, why do you play Haydn? We are not used to hearing him, and we don't like him." Ormandy says he told her that he would play Haydn until she did.

Actually, for all the years of new works, premieres, innovations and experiments, Philadelphia audiences retained a dogged fidelity to familiar repertory. The annual poll for the "request program" in 1948 produced these results for favorite symphonies: (1) Brahms' Fourth (2) Beethoven's Fifth (3) Rachmaninoff's Second (4) Beethoven's Sixth and (5) the Franck D minor. Richard Strauss' *Rosenkavalier* Suite, long an unshakeable Philadelphia favorite, led the list of smaller works. By 1952, Beethoven's Fifth had gained first place, but in 1963, the Franck D minor, a favorite of audiences fifty years earlier, was on top.

Ormandy was no reformer; he was willing to take his audience as he found it. The new works he played were fewer and less far-out than Stokowski's had been, and he was careful to balance them with popular favorites. He frankly said that he liked to send the audience out of the hall whistling or humming the last number on the program.

Besides, the new music supply wasn't quite so abundant as it had been. Stokowski's heyday, much more than Ormandy's, had coincided with a period of great fertility in new music, with Stravinsky creating a new style and school, Shostakovich making his first impact, Schoenberg and Berg challenging accepted styles of writing, and Richard Strauss and Sibelius turning out massive orchestral pieces. Stokowski had eagerly embraced them all. Ormandy undoubtedly was more cautious toward contemporary output, but he also had, on the whole, considerably less substantial and original new music to draw upon. Nevertheless, in Ormandy's early years there continued to be new pieces by Bartók, Hindemith, Kodály, Martinu and Prokofiev, among others. Samuel Barber, born near Philadelphia in West Chester, Pa., headed a list of American composers whose works received their world premieres. In 1947, Ormandy was given the National Music Council Award of Honor for services to American music, in recognition of the American premieres he directed.

And there remained the close working association with Rachmaninoff, who retained his special regard for the Philadelphia Orchestra to the end of his life. In 1938 Rachmaninoff decided to revise his Symphony No. 3 in A minor, which had been premiered by Stokowski two years earlier. Ormandy was to conduct the corrected version, and visited the composer at Huntington, Long Island, to go over it with him. The moment he got there, Rachmaninoff took him to the piano, eagerly handed him the score, and asked that he mark bowings throughout for the strings. They worked all day until 8 p.m., and Ormandy didn't have the heart to tell his distinguished host that he was starved, having eaten nothing since an early breakfast. Later, at the first rehearsal, Rachmaninoff sat in the hall while Ormandy conducted. They had discussed the tempi very carefully, but when he noticed that Ormandy was following the indicated speed exactly, he slipped up onto the stage and began to conduct himself. One of the members of the orchestra stopped playing and said: "Maestro, whom shall we follow, you or Rachmaninoff?" The composer then apologetically admitted that when he actually heard the work he felt different tempi from when he composed it.

In 1939 Ormandy led a Rachmaninoff cycle at which the composer appeared as piano soloist at two concerts and conducted a third himself. In 1940 he composed his *Symphonic Dances,* the first orchestral work he had completed in the United States, and offered it for first performance to Ormandy, who naturally accepted on the spot. The critical reviews of the *Symphonic Dances* were mixed, but they produced at least one indelible memory for the orchestra, for after the first rehearsal Rachmaninoff said to the assembled musicians: "When I was a young man, I idolized Chaliapin. He was my ideal, and when I thought of composition I thought of song and of Chaliapin. Now he is gone. Today, when I think of composing, my thoughts turn to you, the greatest orchestra in the world. For that reason, I dedicated this, my newest composition, to the members of the Philadelphia Orchestra and to your conductor, Eugene Ormandy."

Carefully selected and judiciously spaced as most of the novelties were, there never recurred under Ormandy the disputes over "debatable music" which had proved so enlivening or exasperating— depending upon who was listening—in Stokowski's era. Some, of course, regretted the loss of the excitement and exhilaration, but it cannot honestly be said that attendance at the Philadelphia Orchestra's concerts, either at home or in New York and elsewhere on the road, permanently declined. Perhaps the prevalent view was summed up, somewhat effusively, to be sure, by Edwin H. Schloss writing in the Philadelphia *Record* on September 23, 1945:

> Dr. Ormandy's taste and discretion in selecting "modern" or if you prefer "contemporary" music borders on genius. He carefully avoids terrorizing his customers with extremes of "modernism." He is progressive rather than radical in his choice and what he plays is the best of its kind. He knows as well as anyone that the average concertgoer has his old loves and often holds them as sacred. He also knows that the average hearer doesn't so much know what he likes as like what he knows. And for many seasons past Dr. Ormandy has been cunningly winning over many of his communicants who used to believe that . . . great music died with Richard Strauss or, say, Ottorino Respighi. . . .
>
> Our Herr Kapellmeister is not only the leader of the Philadelphia Orchestra. He is the chief leader of musical taste in our city. He is aware of both those responsibilities. And he discharges both brilliantly.

If Ormandy brought relaxation to his audiences, the state he induced among the board of directors can only be described as euphoria. For the first time in years it was possible for a director of the orchestra association to pick up his newspaper without fearing to find some unexpected pronouncement by the conductor, to encounter sudden fiscal demands for special events or undertakings, or to be caught up in controversies over repertory or programming. Like the rest of the city, the board of directors now settled back to enjoy the music it wanted to hear with an untroubled spirit. Ormandy was content to explore its taste for adventurousness, whereas Stokowski had insisted on exhausting it. Perhaps it was no coincidence that everything settled down just as the orchestra was entering its forties. The era of flaming youth had passed, and the time of mature—and comfortable—middle-age was beginning.

❧ THE WAR YEARS

It was not, however, a time of calm routine. World War II had broken out in Europe, and America's entry in 1941 had its effect upon orchestras and musicians, just as on every other aspect of national life. In World War I the Philadelphia Orchestra had made several contributions: Stokowski had led a concert for 3000 dough-boys at Camp Dix in New Jersey and later a Red Cross concert in Philadelphia which raised $7000; he had also opened every concert by playing his own orchestration of the National Anthem.

But World War II, lasting longer and cutting deeper into the nation's life, had a much more substantial impact. The 1942 season opened with an all-Russian program in tribute to the Soviet troops battling the German invasion of their country. It consisted of Tikhon Khrennikov's First Symphony, Shostakovich's Fifth, and Stravinsky's *Firebird* Suite, thereby encompassing a relative newcomer, an estab-lished Soviet figure, and the greatest of modern masters. Twenty-five concerts during the year were broadcast to troops overseas by short-wave over the Armed Forces Network. Guest conductors included Toscanini, William Steinberg, and Saul Caston. Audiences were invited to be somewhat more casual in their dress, with Harl Mc-Donald announcing that "high hats are out for the duration" and Ormandy adding: "They can come in their overalls if they like." Not many did so, however. Most of the old-time subscribers, as a matter of fact, continued to arrive exactly as before, even to being driven to the curb by their chauffeured limousines. Pleasure driving had been ruled out for the duration by the Office of Price Administra-tion, and OPA inspectors had a field day outside the auditorium grabbing the offending drivers and taking away their gas ration cards. Friday matinee attendances declined for a time as a result.

A restaurant area under the vestibule of the Academy of Music served for a time as the Stage Door Canteen, only to fall into disuse afterwards. A regrettable casualty of the war years turned out to be the long queues of boys and girls who came to youth concerts. For years these enthusiastic youngsters, many of whom continued to come out after Stokowski's departure, had had the custom of gathering in the pre-dawn hours at the Academy for the day's concert. Often they waited all night in line for a front seat in the upstairs amphitheater. In 1942, the local Civil Defense authorities decreed that "in case of alert" it would be "dangerous" to have a crowd of people gathered at night outside the Academy. Accordingly, under new regulations no one was permitted to congregate until 7 a.m. (the box office opened at 9). And so the crowds of young people with their thermos containers of coffee, their blankets and campstools and sandwiches, disappeared from the scene, another bit of excitement gone.

Inside the hall, wartime programs didn't differ basically from those before; there was no talk, for instance, of dropping Wagnerian works. But many American names were represented—the inevitable Harl McDonald, with a piece topically entitled *Bataan,* and Samuel Barber, Paul Creston, Roy Harris, Walter Piston, William Schuman, Virgil Thomson, and others. The orchestra visited USO clubs in the area to play numbers like *Deep River,* the *Toreador Song* from *Carmen, Smoke Gets in Your Eyes* and other numbers adjudged to be acceptable to the soldiery; meanwhile the regular concerts at the Academy ran close to 100 per cent of capacity. On January 23, 1943 the Philadelphia Orchestra played to the largest home attendance in its history, when 3500 people crowded into the Academy to hear the blind pianist Alec Templeton in a program that included Rachmaninoff's Concerto No. 2 in C minor and a set of his own improvisions. This was a special non-subscription event, arranged when a tour by the orchestra had to be canceled.

Touring was a grave problem during wartime, with train schedules curtailed and rolling stock put to military use. The orchestra dropped all its projected long tours, including a twenty-city swing through the south and west. But it did take shorter trips regularly to New York, Washington, Baltimore and Harrisburg. Some of its trips were made in ancient cars with wood-burning stoves for heat. On one stopover in Savannah, Ga., the train was so late arriving that the musicians had no time to change to dress clothes and played the concert in their casual, wrinkled train attire. In 1942 at a concert in Richmond, Va., the orchestra found in the audience one of its own, thirty-four year old Pvt. Allen Farnham, who had been inducted into the service and was now stationed at nearby Camp Lee. A few years before he had been one of the men discharged from (then reinstated in) the orchestra; now, while the audience of 3000 roared its approval, Ormandy invited the GI violinist, in uniform, to the podium to conduct *The Stars and Stripes Forever.*

Ormandy's most notable wartime activity, outside of Philadelphia, was a journey he undertook to Australia at the invitation of the Australian Broadcasting Commission and with the co-operation of the U.S. Office of War Information, to guest-conduct local orchestras there including an "all-star" aggregation especially assembled for him. He had already guest-conducted several summers in Europe, but this was his longest and most sustained stint away from home. Some of his concerts were specially organized for Allied troops in the area, and the entire tour was well-publicized not only locally but in dispatches back to the United States. Critic Neville Cardus said he had dreamed he was in Philadelphia, so beautiful was the playing that Ormandy elicited from his pick-up musicians. Ormandy returned with his reputation considerably enhanced. In fact, he made the *Congressional Record* for the first time on September 1, 1944, when the inevitable Congressman made the inevitable complaint that the taxpayers' money had been spent to send a symphony conductor to Australia. Actually, it hadn't been; the Australians had borne the cost.

The orchestra itself lost thirteen men to the armed forces during the war years, but replacements were found without any noticeable impairment of sound. By 1944 there were six women among the players, though it would be a mistake to ascribe this high proportion entirely to the call-up of men. Actually, both Stokowski and Ormandy pioneered in the engagement of women as regular orchestral musicians. The Philadelphia's first two women were both harpists, Edna Phillips and Marjorie Tyre, but in 1935 Stokowski created a stir when he engaged Elsa Hilger, a cellist. She was the first female instrumentalist, aside from harpists, to join a major symphony orchestra.

Miss Hilger, born in Vienna, had come to the United States as a young girl along with two sisters who played with her in a piano-violin-cello trio. The three of them were guest soloists in Beethoven's Triple Concerto at Robin Hood Dell in 1932, with Henry Hadley conducting. Stokowski knew her work and wanted her for the orchestra, so he phoned her at her home near Freehold, N.J., and asked her to rush down for an immediate audition. "I'm in my housedress," she told him. "Come as you are," he said. She got the job, which was in the last row of the cellos, and moved gradually up through the ranks, until she became associate first cellist in 1944. During the 1950–'51 season she was acting first cellist while Paul Olevsky was in military service; his eventual replacement in the first chair was Lorne Munroe. For years, until her retirement in the spring of 1969, Elsa Hilger's matronly figure and braided hair up front in the cellos were as familiar a sight at Philadelphia concerts as Stokowski and Ormandy themselves. Her entry into the orchestra paved the way for a succession of other women, especially string players, and by 1968 the total had risen to eight, five of whom had husbands who also played in the orchestra.

♪ FLIPPING THE RECORD

Among the casualties of World War II was the American record industry. The availability of shellac, then the basic ingredient of disks, was drastically curtailed, and the production of new phonographs was put aside for more pressing manufactures. But the most crushing blow of all was delivered by James Caesar Petrillo, president of the American Federation of Musicians, who in 1942 imposed a complete ban on all recordings. Petrillo's concern was not with the war effort but with the effect that use of recorded music in jukeboxes and on radio stations was having on the employment of live musicians. He wanted record manufacturers to pay a royalty on every recording sold, the benefits going to unemployed musicians. In the end, he got pretty much what he wanted, through the establishment of the Recording Industry Music Performance Trust Fund, which utilizes the royalties to pay musicians for free performances at schools, parks, charitable institutions and the like throughout the country.

But the war between Petrillo and record companies lasted from 1942 to 1944 (there was a briefer reprise in 1948) and during this time absolutely no records were made by RCA Victor and Columbia, the two major American companies. Symphonic music was an innocent bystander in the battle, since the union's objection basically was to popular music records that put dance bands out of work, but the ban was total. By now the income from the recordings it made for RCA Victor was an important part of the Philadelphia Orchestra's income, and when board chairman Bullitt reported a $26,000 deficit for 1943–'44, he ascribed it to the Petrillo ban.

But even though it had stopped making records, the orchestra continued to think about them—more specifically, about the question of its recording affiliation. Ever since Stokowski's first recordings in 1917 the Philadelphia Orchestra had recorded exclusively for the Victor Talking Machine Company and its successor, RCA Victor. But in 1943 it decided to switch to Columbia. Recording affiliations, like any other business dealings, are always highly pragmatical, and it was obvious that Columbia had offered the orchestra a more profitable arrangement. But there were other factors, too. Everybody knew that the recording ban would some day end, and that the pace would probably be more hectic than ever to make up for the lost time. Ten years earlier the Philadelphia Orchestra had been the main gem in Victor's crown, with first choice in repertory and priority in promotion and advertising.

These conditions had now altered. Besides owning recording rights to the Philadelphia, Victor now also had the Boston Symphony of Koussevitzky and, even more significant, the NBC Symphony of Toscanini, which had been set up exclusively as a broadcasting and recording organization. The Philadelphians and Ormandy felt that they were being pushed into third position, particularly when it came to the selection of repertory to record. Although Columbia had since 1938 undergone a recrudescence of recording activity in the United States, acquiring rights to such aggregations as the Minneapolis Symphony under Mitropoulos, the Pittsburgh under Reiner, the Cleveland under Rodzinski, and the Chicago under Stock, not to mention the All-American Youth Orchestra under Stokowski, there was no doubt that if the Philadelphia came over, it would become Columbia's No. 1 orchestra in prestige, promotion, and in the right to choose repertory. In 1943, the agreement was signed, and it was to endure for twenty-five years.

Accordingly, when the Petrillo interdiction was terminated in November, 1944 a small army of Columbia executives and technicians descended on the Academy of Music. It was a ceremonious beginning, with Edward Wallerstein and Goddard Lieberson representing the record company, and Orville Bullitt the orchestra. Four days were required to install the elaborate equipment, and on November 19 actual recording began, with the opening list including Strauss' *Death and Transfiguration,* Brahms' Fourth Symphony, Beethoven's Seventh, and Lalo's *Symphonie Espagnole* with Nathan Milstein as violin soloist. Ormandy liked to record, and knew how to do it quickly and professionally. His years in radio, with its demands for accurate timing, had almost built a clock into his head; he was co-operative with engineers and technicians; and he knew how to adjust both his own style and the sound of the orchestra to the medium's requirements. Over the next quarter-century, Ormandy and the Philadelphia Orchestra became the foundation of Columbia's orchestral catalogue, putting out more than 300 different recordings, far more than any other conductor or orchestra. The annual revenue to the orchestra association eventually amounted to some $250,000 a year, and the orchestra's sound, name and fame were spread to the farthest corners of the earth. By 1948, Harl McDonald could report that one-fourth the orchestra's total revenue came from recording and broadcasting, and this proportion was to rise even higher as the years went by. When the long-playing record, with its new 33-1/3 r.p.m.

speed, hit the market in 1948, eventually displacing the old 78-r.p.m. system, it was the Philadelphia Orchestra which dominated the new LP release lists.

Ormandy's versatility and adaptability, along with his ability to work at high speed with no impairment of his musicianship, combined to produce recordings unmatched by any other conductor in their range and variety. As high fidelity techniques enabled a wider frequency range to be captured on records, the resplendent sound of the orchestra emerged in a steadily truer likeness. The development of stereophonic sound in 1958 provided the final cachet of authenticity to the "Philadelphia Sound" on records. Three Philadelphia recordings achieved the fiscal distinction of selling $1,000,000 worth of copies apiece, an accomplishment which the Record Industry Association of America chooses to commemorate with the presentation of a Gold Record. It cannot be said, however, that any of the Gold Records represented the orchestra at its musically most significant, since the best-sellers consisted of joint recordings, with the Mormon Tabernacle Choir of Salt Lake City, of an abridged Handel's *Messiah* and *The Lord's Prayer*, *The Glorious Sound of Christmas* with the Temple University choir. These may not have added much artistic luster to the Philadelphia's status, but they helped pay the bills.

♪ NEW FACES

In 1945 Ormandy signed a new contract with the orchestra which would take him through the 1950–'51 season. If anyone had doubts he was in Philadelphia to stay they surely were dispelled by now, and gradually the orchestra began to reflect his methods and personality. Virgil Thomson in the New York *Herald Tribune* for October 19, 1952, wrote after a Carnegie Hall concert that "a remarkable amplification" of the sound qualities of the orchestra had taken place under Ormandy.

"The Philadelphia Orchestra, believe it or not, is a better orchestra than it used to be," he declared. Then he went on:

It is even better, I think, than any other orchestra has ever been. There has never been, in the memory of living persons, a sound like that or a flexibility like that. Under Stokowski himself it was rougher, throatier, less agile. Orchestral execution at its best has not altered much in the last thirty years. . . . It has been assumed by all that no radical improvement was possible.

Nevertheless, one has been achieved by Philadelphia. And it has been achieved through no radical method. No miraculous laying-on of hands, no wonder-cure has done it. Nor has any striking personality galvanized the players. A straightforward, a modest (though highly expert) musician, Eugene Ormandy, has achieved the seemingly unachievable. From now on, the musicians and music lovers of this world must look to the Philadelphia alone for their standards. . . .

The qualities most remarked in the Philadelphia's playing, which are a certain velvet-like down on the surface of the string tone and an unequaled sensitivity of all the players to their conductor's slightest and most spontaneous wish, these were exactly the qualities that Leopold Stokowski strove for, achieved, and left as a legacy to his successor. He also left an expert personnel, accustomed to using these qualities. Ormandy made no radical changes. He merely kept up the quality of the personnel through the normal replacements necessary to meet the demands of the war and the need of keeping everything first-class, very much as a wine-buyer replenishes his cellar. . . .

Eugene Ormandy has a fine ear and he knows what he wants. He wants beauty of sound and virtuosity of execution, both of them at the service of music in complete humility. His achievement toward this ideal with the Philadelphia Orchestra is one of the notable achievements in contemporary music-making.

Ormandy, as Thomson noted, restocked the orchestra slowly, relying on the normal attrition that changes the face of any 100-member organization—deaths, retirements, attractive opportunities elsewhere, and the host of other reasons that lead people to leave even good jobs. Gradually new faces appeared in the orchestra, and some of the old faces appeared in positions of greater responsibility and authority.

Alexander Hilsberg was one of these. Born in Warsaw in 1900, he set out to be a violin virtuoso, undertaking a tour of Siberia and Manchuria as a young man, and winding up finally in the United States by way of Japan. In 1926 he joined the Philadelphia Orchestra after a tryout at which, he recalled, he played through a bathroom door while Stokowski, never one to stand on ceremony at auditions, splashed about in the tub. Stokowski made him concertmaster in 1931, and in 1945, when Caston left to become conductor of the Denver Symphony, Ormandy named Hilsberg as assistant conductor of the Philadelphia. He acquitted himself in his new post with distinction and decisiveness. When José Iturbi, scheduled to conduct on a Friday afternoon, arrived a few minutes late at the Academy, he found to his astonishment that Hilsberg had already launched into the opening overture. In 1946 and again in 1949 when Ormandy was unable to conduct important concerts first because of a strained shoulder muscle and later because of a virus attack, Hilsberg filled in with such aplomb that one New York critic was impelled to call him "a conductor of exceptional accomplishments." He developed quite a personal following in Philadelphia, and so impressive were his appearances on the podium there that in 1951 the New Orleans Symphony engaged him as its conductor, and he led a distinguished career until his death in 1961.

One of the primary sources of the orchestra for new young players was Philadelphia's foremost conservatory, the Curtis Institute of Music. Founded in 1924 with an endowment by Mrs. Edward Bok, the school from the start drew on the orchestra for many of its faculty and advisors. Stokowski, of course, had been deeply interested, taught there, and conducted the student orchestra. Some of the orchestra's first chair men took faculty posts, and Josef Hofmann was the first head of the piano department, later becoming director of the school. His successor in 1941 was the violinist Efrem Zimbalist, who subsequently married Mrs. Bok. The present director is Rudolf Serkin. In 1928 tuition fees were abolished, and since then Curtis has been entirely a scholarship operation, which means, of course, that only students of the highest potentialities are accepted.

With Curtis contributing, far more than any other single institution, to the orchestra's personnel, and with its students closely influenced by either the presence or the proximity of the Philadelphia's players, continuity of the orchestra's style and sound from generation to generation was considerably assisted. Curtis also gave the orchestra a goodly number of its individual stars and personalities. Mason Jones joined the orchestra as third horn in 1938 at the age of nineteen straight out of Curtis; within two years he was first horn and one of the most distinguished orchestral musicians in the country, eventually becoming personnel manager of the orchestra while continuing as a player. When Edna Phillips retired as harpist she was succeeded by a Curtis girl, twenty-one year old Marilyn Costello, an Ohioan who came to Philadelphia to study. In the same class was a young fiddler named Isadore Schwartz who joined the second violins of the orchestra and forthwith became one of its most envied members, for reasons only partially musical. Izzy Schwartz was torn at an early age between two great loves, playing music and playing the horses, and far better than most men who lead a double life, he was able to reconcile them both. In fact, he achieved such proficiency in his second occupation that he eventually became a horse-owner himself, naming one of his thoroughbreds Maestro Gene, in honor of the Philadelphia's conductor. But his greatest pride was his daughter, pianist Susan Starr, one of the brightest young American concert artists, who placed second in the Tchaikovsky International Competition in Moscow in 1962 to Vladimir Ashkenazy and John Ogdon, who tied for first. Miss Starr, like her father a Curtis graduate, made several solo appearances with the Philadelphia Orchestra, working her way up through children's and youth concerts to a full-fledged performance during the regular season. Schwartz is one of the few fathers who have literally played second fiddle to their daughters, and is proud of it.

TELEVISION AND TRAVELS

The beginning of the post-war era enabled the orchestra to broaden its musical scope, resume its travels, and again play an important role both nationally and internationally. Even before the war ended, in 1944 the men of the orchestra had extended a hand to the musicians of the Soviet Union by sending to the Leningrad Philharmonic, whose facilities had been wrecked and supplies depleted during the long Nazi siege, a shipment of instrumental parts—strings, bows, mutes and reeds. It was a gesture not forgotten by the Leningraders when the Philadelphians visited Russia years later.

In the seasons immediately after the war Ormandy began to program more new works, particularly by foreign composers. Martinu, Antheil, Khatchaturian and Walter Piston, along with the first American performance of Prokofiev's *Alexander Nevsky* in its cantata form, were on the 1945 schedule. In 1946 American premieres were given to Prokofiev's *Ode to the End of the War* and Manuel Rosenthal's *Saint Francis of Assisi,* neither of which proved a durable contribution to the repertory. Also played was a Flute Concerto composed by Louis Gesensway, a member of the orchestra since 1926. Violinist Gesensway, also a Curtis graduate, had already had several of his pieces played by the orchestra. Most of the critics found his Flute Concerto an admirable vehicle for soloist William Kincaid.

During the regular season Ormandy, more than most conductors, prefered to remain with his own orchestra rather than taking engagements elsewhere; as a result, the Philadelphia Orchestra tended to have fewer guest conductors than most similar organizations. Late in 1946, however, he suffered a muscle strain in his right shoulder. Ormandy says that he has been incapacitated temporarily three times in his career; each time the same muscle has been responsible; and each time it has popped during Tchaikovsky's Fifth Symphony. In any case, he was advised to rest a while. His immediate replacement was Hilsberg, but guest conductors also helped to fill the gap. They included Dimitri Mitropoulos, now at Minneapolis after two summers at Robin Hood Dell; George Szell, on the verge of a distinguished career in Cleveland; Igor Stravinsky, no longer regarded as quite the wild man of his previous visit in 1925; and Zoltan Kodály, Ormandy's old teacher at the Budapest Academy of Music and now on his first visit to the United States.

Ormandy's reunion with Kodály was particularly moving for him. The Hungarian composer was sixty-four years old, and had been professor of Music Theory and Composition at the Budapest Academy when Ormandy was a student there. Ormandy remembered, at the age of ten, handing him a composition for evaluation and being asked what it was. "This is a modern composition," the young student replied. Kodály handed him back the paper and said: "First go home and learn about the triad." Now the old master and his successful pupil had a genial reunion at Ormandy's home, and the composer led the orchestra in the first American performance of his *Peacock Variations.* Before he left, Kodály, on his way back to Hungary, said to Ormandy, "Jenö, when are you coming home?" Ormandy quietly replied: "I *am* home."

Still newer names appeared among the guest conductors of the next few seasons: Leonard Bernstein, not yet the music director of the New York Philharmonic; Ernest Ansermet of l'Orchestre de la Suisse Romande on his long overdue first American visit, and Guido Cantelli, Toscanini's gifted protégé who died tragically in an air crash in 1956.

In the spring of 1946 the orchestra resumed its long-haul touring, which had been interrupted by the war. A forty-two day excursion was made across the United States and into Canada, the longest journey since 1937. Officials estimated that a total of 450,000 people had attended live concerts by the Philadelphia Orchestra during the year, an all-time record for any orchestra. However, all this exposure resulted in a season's deficit of $24,000, and the following year the orchestra launched a $200,000 campaign to pay off its debts.

Ormandy was also managing to do considerable touring of his own during the summer months. In June, 1944, after his return from Australia, Toscanini invited him to New York to guest-conduct the NBC Symphony. The timing of the invitation raised a few eyebrows, because Leopold Stokowski had just been dropped as co-conductor of the NBC orchestra, reportedly at the insistence of Toscanini, who didn't like such Stokowskian touches as the reseating of the orchestra and the introduction of free bowing.

In 1947 Ormandy extended his activities to the West Coast,

when he accepted an invitation to conduct the Hollywood Bowl Orchestra for a concert by Margaret Truman, the daughter of the President of the United States. The visit had unexpected results, for while there he also conducted a straight orchestral concert in the Bowl with such effect that he was promptly engaged as music director of the Bowl for the 1948 season. When he got there, he gave the Californians more than they had bargained for—a full-scale performance of Mahler's Symphony No. 8 in E-flat—the same *Symphony of a Thousand* with which the young Leopold Stokowski had stunned Philadelphia in 1916. Even Hollywood had never heard anything so spectacular, and the newspapers resounded with Ormandy's praise for days afterwards. In the Bowl, he also conducted his first opera, Puccini's *Madama Butterfly*.

Although Ormandy was never responsible for technological or electronic innovations, he certainly responded to them with alacrity. He directed the Philadelphia Orchestra in recording the movie soundtrack for Robert Flaherty's fine movie documentary *Louisiana Story*, and later played a suite drawn from Virgil Thomson's score at concerts in the Academy. But his most spectacular venture into twentieth century technology at this time came in his race with Toscanini to see which could conduct the first symphonic concert for the new entertainment medium, television. In 1948 there were only about 5,000,000 TV sets in the United States (by 1968 the total was 80,000,000) and presumably very few of their owners cared about seeing a symphony orchestra perform on the tiny screen with tinny sound.

Nevertheless, considerable excitement was engendered by the prospect. Television had begun experimentally twelve years before, and by now its possibilities were apparent almost to every one. Besides, this was to be the first time in three years that live music *of any kind* had been heard on television because of a ban imposed by the ever-resistant Mr. Petrillo. Great rivalry existed, of course, between the National Broadcasting Company and the Columbia Broadcasting System in television as in all other aspects of broadcasting, and it was NBC which seemed ready to take the lead in symphonic telecasting. It announced that on Saturday, March 21, 1958, from 6:30

to 7:30 p.m. Arturo Toscanini would conduct the NBC Symphony in a televised all-Wagner concert which would originate in Studio 8-H in New York and be carried by channels in New York, Washington, Philadelphia, Schenectady and Buffalo.

CBS promptly countered by announcing that Ormandy and the Philadelphia Orchestra would be put on television the same day, but at 5 p.m., or ninety minutes in advance of the NBC broadcast. And so it was, with the Ormandy broadcast being carried by coaxial cable to the CBS outlet in New York. Most viewers agreed that the NBC telecast was visually more expert, with facial close-ups of Toscanini, slow dissolves from one section of the orchestra to another, and other attempts to provide photographic variety. The hastily arranged CBS program on the other hand, was unimaginatively photographed, with little camera movement, much in the manner of an unvarying view of an actual concert. The Philadelphia Orchestra, however, could claim that it had actually made the first symphonic telecast in all history, since its show was over before Toscanini's began. Moreover, it did have a shade more musical interest, since Ormandy had played Rachmaninoff's Symphony No. 1 in D minor, Op. 13, written in 1897 and shelved after its first performance in St. Petersburg—and so, to all intents and purposes, a "new" work.

One more Ormandy exploit of the late 1940s deserves to be mentioned—his first and only excursion into motion pictures. He was signed, with pianist Artur Rubinstein, to appear in a tear-jerker of an RKO movie, all about a blind night-club musician with a great concerto racing through his head who eats his heart out trying to get it played with Rubinstein at the piano and Ormandy on the podium. Needless to say, he succeeds. Included in the cast were such luminaries as Ethel Barrymore, Merle Oberon and Dana Andrews, and an actual concerto was composed for the picture by one Leith Stevens. The movie underwent a number of vicissitudes, including three changes of title, *Counterpoint, Memory of Love* and *Night Song.* By any other name it smelled as sweet. Reviewing the picture in the New York *Times,* Bosley Crowther termed the music "a scrappy and meaningless jangle" and commented: "If Mr. Rubinstein and Mr. Ormandy can swallow it, along with their pride, they must have pretty strong stomachs." As a Hollywood actor, at least, Ormandy proved to be no Stokowski.

⸙ THE BRITISH TOUR

On one occasion when the Philadelphia Orchestra was pulling into the Thirtieth Street Station (some versions of the story make it the Philadelphia International Airport) Eugene Ormandy is reputed to have remarked to his concertmaster: "This looks like a nice town. Why don't we play here?"

For all the time it has spent in the Academy of Music—and its home seasons last as long as anybody else's—the Philadelphia has traveled farther, longer and more persistently than any other American orchestra. Almost from the start it has been an orchestra on wheels, and Ormandy's quip is easy to understand.

But the first big foreign trip didn't come until 1949. Stokowski, it may be remembered, had been agitating and planning for a European visit for years. False alarms about the imminence of the voyage were spread in 1924, 1927, 1934 and 1936. Always the plans fell through, and when Stokowski did go abroad, he went alone. But on May 13, 1949 the orchestra, 110 strong, finally set sail from New York on the Cunard pocket liner Parthia, bound for Liverpool and a month in Britain.

Why Britain? The answer was simple. A twenty-nine year old British impresario named Harold Fielding had been found who was willing to underwrite the entire expedition. The orchestra association took out a special policy with Lloyd's of London, insuring it against any losses, such as from cancellation of concerts. The itinerary called for twenty-eight concerts in twenty-seven days, with ten in London and eighteen in the provinces. Ormandy took along a considerable repertory, including eight American works: Barber's *Adagio for Strings,* Griffes' *The White Peacock,* Gershwin's *Rhapsody in Blue,* Kent Kennan's *Night Soliloquy,* Harl McDonald's *Rhumba* and *Mission,* Sousa's *Stars and Stripes Forever,* and the Passacaglia and Fugue from Thomson's *Louisiana Story.* British music was excluded at the request of impresario Fielding. Each city on the tour was offered its choice of twenty programs, representing a total of seventy compositions. Soloists included two pianists, Eileen Joyce and José Iturbi, and there were two concert performances of *Madama Butterfly,* with the Australian soprano Joan Hammond and the American tenor Eugene Conley in the leading roles.

On arrival, the orchestra was greeted with discouraging word about the advance sales. Ticket prices had been steeply scaled and hadn't been going as well as expected; it was said that Fielding stood to lose as much as $140,000 (actually his eventual loss was about two-thirds that figure). But the opening, at Albert Hall on May 24, was a brilliant success both musically and socially. Queen Elizabeth (now the Queen Mother) attended in a crinoline-styled gown and a diamond tiara, remarking after the concert: "Superb—we have never heard such lovely music." The London *Times* told its readers that no British orchestra could equal the Philadelphia for its "precision of ensemble, refinement of tone, sheer virtuosity of execution, and subtlety of control." Later on *The Times* complained briefly "of a lack of penetration beneath the surface of the music with which Mr. Eugene Ormandy appeared always to be content"; this was virtually the only even mildly sour note which the orchestra heard on its entire trip through England and Scotland. Sir Thomas Beecham, who conducted one tour concert (Iturbi directed another, Ormandy took all the rest), said: "Of all the American orchestras I have conducted in recent years, yours is by far the greatest. It has beauty of tone, youthful enthusiasm, exquisite balance. It is even a greater body than when I conducted it some nine years ago."

The Philadelphia was the first American orchestra to undertake such a foreign journey since the distant year of 1930, when Toscanini had taken the New York Philharmonic; it was known to European music lovers not only through its reputation but its recordings, and as it progressed through England and Scotland with steadily growing praise, great crowds turned out to greet it and to purchase tickets to hear it. Where there were empty seats they were always in the highest-priced areas, and as Fielding began to reduce his steep rates the halls quickly became filled. When the orchestra reached Man-

chester, 6000 people jammed Belle Vue Auditorium, and so many
were turned away that another concert had to be scheduled for the
next day; it was sold out within four hours. In the end nineteen of
the twenty-eight concerts were sold out, including four in London's
Harringay Arena, which seated 10,000. The final Harringay concert
consisted of works played in the movie *Fantasia,* and drew a record
admission of 10,323, with 5000 others unable to gain entry. In some
instances stage seats were arranged in tiers behind the musicians,
so that when Ormandy looked at his ring of double-basses he found
audience legs behind them. Another time, when violinist Lois Putlitz
left her place among the fiddles to play the celesta, on which she
doubled, one of the customers slipped into her chair.

Needless to say, the orchestra, accustomed though it was to
success wherever it went, was overwhelmed by the public adulation
it received, as well as the foot-stamping and cheering which its
playing evoked from the supposedly staid British audiences. The
heavy performance schedule didn't permit much sightseeing, but the
trip was nevertheless just as much of an eye-opener for many of the
players as it was an ear-opener for many of the listeners. A literary
contingent from the orchestra, headed by violinist Schima Kaufman,
even attempted to make a call on George Bernard Shaw at Ayot
St. Lawrence, remembering that the great playwright had, in his
early days, been a music critic, and a good one, under the pseudonym
of Corno di Bassetto. They sent him a message asking that they
be permitted to pay their respects, and received this Shavian communication in reply:

> The average age of orchestral players who can remember
> Corno di Bassetto must be above eighty. Corno himself is ninety-
> three and cannot possibly entertain a full orchestra of decrepit
> players in this remote and tiny village. He can give them a
> friendly wave of the stick he hobbles on and wishes them all a
> happy funeral.
>
> —G. BERNARD SHAW.

In all, the Philadelphia Orchestra played to a total of 125,000
persons during its twenty-seven days in Britain, far more than any

In 1962 the Academy of Music, at the corner of Broad and Locust, was designated a National Historical Monument by the U.S. Department of the Interior. Opened in 1857, it is the oldest auditorium in the country still in use in its original form for its original purpose.

The Academy's architects based their interior design on La Scala, Milan. Curvature of walls and dry "well" beneath the floor contribute to excellence of acoustics. Chandelier originally had 240 gas burners, was electrified in 1900.

Friday afternoon audiences are traditionally "Old Philadelphia" feminine. View is of Broad Street entrance as typical matinee crowd arrives.

Saratoga Performing Arts Center in upstate New York, where the orchestra has been playing every August since 1966. The $3,600,000 structure seats 5100, and thousands of others can see and hear from the grassy slopes.

A children's concert brings forth some feline participants. The orchestra is being directed by assistant conductor William Smith.

Part of the more or less rapt audience. Philadelphia's schools co-operate in encouraging young listeners.

Miss Frances Wister, flanked by Orville Bullitt (left), board president from 1938 to 1955, and Ormandy. Miss Wister typified energy, devotion and persuasiveness of women's committees; was star performer at orchestra's annual awards of watches to players with twenty-five years' service.

Harl McDonald checking time schedule. McDonald was manager of the orchestra from 1939 until his death in 1955, a tenure exceeded only by Arthur Judson. McDonald's compositions were also played frequently both by Stokowski and Ormandy.

Cellists at rehearsal. Wearing eyeshade, pocketbook beside her, is Elsa Hilger, a familiar figure for thirty-four years. At right is principal cellist Samuel Mayes, one-quarter Cherokee Indian. At rear, wearing dark jacket and tie, is new member Lloyd Smith.

Famous Philadelphians of the past. From left are concertmaster and assistant conductor Alexander Hilsberg, flutist William Kincaid and oboist Marcel Tabuteau, conferring with Ormandy.

The orchestra listens at a rehearsal as Ormandy goes over a point.

Horns. Mason Jones, principal hornist who doubles as personnel manager, and his associates.

Harps. Marilyn Costello (right) and Margarita Csonka.

First-desk woodwinds. In center, principal flutist Murray Panitz (in light shirt). Alongside him, at right, principal oboist John de Lancie. Behind de Lancie is principal clarinetist Anthony Gigliotti, with principal bassoonist Bernard Garfield beside him. In front of Panitz is violist Gabriel Braverman.

Brothers. The de Pasquale Quartet: Robert, second violin; Joseph, viola; Francis, cello; William, first violin.

The orchestra on stage at the Academy. The organ, which weighs 200,000 pounds, was installed in 1960.

Husbands and wives. From left, William and Barbara de Pasquale; Stephane and Cathleen Dalschaert; Glenn and Julia Janson; Donald and Margarita Csonka Montanaro; Samuel and Winifred Mayes.

Among array of great soloists who appeared with the orchestra over the years was Fritz Kreisler, seen here (second from left) with Ormandy, first violist Samuel Lifschey, and oboist Tabuteau (reed in mouth).

Pierre Monteux, who gave world premiere of Stravinsky's *Firebird* in Paris in 1913, stirred up a storm when he criticized Philadelphia audience after it walked out on his performance in 1928.

Lauritz Melchior and Kirsten Flagstad rehearse for appearances with the orchestra at the May Festival in Ann Arbor, Mich. in 1937. With them is Charles O'Connell, former Victor recording director and also guest conductor on the 1936 national tour.

Marian Anderson, born and raised in Philadelphia, confers with Ormandy prior to an appearance.

Tabuteau and Toscanini during the Maestro's guest-conducting and recording stint at the Academy of Music in 1941.

Violin talk. Isaac Stern, rehearsing for a solo appearance, has a musical discussion with the violin section. Seated left to right are concertmaster Norman Carol, associate concertmaster William de Pasquale, Morris Shulik (leaning on stand), and associate concertmaster David Madison.

Conductor and composer. Ormandy with Dimitri Shostakovitch, during Soviet
musician's visit in 1959.

Conductor and politician. Adlai
Stevenson was reader in 1962
performance of Aaron Copland's
A Lincoln Portrait.

Van Cliburn records the Grieg A minor Concerto in session held at Saratoga Springs, N. Y.

Artur Rubinstein performs at the Academy. He made his American debut with the orchestra under Fritz Scheel in 1906, at the age of twenty.

Igor Stravinsky sits in with the orchestra. Behind him is Anshel Brusilow, concert-master who left in 1966. Many Stravinsky works were premiered in Philadelphia.

With Ormandy is Polish avant-garde composer Krzysztof Penderecki. Orchestra gave his *Threnody for the Victims of Hiroshima* its Philadelphia and New York premieres in 1969.

Maestro of the Philadelphia. Eugene Ormandy at the Academy of Music.

other foreign orchestra. Impresario Fielding, totalling up his books, found he had lost £23,900—about $96,000. With admirable sang-froid, he declared he had expected to lose money all along but had achieved his objective "to let the people of Britain hear in person the world's greatest orchestra." Not only that—he invited them back.

♣ JUBILEE AT THE ACADEMY

The excitement of the orchestra's success abroad seemed to take some of the edge from the forthcoming celebration at home of its fiftieth anniversary in the course of the 1949-'50 season. Little of a commemorative nature was planned for the golden jubilee aside from the issuance of a handsome and useful sixty-four page souvenir brochure edited by Donald L. Engle, and a repeat of Fritz Scheel's opening program on November 16, 1949, this time with William Kapell as soloist in the Tchaikovsky Piano Concerto No. 1. Kapell, who was later to die in a plane crash, was one of many young artists like Eugene Istomin, Eugene List, Susan Starr, Jaime Laredo and Anna Moffo who found their careers materially assisted by Ormandy's interest.

The most significant event of the year 1950 didn't take place until December, and it had nothing directly to do with the orchestra or with Ormandy who, at the moment, was busy in New York preparing to direct the Metropolitan Opera's production of Johann Strauss' *Fledermaus* for Rudolf Bing, the Met's new general manager.

On December 15 it was announced that the Philadelphia Orchestra Association had bought a controlling interest in the Academy of Music with the intention of preserving the edifice as a home for the orchestra. This meant that the orchestra had finally decided to give up its sporadic investigations of the possibility of finding a new home site for the orchestra; for years there had been talk of one on the Benjamin Franklin Parkway, near the Philadelphia Art Museum. Until the purchase of the hall, the orchestra had had to pay rent there like any other tenant, and there were times when it found its rehearsal and similar activities hampered by rental of the facilities to others.

Stockholders of the corporation that owned the Academy also had the privilege of sitting in a special roped-off section for any and all concerts, which cut down somewhat on ticket-sale revenue available to the orchestra. With the advent of Stuart F. Louchheim in 1952 as head of the new corporation running the hall under the aegis of the orchestra, an extensive program of refurbishing and modernizing the ancient hall was instituted—a process that was to continue for years, with more than $3,000,000 spent by 1968.

Actually, the Academy of Music had served both the city and the orchestra handsomely for years. Even when it was completed in 1857 it was regarded as something special. Napoleon Le Brun and Gustavus Runge, the architects (both Philadelphians, despite their foreign-sounding names), had $250,000 to spend, and since for this sum they could not build an edifice that was beautiful both within and without, they decided to concentrate on the interior and leave the outside "plain like a market house." Eventually, a marble facing was to be added to the exterior, but eventually has never come.

Originally, the Academy was to be an opera house, and its design was taken from La Scala, Milan, which Le Brun visited for a personal investigation before building. Remembering the fiasco of the opening night of Philharmonic Hall in New York's Lincoln Center in 1962, one is startled to learn that Le Brun's auditorium was pronounced an acoustical marvel from the start. Several explanations for the fine sound are given. Some authorities ascribe it to the fact that during construction the shell of the building was allowed to stand open for a full year without a roof, thus allowing it to "weather"—that is, to attain an imperviousness to dryness or dampness. Others say that the combination of the shape of the auditorium and its ancient wood and plaster simply makes for rich, warm sound. Still another group gives the credit to a dry "well" beneath the parquet floor which allegedly contributes in some mysterious way to the hall's resonance. The "well" is indeed there, and visitors, after sufficient importuning, are sometimes taken down to view it—a five-foot high, circular structure consisting of a whitewashed brick wall, open at the top and with absolutely nothing within it.

The orchestra fitted comfortably into the Academy of Music for its first concert in 1900 and has remained so ever since. It would be impossible to build a hall today that could accommodate 3000 people and yet remain so intimate, if for no other reason than modern building codes would simply require different arrangements. In addition to its auditorium, the Academy is liberally supplied with imposing staircases, a spacious and quietly elegant ballroom, and various subsidiary chambers. The catacombs beneath the hall, housing the orchestra's archives and various other appurtenances of history, are worthy of the Paris Opéra in their intricacy, massiveness, and general air of secrecy.

Of course, substantial changes have been made in the Academy over the years. Although it retains enough of an appearance of antiquity to have been designated a National Historic Landmark by the United States Department of the Interior, it has been substantially modernized. An acoustical shell was installed in 1922 to enhance the orchestra's sound; it was replaced in 1964 with a still newer one made of hardwood. In 1960 a 200,000 pound organ was presented by Mrs. Efrem Zimbalist (formerly Mrs. Edward Bok) in honor of her father, Cyrus H. K. Curtis. In 1968 two new improvements illustrated its past traditions and its future usefulness. Outside the hall handsome ornate gas lamps were installed at each of the entranceways by the Philadelphia Gas Works—exact replicas of the original lamps on the building. At the same time, within the hall a new $1,000,000 air-conditioning system began operations, permitting year-round use of the building.

In 1957 the Academy's 100th anniversary was marked with a gala concert and ball, with tickets scaled from $25 to $250. Ormandy conducted the orchestra and the variegated guest list included Marian Anderson, Danny Kaye, Artur Rubinstein, Dinah Shore and Isaac Stern. So successful was the affair socially and financially that Louchheim made it an annual event, with the proceeds (over $150,000 a year) applied to improvements in the hall. In a little more than a decade, the Academy Ball has become one of the great events of the Philadelphia social calendar.

Toward the end of 1968 the Academy took a final step forward toward assuring its future usefulness. Having acquired a parking lot directly behind the theater, it sold it to a group of builders who proposed to erect a triple-tower, thirty-three story luxury apartment complex on the site. But it was stipulated in the agreement that the new buildings would also constitute a direct addition to the Academy itself, providing an entire new backstage area including a rehearsal hall larger than any the orchestra had previously enjoyed, special recording facilities, vast storage space, loading docks, and offices for the orchestra association, which had previously been located at 230 South Fifteenth Street, a block away. The site would also include a theater-café and restaurant, a sculpture garden, and an underground parking garage, and the new additions would in no way alter either the exterior or the interior of the Academy. According to Louchheim, the $16,000,000 project would take care of the Academy's backstage needs for 100 years to come.

In its years of existence, the "Old Lady of Locust Street" has seen the rise and fall of many another famous edifice, such as the not too dissimilar Metropolitan Opera House in New York, which was born in 1883 and died in 1966, barely into its seventies, and almost a child, as venerable theaters reckon their age. With its interrelation with the Philadelphia Orchestra now assured in perpetuity, and its facilities replenished and refurbished, the Academy of Music is living proof that the first hundred years are, indeed, the hardest.

℥ CIVIC INSTITUTION

Typical of the unique civic status held by the Philadelphia Orchestra was its participation in April, 1952 in ceremonies attendant on the demolition of the Broad Street Station of the Pennsylvania Railroad. When New York's Pennsylvania Station was razed some fifteen years later, the New York Philharmonic (like most other New Yorkers) couldn't have cared less; and if the Back Bay Station is ever decommissioned it seems hardly likely that the Boston Symphony will be there to bid it farewell.

But when the acetylene torches and wreckers' balls were about to be applied to the sooty, Gothic Broad Street structure, Ormandy and the orchestra were on hand. As a matter of fact, they were on board, for the last train to leave Broad Street, hauled by locomotive No. 4800, was the Philadelphia Orchestra special, bound for the annual spring concert tour. Before their departure they played the *Star-Spangled Banner, Stars and Stripes Forever, Finlandia* and *Auld Lang Syne,* with Ormandy conducting a crowd of 5000 citizens who filled the station and joined in the singing. The Broad Street Station went out in style, and with it went the "Chinese Wall" or tracks that paralleled Market Street to the Schuylkill River, cutting the center of the city in two.

Civic celebrations and municipal recognition were no novelties to the orchestra. A grand reception was tendered upon its triumphal return from Britain, and festivities of various sorts were held, frequently at Wanamaker's or Gimbel's department stores. Ormandy, too, was showered with honors. He received honorary doctorates enough to take up almost an inch in *Who's Who in America,* including a Mus. D. from the University of Pennsylvania in 1937 and again from the Curtis Institute in 1946, and an LL. D. from Temple in 1949. A half a dozen foreign countries conferred orders of merit on him; in 1957 Boston University gave him its citation for distinguished service to music; and in 1968 he received the Pennsylvania Award for Excellence in the Performing Arts.

Local pride—as distinguished from local provincialism—also played a considerable part in making the orchestra and its activities representative of the city. Philadelphia was the home grounds of many expert performers both on the solo and orchestra levels, with a distinguished musical citizenry ranging from Marian Anderson, the great contralto, who was born there, to Efrem Zimbalist, the violinist who emigrated from Russia to the United States, became head of the Curtis Institute, and married Mrs. Edward Bok in 1943. Through Curtis, one native Philadelphian after another found his way into the orchestra's ranks. Most composers from the area, such as Samuel Barber and Gian Carlo Menotti, gravitated toward New York, but there were those who remained, and whose music was played. In the 1954 season two world premieres of works by Philadelphia composers were given, Louis Gesensway's *The Four Squares of Philadelphia* and Vincent Persichetti's Fourth Symphony.

To a greater extent than in other cities, the players of the orchestra also became minor celebrities. The departure of a musician from the orchestra, or the hiring of a new one, was invariably an item of news interest in the press, and one paper, the Philadelphia *Record*, adopted for a time the disconcerting habit of genially referring to the orchestra as the "Village Band." Most of the papers at one time or another ran articles on the individual players, their habits, hobbies and families. Thus it became possible to learn which instrumentalist worked out at the local gym and how often, which hunted and which fished, which collected art and which kept guppies.

None of the players adopted a more practical pastime than Adrian Siegel, the cellist. Siegel's gifts as an actor had already been displayed on the occasion he impersonated Charlie Chaplin at a children's concert, but he also turned out to be a talented photographer and developed the habit of keeping his camera by his side as he played. Siegel, who joined the orchestra in 1922, compiled one of the greatest portfolios of musical photographs in the country, with thousands of candid shots of Stokowski, Ormandy and virtually all the guest conductors and soloists who appeared with the orchestra. He even managed to get one photo of Stokowski and Ormandy together following the former's departure; it is believed to be the only such picture in existence.

Many of Siegel's photographs were taken without the subject's knowledge, but when artists discovered he was working on them they were extremely co-operative. Once he asked Fritz Kreisler whether he might photograph him during a performance and the great violinist unhesitatingly replied: "Any time, of course. If you do not have good light I can hold still for as much as four seconds." During Toscanini's visit with the orchestra in 1941 Siegel snapped him as unobtrusively and surreptitiously as possible from his chair in the cello section during performances, knowing of the weak-eyed conductor's aversion to having cameras pointed at him. Afterwards Siegel happened to be at the stage door when Toscanini came out, and joined a group which was helping the maestro into a cab. Toscanini suddenly spotted him. Talking to no one in particular, he said: "He plays cello. What does he take pictures for?" Then, turning to Siegel:

"Please let me have some if they are good." Later on, when he retired from playing, Siegel was appointed the orchestra's official photographer, and his pictures have illustrated countless articles and publications about the Philadelphia Orchestra, including this book.

Along with the activities of current members of the orchestra, the press also had several sad events to report during the 1950s. For the only time in the Philadelphia's history, a death occurred on stage when, on April 2, 1951, pianist Simon Barère, fifty-four, suffered a heart attack, rolled off the stool, and fell to the floor of Carnegie Hall in New York while playing Grieg's Piano Concerto in A minor during a special concert given under the auspices of the American-Scandinavian Foundation. A few moments before starting, Barère had remarked to Ormandy: "You know, this is the first time I have ever played with you; I hope I may come back again," and Ormandy had replied, "Of course."

Harl McDonald died unexpectedly at Princeton, N.J. March 30, 1955, being succeeded as manager by Donald L. Engle. A year later, on March 18, 1956, came the death of one of the great ladies of Philadelphia, Miss Frances A. Wister, at the age of eighty-one.

No one, man or woman, had worked with more love, loyalty and understanding for the orchestra than Miss Wister since its inception in 1900. It was largely through her efforts that the women's committees had come into being and contributed so much, and in a book entitled *Twenty-five Years of the Philadelphia Orchestra* she had chronicled the orchestra's early years with scrupulous accuracy and no little literary style. Miss Wister became known to the orchestra's administrators, musicians and audiences alike as something of a character about the Academy, capable of moments of sternness and flashes of humor. When Elsa Hilger came into the orchestra Miss Wister was said to have gone to one of the directors and complained that the new cellist was showing too much ankle as she sat on stage. She watched over orchestral and Academy doings with a close eye. Perhaps her greatest moment came each year when she stood on the stage in high-buttoned shoes and a huge hat with a rose in the center to present a gold watch to each member of the orchestra who had attained twenty-five years' service that season. This annual ceremony was rehearsed as thoroughly as any of Ormandy's concerts; Miss Wister would ask Joseph Santarlasci, the orchestra's assistant manager, to sit in various places in the house, especially its nethermost reaches, while she tested the carrying power of her voice. Her presentation speeches were always thoroughly prepared and personalized, according to the instrument and the hobbies of the recipient of each watch. It was a performance always deeply appreciated by the Friday matinee audience.

During her life Miss Wister exhibited no outward show of wealth, but she left a bequest of $100,000 to her beloved orchestra. Ormandy led a special performance of Bach's *Air for the G String* in her memory, while the audience stood. Miss Wister's successor was Mrs. James S. Hatfield, who continues in that post to the present, thus providing a continuity in the directorship of the women's committees that parallels the orchestra's continuity of conductors.

Substantial changes within the orchestra were going on in these years, as "Stokowski men" gradually departed or were retired at the compulsory age limit of sixty-five, and "Ormandy men" came in to take their places. Hilsberg's departure at the end of the 1951 season brought Jacob Krachmalnik, twenty-eight years old, from Cleveland as concertmaster, with David Madison continuing as associate concertmaster, a post he had held since 1940. Another new arrival was William Smith, appointed assistant to the conductor in 1952. After a year, the preposition in his title was dropped and he became assistant conductor, the same job held by Hilsberg. Smith, a native Philadelphian who had studied composition with Harl McDonald at the University of Pennsylvania, has remained assistant conductor from 1952 to the present, also playing the celesta, piano and organ for the orchestra. Smith took over the children's concerts and also conducted several subscription concerts annually; he also became the program annotator and broadcast commentator, and served as Ormandy's deputy and general assistant. Another native Philadelphian, a brilliant twenty-four year old violinist named Norman Carol, made his solo debut with the orchestra in 1954, playing the Mendelssohn Concerto; twelve years later he would return as the Philadelphia's concertmaster. Even when some of the orchestra's greatest players retired at sixty-five, top-quality replacements were always there to step into their place;

thus Marcel Tabuteau's pupil, John de Lancie, succeeded him as first oboist in 1954.

The financial state of the orchestra at this time was reasonably satisfactory, with the Philadelphia getting at least a share of benefits from the booming post-war economy. For the 1950–'51 season the annual deficit was announced as totalling exactly $23, though by 1951–'52 it had risen to a more normal $20,000. In January of 1955, C. Wanton Balis, Jr., head of the insurance firm of Balis & Co., succeeded Orville Bullitt who, after sixteen years as president of the orchestra association, became its board chairman. Balis didn't exactly find the orchestra swimming in black ink, but the annual report could at least point out that among the ten leading American orchestras, the Philadelphia had the lowest operating deficit.

⸓ TWO GRAND TOURS

Like Stokowski before him, Ormandy always was a believer in the need for the orchestra to travel, and he made it clear that he intended to keep the Philadelphians on the move. "A great symphony orchestra is a national, not merely a local asset," he said. "We regard it as a duty to travel to other cities, for although our recordings distribute our music to millions everywhere, it is still important to the life of an orchestra that it be seen and heard 'living.'"

The year 1955 seemed like an especially good time for a trip to Europe. The Continent had had a decade to repair at least the physical ravages of war; air travel had become a normal means of trans-Atlantic transport; and in Paris an American "Salute to France" had been organized as a cultural showcase to demonstrate to the presumably still skeptical Europeans that America really had other accomplishments to display besides central heating and universal plumbing.

The Philadelphia Orchestra, accordingly, became the first symphony orchestra to be sent to Europe as an officially designated group, being sponsored by the International Exchange Program of the American National Theater and Academy (ANTA) and the United States Information Agency. Prior to the departure, Ormandy had a White

House meeting with President Dwight D. Eisenhower who instructed him, according to press reports, to convince the Europeans that America had a great cultural life. This time the trip was made in three KLM airliners, with a Skymaster DC-4 carrying the instruments, and the musicians divided between a Constellation and a DC-6. Mrs. Ormandy and thirteen orchestra wives went along. The tour lasted from May 15 to June 20, when the orchestra was due back to give its summer series at Robin Hood Dell.

Three concerts were played in Paris, one at the Opéra, two at the Palais de Chaillot, with sold-out houses applauding such works as Tchaikovsky's Symphony No. 4 Moussorgsky's *Pictures at an Exhibition,* Berlioz' *Roman Carnival* Overture, and Norman Dello Joio's *Epigraph.* American works Ormandy took along with him included Barber's *Second Essay for Orchestra,* Howard Hanson's *Sinfonia Sacra,* Harl McDonald's *Santa Fe Trail,* Thomson's *Louisiana Story,* and the *Armenian Suite* by Richard Yardumian, another Philadelphia-born composer. In all, twenty-eight concerts were given in eleven countries—Belgium, France, Portugal, Spain, Italy, the Netherlands, Switzerland, Austria, West Germany, Finland and Sweden. None had ever heard the Philadelphia play live before, and in all, its sound and style were greeted as a revelation in orchestral music.

By all odds, the most memorable episode of the trip came when the orchestra decided to pay a call on Jan Sibelius in Finland. As far back as 1937, on a guest-conducting visit to Europe, Ormandy had conducted the Stockholm Konserförening Orchestra in Sibelius' Symphony No. 2 in D to such effect that the composer, hearing it over the radio, telegraphed the conductor: *"Es ist wunderbar"*—it is wonderful. Now, in 1955, with the conductor and entire orchestra actually in Helsinki to partake in a Sibelius Festival, the time seemed propitious for a personal visit.

Sibelius was eighty-nine years old, he lived in a small rural villa called Ainola, forty miles from Helsinki, he hadn't attended a concert for twenty years, and he remained in virtual isolation, never receiving large groups of visitors. But he invited the Philadelphians to come, and though all 100 members of the orchestra couldn't crowd into the glorified log-cabin that was his home, they stood outside while the old composer, well wrapped-up and leaning on a stick, came out to greet them with the words in English: "I am very happy to see you. You are all great artists." Ormandy, standing on the porch with Sibelius, told him, "There are many members of this orchestra who once played your music for the first time in the United States, who actually introduced you to American audiences." Sibelius' pale face lighted up and he waved his hand and repeated, "I am so glad to see you." The visit to Ainola produced one unexpected by-product: Sibelius had steadfastly refused to be photographed for twenty-five years. But he posed smilingly while Adrian Siegel and other camera-carrying musicians snapped away, and when the orchestra returned home it was with a rare collection of Sibelius photos.

Overseas henceforth ceased being a novelty to the Philadelphia Orchestra. In fact the following year there was talk of a trip to Soviet Russia, with the State Department endorsing the idea. The orchestra's management was willing, but the musicians demurred. For years they had been chafing at the rule on compulsory retirement at sixty-five, and now they decided to make the Russian trip conditional on the reinstatement of two senior musicians the management had said would not be permitted to return next season. Although the two questions were totally unconnected, the musicians were adamant, and the tour was canceled. Instead, the distinction of being the first American orchestra to visit Russia went to the Boston Symphony, which was touring the European continent in the summer of 1956 and was asked to extend its stay for a week, permitting a visit to the U.S.S.R. from September 5 to September 10.

But two years later, the Philadelphia Orchestra did get to Russia as part of its most extensive journey yet. For eight weeks in the spring and summer of 1958 the Philadelphia Orchestra, after crossing the ocean in three KLM planes, traveled through fourteen countries, visited twenty-five cities, and played forty-three concerts, again under the aegis of President Eisenhower's cultural exchange program, with the assistance of a generous contribution from the Rev. Theodore Pitcairn. Included were a triumphal return to England, with twelve curtain calls at Royal Festival Hall, the first visits ever to Germany and Austria, and an audience with Pope Pius XII at the Vatican. The grand finale was a three-day appearance at Europe's biggest event in years, the Brussels Fair, on July 2, 3, and 4, America's "national days" there, with Isaac Stern and Van Cliburn joining in the concerts.

But the most exciting aspect of the trip was the visit to the Soviet Union and other Communist-bloc countries. The Boston Symphony's visit, after all, had been a hasty, improvised affair; the Philadelphia's was extensive and carefully planned, with twelve concerts in Russia (Moscow, Leningrad, and Kiev), six in Poland, and two each in Romania and Yugoslavia. At the inevitable Philadelphia civic luncheon that sent the orchestra off, Ormandy was given a present to take to the Russians: a letter written by Tchaikovsky to an American friend sixty-seven years before, and now to be returned to its country of origin. The conductor was also carrying along his own bagful of novelties, for he had announced that each program on the tour would include at least one American composer: Barber, Harris, Dello Joio, Copland, Thomson, William Schuman, Creston, Keñaň, or Gershwin.

The audiences everywhere were demonstrative, but nowhere more so than in Russia. In Leningrad the musicians of the Philharmonic remembered the gift of instrumental parts the Philadelphians had sent them during the war; in Moscow crowds clustered in hotel lobbies and around entrances to greet Ormandy and the players; within the halls in both cities audiences cried "Bis, bis!" and stamped their feet in the loudest and longest demonstrations the musicians had ever heard. In Kiev, the Ukrainian capital, the orchestra had the unusually moving experience of playing on its home grounds Moussorgsky's *Pictures at an Exhibition,* whose climax is a sonorous depiction of that city's renowned legendary gate. Ormandy might understandably have feared that bringing the Great Gate to Kiev would be like carrying coals to Newcastle, but the audience, which had sat rapt throughout the lengthy piece, burst into unrestrained cheering and stamping at the end. Incidentally, among the spectators in that hall was one unexpected listener, an American conductor who had been invited to Kiev to guest-conduct the local orchestra the following week. He had not been to a Philadelphia Orchestra concert for seventeen years, and what he heard that night interested him. He was Leopold Stokowski.

ϟ EVENINGS IN THE DELL

As a result of its lengthy European trip, the orchestra was two weeks late in returning home for its scheduled summer concerts in Robin Hood Dell. This contingency had been foreseen, and the Cleveland Orchestra had been engaged to play the beginning of the Dell season. The Dell had long since become, and remains today, an integral and indispensable part of both the orchestra and the city's life. But it had had to survive more than one financial crisis, and there had been moments through its history when its survival seemed very dubious indeed.

Robin Hood Dell is a natural amphitheater in Fairmount Park, which is certainly one of the most beautiful and best-kept urban parks in the United States. The Dell area draws its name from an ancient hostelry called Robin Hood Tavern which stood there in the early eighteenth century. In 1930, when it presented a far more rustic and primitive appearance than it does today, the players of the Philadelphia Orchestra decided to organize an eight-week series of summer concerts there. They did so on their own, without any involvement by the orchestra association, hiring conductors and soloists, and taking their remuneration from the gate receipts. Alexander Smallens was the principal conductor, and Ormandy, until then totally unknown in Philadelphia, guest-conducted three concerts the first summer, and seven the second. At the Dell musical standards were as high as at any other summer symphonic series in the country; in 1944, for example, Dimitri Mitropoulos was appointed permanent conductor. But its financial vicissitudes were considerable, and in the summer of 1948 the Dell was forced to close down at the halfway point, owing $27,000 to the musicians and $27,000 to its patrons. Due to the benefactions and leadership of a music-loving industrialist, Fredric R. Mann, concerts were resumed. However, there was a general feeling that the Dell would be doomed unless a new basis of operations was found, preferably with the city of Philadelphia participating.

Actually, while the city fathers had preened and prided them-

selves for half a century over the famous orchestra in their midst, and
the citizens jokingly spoke of it as "Philadelphia's greatest export," the
municipality had contributed nothing in the way of hard cash to its
support. The City Council, finally recognizing that something in the
way of a municipal gesture was necessary, granted $50,000 in return
for four free concerts to be given at the city's massive Convention Hall.
Tickets were distributed through schools and newspapers and the first
series brought an outpouring of 60,000 listeners, most of whom presumably had never heard the orchestra before. Eventually the subsidy
plan was dropped when the orchestra, in effect, found that the cost
of giving the concerts was surpassing the total of the grant.

In 1953 the city joined in assisting operations at the Dell. The
summer before several concerts had been held experimentally with
no admission charged. Crowds of 20,000 and 25,000 had turned out,
sitting on the grassy slopes, since the seats accommodated only 10,000.
Accordingly, it was now decided to give all Dell concerts free of
charge, with the municipality and the Friends of the Dell, Inc. sharing the costs of the season. Three years later, the physical set-up at
the Dell was completely rebuilt, with a new fan-shaped amphitheater,
a new acoustical shell for the orchestra, ramps in place of the old
steps, and additional comforts and conveniences. The city and the
Friends divided the reconstruction costs of $350,000, and also the
seasonal operating budget of $150,000. Technically the Dell "leases"
the orchestra from the orchestra association each summer, so the Dell
pays 87½ percent of the men's salary for the Dell Season, with the
association paying 12½ percent.

The first six-week season in the new quarters was inaugurated
with Rudolf Serkin as piano soloist on June 18, 1956, and a gala
affair it was. Ormandy himself conducted an all-Beethoven program,
and the ribbon-cutting was achieved by an intricate operation worthy
of Rube Goldberg. Concertmaster Jacob Krachmalnik sounded an A
on his fiddle, and the resulting vibrations of 442.6 cycles per second,
by means of an electronic device, exploded a ribbon made of mag-
nesium tape in a puff of smoke. The Dell has been going strong ever
since, and is one of the compensations of a summer in Philadelphia.

The Dell concerts, of course, stayed close to standard repertory, but during the regular winter season at the Academy Ormandy managed to program an average of perhaps a dozen new works a year—a slower rate than Philadelphians had had in the Stokowski years, but still a substantial element of the yearly schedule. Similarly, although the usual leading soloists continued to return for Academy programs, distinguished new names also appeared. The autumn of 1955 was a great time for Russians. On October 3, the pianist Emil Gilels made one of the most sensational American debuts in years, playing the Tchaikovsky Concerto No. 1 with the orchestra first in Philadelphia, then in New York. The critics called him phenomenal, and Howard Taubman in the New York *Times* singled out Ormandy's contribution by noting: "One would have thought that soloist and conductor had played the work together at least fifty times." On November 25 and 26 more excitement, when Soviet violinist David Oistrakh made his United States orchestral debut in Philadelphia, playing the Brahms Concerto and the Prokofiev D Major Concerto. Praise was also showered on Oistrakh, and when he returned to Russia he unexpectedly reciprocated, writing an article in which he praised the Philadelphia Orchestra above all others: "There is hardly another orchestra in the world which may be compared in beauty of tone, flexibility, harmonious ensemble, and abundance of variety, nuances, and color . . . It is very difficult to imagine that anyone else could fit in as conductor for this orchestra except Eugene Ormandy." Still another new Russian name appeared on November 9, 1959 when the cellist Mstislav Rostropovitch played a new concerto by Dimitri Shostakovich. A large delegation of Soviet musicians, including Shostakovich, were making a group visit to the United States, and on hand for the concert, all listening intently, were Shostakovich himself, Dimitri Kabalevsky, Tikhon Khrennikov and others. It should have been a moving experience for Shostakovich, for he was sitting in the hall where some of his music had been exposed to Americans for the first time; indeed, the audience that night might well have included some of the very same people who had left early to avoid hearing it played years before.

In any case, the concert produced an ovation for both the composer and the performer, and the newspapers were full of interviews with the traveling Russians. But the excitement was as nothing to that which was building up in the wake of a startling announcement by the orchestra: Leopold Stokowski was coming back.

❧ THE RETURN

It had been a long time—nineteen years, to be exact. Stokowski literally hadn't set foot in Philadelphia in the intervening time. Nor had he established a long-term connection any place else. He had created and directed the All-American Youth Orchestra and led it triumphantly through Latin America, he had conducted at the New York City Center, he had been co-conductor of the NBC Symphony with Toscanini for a year, he had been active with the New York Philharmonic, and some thought he would be named its musical director, but the job went to Mitropoulos. His latest post was as conductor of the Houston Symphony. And, of course, he had guest-conducted around the world, including the stop in Kiev where he had heard his old orchestra give a concert, and, as he confided afterwards to friends, been deeply impressed.

Stokowski's return to the orchestra was largely the work of Ormandy, who had wanted for years to invite him back. For a long time the Board resisted, but they finally told him to go ahead and try. The invitation was extended at the beginning of 1959, with the suggested dates of February 12, 13, and 15, 1960 in Philadelphia, and February 16 in New York. When Max de Schauensee, critic of the Philadelphia *Bulletin,* interviewed Stokowski in his apartment on New York's Fifth Avenue, high over the Central Park reservoir, and asked him: "Are you pleased to return to Philadelphia next year?", the seventy-eight year old conductor replied: "Yes, I am very pleased. But it took a long time, didn't it?"

As might be expected, Stokowski's return was an emotional experience, for him, for the orchestra, and for the city. He spent some hours traveling around the town, trailed by reporters, and praising the improvements he noticed. He paid a special visit to a life-sized metal goat in Rittenhouse Square, and observed with delight that it was still shiny from being rubbed by generations of children.

When he strode out onto the stage of the Academy, his once golden halo of hair now thinned out and white, the audience rose in a standing reception. So prolonged was the applause that he had to hold up his hand to stop it. When the house quieted down, he began: "As I was saying nineteen years ago . . ." upon which everyone exploded in laughter. Then he went on to express his thanks to Ormandy and the orchestral management for "making this occasion possible."

It was not a strange orchestra which Stokowski stood before, for no fewer than thirty-six of "his" players were still in it. Even more reminiscent of old times, he had rearranged the orchestra seating, bringing the winds forward on the front right, and moving the cellos toward the rear. In typical Stokowski fashion, he was introducing a new young solosit, mezzo-soprano Shirley Verrett, who sang in de Falla's *El amor brujo*. Mozart's *Marriage of Figaro* Overture was the opening number, and the rest was vintage Stokowski—Respighi's *The Pines of Rome* and Shostakovich's Fifth Symphony. A few days later he took the same program to New York and once again received a tumultuous reception. In fact, it was such an exhilarating reunion that Stokowski was invited back for next season, and promised to return with nothing less than Schoenberg's *Gurrelieder*. He also appeared at the Dell that summer, drawing a tremendous crowd of 31,000. When a plane roared overhead he didn't even look up, leaving people who remembered how he had walked out on a sneeze to marvel at how the old man had mellowed.

Ormandy had an unexpected celebration of his own at about this time, because when he raised his baton for Beethoven's *Prometheus* Overture the orchestra played "Happy Birthday" instead, and the audience joined in. It was his sixtieth birthday, and he had been the orchestra's conductor for twenty-three years. By now he had become one of its pillars of stability, remaining steady and secure while various changes went on around him. Engle left as manager to become director of the Martha Baird Rockefeller Fund for Music, and his successor as manager became Roger Hall. Krachmalnik departed in 1958 to attempt a solo career, and the orchestra got a new concertmaster in thirty-year-old Anshel Brusilow, who had been associate concertmaster in Cleveland. William Kincaid, the great flutist, retired at the end of the '59–'60 season, another casualty of the over-sixty-five rule. His final concert was a gala affair, for he appeared as soloist in the Mozart G Major Concerto, and, on behalf of the Women's Committees, Mrs. James Hatfield presented him with an elaborate telescope, astronomy being one of his hobbies. Kincaid left behind him not only the memory of a uniquely beautiful sound but a generation of pupils he had trained, including two famous woman players, Doriot Anthony Dwyer and Elaine Shaffer. Replacing Kincaid proved to be an arduous task, the post of first flute finally going to Murray Panitz, a product, for once, not of Curtis, but of the Eastman School in Rochester, New York.

Ormandy's twenty-fifth anniversary year, 1960, almost became tragic for him when he was badly injured on December 20 in a three-car highway accident near Great Barrington, Massachusetts. His car was demolished, his wife's skull was fractured, and he lay unconscious half an hour and suffered cuts that required considerable stitching. Although his recovery was complete from the injuries, the accident served to aggravate a childhood hip-joint ailment, epiphysitis, and from then on he walked with a limp. Two weeks after Ormandy's accident, Leopold Stokowski broke *his* hip while playing with his two young sons. This necessitated a shift in schedule, and William Steinberg of the Pittsburgh Symphony was asked to do some guest-conducting in Philadelphia. Stokowski, however, had promised *Gurrelieder,* and he arrived in March to do it, walking on crutches, sitting on a stool, and directing a vast ensemble that included Rudolf Petrak, Nell Rankin, and Margarita Zambrana as soloists.

Accidents, changes, the passage of years in general—nothing seemed able to diminish the quality of the Philadelphia Orchestra, or to lower the esteem in which it was held by its audiences and its competitors. And yet as the orchestra entered the 1960s it was plagued, as other American orchestras were, with steadily deteriorating labor relations, urgently raising questions not only of wages and hours, of benefits and deficits, but of survival itself.

♪ DISCORD OVER DOLLARS

Earning a living in music has never been easy. Bach just about scraped his way through, Mozart borrowed money from all his friends who had it, Schubert died with barely a penny to his name. These were great composers and performers. Orchestral players, the great unknowns of music, have traditionally suffered not only from low pay, but from short seasons, and from almost total lack of security. Today, much of this is changed. A musician in the Philadelphia Orchestra works fifty-two weeks a year, receives minimum pay of nearly $15,000 (many get more), and cannot be discharged (after the first year) except for the most gross offenses, and then only after a full hearing. Yet the memory of the old days persists, and musicians, like the rest of organized labor, have never stopped trying to consolidate and expand their gains. The result has been a series of labor crises for the Philadelphia Orchestra, which have grown increasingly sharper and more serious with the passage of the years.

In the mid-1920s minimum pay for a Philadelphia musician was $60 a week, though there were always some who received more. This rose somewhat over the next decade, but two Depression salary cuts helped keep the figure down. Even though salaries again began to rise, the orchestra's labor relations were not helped by the summary dismissal of eight players from the orchestra in 1940, despite the subsequent reinstatement of four of them; in fact, the case gave urgency to union demands for stronger security and larger pensions. In 1943, Local 77, the Philadelphia unit of the American Federation of Musicians, put up such a stiff battle for its wage demands that a settlement was not reached until the day before the season's opener, which meant there was only one day's rehearsal for the first concert. The pattern was repeated in 1948, with the union demanding a $125 minimum weekly salary and the association offering $110. The compromise agreed upon was $115, but once again the season had to start with only one day's rehearsal.

In 1954 the season began with no rehearsal at all; in fact, it began four days late. When no contract agreement had been reached by the opening date of Friday, October 8, the entire weekend of concerts was canceled. Finally, on Tuesday, October 12, a three-year agreement was negotiated providing for annual rises of $2.50 to a minimum of $147.50. A concert was hastily scheduled for that night; the musicians, who had heard the settlement news on the radio, rushed to the hall, where they played the concert in their street clothes. The Academy was only half-filled, but those who heard the program—an all-Russian one—said it was one of the most exciting and exhilarating the orchestra had ever given.

By now it had become apparent that pay was not the only problem at issue in the negotiations. Demands were made that the orchestra "receive more money, play fewer concerts and travel less." Objections were raised to the large number of "run-outs"–the musicians' term for same-day round trips to give concerts in New York, Washington, and elsewhere. The over-sixty-five retirement rule came increasingly under fire, although the management argued strongly that, with discharges made almost impossible, mandatory retirement of older players provided the only method left of replenishing the orchestra with young ones.

In 1961 the orchestra was hit by its first protracted strike. It lasted twenty days, being interrupted only so that a scheduled United Nations concert in memory of Secretary-General Dag Hammerskjold could be given in New York. Strife was endemic in the music world that year, with the Metropolitan Opera Orchestra walking out, in a dispute eventually arbitrated by Secretary of Labor Arthur Goldberg. The Philadelphia strike ended in a minimum salary of $190 a week for a thirty-five week season, increased pensions,* and a reduction from nine to eight in the weekly "services" by the musicians—a "service" being either a concert or a rehearsal.

The 1961 strike had been settled with a two-year agreement, so

---

* The pension plan has been improved gradually over the years, with both orchestra members and management contributing. Benefits vary according to length of service and other factors. But, as of the 1968–'69 season, the average player retiring at age sixty-five after thirty-five years of service, could expect a lifetime pension of approximately $4000 a year, exclusive of Social Security.

in the spring of 1963 another round of contract negotiations began. This time the union negotiating committee raised a demand which not only took management aback but also seemed to startle many of the musicians: that the orchestra members have the right to fire the conductor if 75 per cent of the players voted in favor of doing so. Naturally, the orchestra association refused to entertain such a demand, but even more impressive was the reaction of the rank and file of the musicians themselves. When Ormandy entered to conduct the next concert, the entire orchestra rose in its place in a demonstration of support. Further, the orchestra subsequently voted 78 to 21 to accept the resignation of a union lawyer who was said to have set forth the demand.

As it turned out, the 1963 contract represented a landmark in the economic advancement of symphony musicians in the country. For the first time in history an orchestra was given fifty-two weeks' employment a year, including four weeks of paid vacation. In the third year of the three-year agreement, the minimum rose to $200 a week. When the musicians were guaranteed an additional $2,000 a year in recording fees, this meant that no one in the orchestra would be making less than $12,400 a year. Ormandy was elated with the fifty-two week aspect of the contract; he called it the "realization of a lifetime dream." Speaking for the association, Balis said: "We have broken the pattern of labor strife." At the time, it seemed like a reasonable assumption.

♀ WITHIN THE FAMILY

The orchestra may have been making labor history in the early 1960s, but it also was making music. Some of the events in which it participated were commemorative or ceremonial. In September, 1962, it was invited to join the week of special concerts that inaugurated Philharmonic Hall, the first building of the Lincoln Center cultural complex in New York. The Philadelphia's sound, like that of all the other participants in the festivities, was adversely affected by the disastrous acoustics of the new $17,000,000 hall. After the concert

Balis remarked: "At least now we have our answer for the people who ask us why we spend our money refurbishing an old hall like the Academy instead of building a new one."

On February 9, 1963, a strictly Philadelphia anniversary was celebrated when Stokowski was invited to repeat his inaugural program of fifty seasons before. Just as on October 11, 1912, he stood before the orchestra at the Academy and led it in Beethoven's *Leonore* Overture No. 3, Brahms' First Symphony, Ippolitov-Ivanov's *Caucasian Sketches*, and Wagner's *Tannhäuser* Overture. Only the *Caucasian Sketches* seemed a little dated, and even it was roundly applauded by the nostalgic audience. Philadelphia's tastes hadn't altered much over the years: the "request program" for 1963 included Franck's D minor Symphony, Brahms' Academic Festival Overture, Debussy's *Afternoon of a Faun,* and what had now become the hardiest of Philadelphia perennials, Richard Strauss' *Rosenkavalier* Suite. On somewhat more adventurous paths, Ormandy stimulated widespread interest with performances of Tchaikovsky's "Seventh" Symphony, a reconstruction put together by a Russian musicologist named Semyon Bogatyrev, and Mahler's Tenth, left incomplete by the composer but finished from sketches by the English musicologist Deryck Cooke. Both these works were subsequently recorded.

Personnel changes continued to be made gradually, as the orchestra moved toward the shape it was to have at the end of the 1960s. Roger Hall resigned as manager in 1963 to go to RCA Victor as director of artists and repertory; his eventual successor, Boris Sokoloff, came from Minneapolis in 1964 and has remained in the job to the present, making his tenure the third longest in the orchestra's history. Within the ranks of the orchestra, Lorne Munroe, first cellist since 1951, left in 1964 for the same post in the New York Philharmonic. His successor was Samuel Mayes, who after leaving the Philadelphia in 1948, had taken the first chair of the Boston Symphony and held it with distinction. With Mayes came his wife Winifred, also a cellist, contributing toward a trend of the Philadelphia to becoming a kind of family orchestra. By 1968 there were no fewer than five married couples within its ranks—the two Mayes; William and Barbara de

Pasquale, violinists; Stephane and Cathleen Dalschaert, violinists; Glenn and Julia Janson, French hornist and violinist; and Donald and Margarita Csonka Montanaro, clarinetist and harpist.* In addition the orchestra boasted even a greater rarity, an entire string quartet of brothers, the de Pasquales—violinists William and Robert, violist Joseph, and cellist Francis. The de Pasquale Quartet made occasional concert appearances on its own apart from the orchestra.

It was not, however, the only string quartet formed within the ranks of the Philadelphia Orchestra. In the early '60s four players organized themselves into a group called the Philadelphia String Quartet—Veda Reynolds and Irwin Eisenberg, violins; Alan Iglitzin, viola, and Charles Brennand, cello. After some five years of giving chamber music concerts on the outside, in 1966 they announced their resignation *en masse* from the orchestra to take up residence as performers and teachers at the University of Washington in Seattle. Naturally the sudden pulling out of so substantial a group posed problems, and the orchestra association went to court in an effort to contest their action. The rulings, however, went against the management, and the players remained in Washington State.

The entire question of outside work by musicians seemed to be exacerbated by the instituting of the fifty-two week season. Previously it had been a norm for players to seek to supplement their income by outside engagements, provided these did not interfere with their orchestral work; now, however, the management tended toward an attitude that year-round employment at high wages should be followed by a lessening, if not an elimination, of appearances with other organizations. The result was a controversy which a local wit labeled the "Moonlighting Sonata."

Several outside musical organizations were involved at various stages of the dispute. But it came to a head with the resignation in 1965 of Anshel Brusilow, an extremely talented violinist who had succeeded Krachmalnik in 1958 as concertmaster. Brusilow, a native

---

* Two other family duos were the Gorodetzer brothers, cellist Harry and double-bassist Samuel, and the two Lanzas, violinists Joseph and Louis. In the late 1920s twin brothers, John and Alexander Gray, played cello and viola.

Philadelphian, had ambitions to lay aside his bow for a baton, and became the conductor of a group called the Philadelphia Chamber Orchestra.

Now, the fifty-two week contract signed by the Philadelphia Orchestra Association and Local 77 in 1963 had a "no-moonlighting" clause which permitted members of the orchestra to teach, to give solo performances and to play in chamber groups of six players or less, but otherwise retained exclusivity of their services. Brusilow's work with the Philadelphia Chamber Orchestra, which had thirty-five members, came into question, and he announced he would resign from the Philadelphia Orchestra, later explaining: "No one could tell me that I couldn't conduct another orchestra." In any case, his departure was not precipitate, for he agreed to stay on until August 1, 1966, when Norman Carol came from the Minneapolis Symphony to take his place.

℘ THE EIGHT-WEEK STRIKE

The strike that hit the orchestra in 1966 was, everybody agrees, one of the most unpleasant episodes in the history of the Philadelphia Orchestra. It silenced the orchestra for fifty-eight days, it generated a great deal of antagonism and animosity, it produced charges and counter-charges that occupied columns of space in the Philadelphia newspapers, it embroiled Leopold Stokowski in still another controversy, it split the musical public into two camps. All that could be said in its favor was that it in no way affected the apparently unassailable excellence of the orchestra when it returned as a playing unit, and that it left hope that once the rancor had cleared away, a better and brighter era of labor relations might come into being. This was a hope, however, which remained to be tested at regular intervals in future contract negotiations.

Before the 1966 season began, the players demanded a new weekly minimum of $275 a man, $75 more than they were getting. The association's offer was for a five-year-contract culminating in a yearly minimum remuneration of $14,090, including recordings. There were other differences as well: how many "services" a week to be performed by the players; the permitting of "moonlighting"; the sixty-five retirement rule; touring schedules, and virtually all the other points of contention which had come up through the years.

The strike began on September 19, and the positions of both sides hardened as the weeks passed and concert after concert was canceled. Recriminations were sharp, and the quarrel extended beyond the immediate circle of the orchestra until the press and public were drawn into it. One editorial in the *Inquirer* melodramatically depicted the strike as a struggle between "power-play unionism" on the one hand and a "philanthropic organization which operates always at a deficit made up by voluntary contributions from lovers of fine music" on the other. The management put out statements alleging that the instrumentalists worked only eighteen hours during a typical week, and the union countered by saying that they worked seventy-two hours. It turned out that the difference lay in whether such items as practice time at home and travel time to out-of-city concerts were included in the working hours.

Perhaps the most apt appraisal of the various charges and counter-charges was that written by critic Max de Schauensee in the *Bulletin* after the strike ended. Commenting that the orchestra "over the last fifteen years has one of the worst strike records . . . of any major orchestra in the country," de Schauensee chided the orchestra men for complaining about their heavy away-from-home schedule. Travel, he said, was one of the hazards of the entertainment field, as was well known to everyone going into it. However, he wrote, "there seems to have been a lack of general communication on both sides of the wall. Sometimes a human approach and a few little personal touches in relationship can avoid a heap of trouble and forestall disaster. In this it would appear that the management fell somewhat short."

During the strike Ormandy went to Europe to fulfill previously contracted guest-conducting engagements. "I feel so helpless," he said. "It's between the union and the orchestra's board and I have been asked to stay out of it."

Stokowski, however, was asked to come into it. The men invited him to conduct a special strike benefit concert at the Convention Hall and, to the annoyance of the management, he accepted. An audience of 9000 paid $17,500 to hear Stokowski conduct Beethoven's Seventh and three shorter works, then add four encores. A speech, of course, was inevitable; in it, he praised a special acoustical shell built by the orchestra members at a cost of only $1200, and urged the audience to "do something" about the strike deadlock, although he did not say what. For its part, the city of Philadelphia attempted to intervene in the strike, with Mayor James H. J. Tate appealing to both sides to reconcile their differences and appointing a three-man "Board of Public Accountability" to look into the issues.

The strike finally ended on November 15, after thirty-five concerts had been canceled. The agreement provided for a minimum wage rising in three stages to $237.50 by 1968 and a limit of eight "services" per week. No more than six weeks of touring was to be permitted in the course of a year. Limits were placed upon the total number of concerts and the number of out-of-town trips each week. The sixty-five retirement rule remained, but the restrictions on "moonlighting" were lifted. The settlement was approved by the orchestra by a vote of 65 to 33. Since Ormandy was in Europe when the strike ended, the first few concerts were directed by assistant conductor William Smith, followed by a series under the baton of Lorin Maazel, who had been scheduled as guest conductor during the period.

The musical public was relieved when the strike ended, and it rejoiced further when it became apparent that the eight weeks of inactivity and acrimony had not in the least affected the Philadelphia's standards of execution or its distinctive tone. With the new contract signed, the orchestra was able to go back to work with all its old-time pride and professionalism—at least for another three years.

⸘ SARATOGA SUMMERS

Not least of the problems posed by the establishment of the fifty-two week work-year was that of how to keep the orchestra busy during the summertime. Since it was paying the men the year round, the management not unreasonably expected them to work the year round, except for a six-week vacation period. The question was: where?

For years, of course, the musicians, sharing with other mortals the desire to eat all year long, had been making their own arrangements for summer employment. In the earliest days, many of the Philadelphia instrumentalists had played in the orchestra of the Bach Festival at Bethlehem, Pennsylvania. The concerts at Robin Hood Dell had first started as a summer self-employment project by members of the orchestra. Even before the fifty-two week year was formalized, the management had extended the season systematically by engaging the orchestra to play at various festivals, such as the spring festival at Ann Arbor, Michigan, and a fall festival in Worcester, Massachusetts (visits to the latter were dropped in 1957). But the summer months, once the Dell season had ended, remained a gap, both musically and economically, and it was evident that it had to be filled if year-round salaries were to be feasible.

The answer was found in 1966 when the orchestra became a participant in the Performing Arts Center at Saratoga Springs, New York. Originally, the New York Philharmonic was to have joined in this project established in the rolling green country north of Albany, the state capital. But when the Philharmonic decided against participation, the Philadelphia was approached and agreed to come in, with George Balanchine's New York City Ballet Company as the other principal constituent.

The Performing Arts Center constructed at Saratoga at a cost of $3,600,000 was a gracefully semi-circular two-level auditorium seating 5100 and accommodating 7000 others on a lawn that sloped upward behind the last rows of seats. Set in the vast Saratoga State Park amid grassy promenades, ancient shade trees, and elegant refreshment facilities, the Performing Arts Center was immediately recognized as one of the most attractive summer music establishments in the world. The rustic nature of the surroundings was emphasized when it was found necessary to divert a nearby brook during the performances, as its gurgling proved distracting both to the performers and the audiences.

The Festival was set up to run for two months, with the New York City Ballet on hand in July, and August reserved for the orchestra. August traditionally is the highlight of the year in Saratoga, since it is the month in which horse races are held at the Saratoga

Race Track. This helped turn the orchestra's stay in Saratoga into a gala social season, but it also made accommodations difficult and expensive to come by for prospective visitors to the Perfoming Arts Center. The question of housing for the orchestra members and their families was solved with the use of spacious and comfortable dormitories on the new campus of Skidmore College just outside of Saratoga town. But most of the audiences for the first few years of the Saratoga operation came from the surrounding areas, including the Albany Capital District, rather than New York City, 200 miles away, or Philadelphia, about 300. To a considerable extent, this was a brand-new audience for the orchestra, and one which had known it previously on recordings, if at all. In common with most summer festivals, the programs arranged were not especially adventurous; Saratoga concert-goers heard a standard cross-section of the repertory. They also heard a good variety of guest artists, with Van Cliburn a regular visitor. Ormandy shared the podium with guest conductors, including such luminaries as William Steinberg, Seiji Ozawa and Julius Rudel. Opera was given in concert form, and one of the most memorable productions was a performance of Bizet's *Carmen* in 1968, with Rudel conducting and the mezzo-soprano Shirley Verrett giving a preview of her subsequent Metropolitan Opera debut in the title role.

In its first three years at Saratoga, the Philadelphia Orchestra seemingly had established a new home for itself. Talk continued to be heard of a festival base closer to Philadelphia, and a site in the Poconos was suggested as a possibility. But barring unforeseen development, the orchestra appeared to be a continuing part of the Saratoga summer scene.

Establishment of the Saratoga base in no way cut down on the orchestra's penchant for travel. Time was found for summer appearances at the Garden State Festival in New Jersey, the Long Island Festival at Brookville, New York, and at the Caramoor Festival at Katonah, New York, with the orchestra enthusiastically received at each site.

The orchestra's two major overseas excursions of the 1960s were a ten-nation tour of Latin America sponsored by the State Department in June, 1966, and a visit to Japan the following year. The Latin

American tour, which brought a letter of commendation from President Lyndon B. Johnson, found huge crowds wherever the orchestra played, including a capacity house of 4000 at the Teatro Colon in Buenos Aires, and a throng of 12,000 at the final appearance in Mexico City.

The Far Eastern tour was even more of a triumph. With a party of 150 that included Mrs. Ormandy and 36 orchestra wives, the Philadelphians spent three weeks in Japan and another three playing in Alaska and on the American West Coast. Five concerts were given at the Osaka International Festival and eight in Tokyo. The orchestra received reviews that can only be described as rapturous. Speaking to an overflow audience at the last concert in Tokyo, Ormandy said: "This has probably been the happiest three weeks I have spent with the orchestra on tour." Among the works played was one by a Japanese composer named Ikuma Dan, who told Ormandy afterwards that he never dreamed his music "could sound like that."

In Japan the musicians were besieged by autograph seekers. Ormandy was astonished to be asked by one old-time music-lover to autograph one of his Minneapolis Symphony 78-r.p.m. albums, made thirty-five years previously. Presents poured in on the musicians, and what they weren't given they purchased, acquiring enormous quantities of kimonos, cameras, tape-recorders, and Japanese prints. In its six weeks tour, the orchestra was heard by 100,000 listeners at concerts, and countless others during two television broadcasts in Japan.

CHALLENGE AND CHANGE

No orchestra, no matter how high its accomplishment or firm its foundation, can avoid looking toward the future. As it neared its seventieth anniversary date, the Philadelphia began to show signs of new directions it might be taking both musically and structurally in the years immediately ahead.

It became evident, in the first place, that programs were beginning to become somewhat more adventurous and forward-looking in content than had been the case for many seasons past—although it remained to be seen how far audience toleration, which had been the decisive factor in Philadelphia program planning for many years, would be stretched. After a rather conservative year in 1967–'68, the 1968–'69 season included such names relatively unknown to Philadelphia subscription audiences as Alberto Ginastera, Hans Werner Henze, Krzysztof Penderecki and Toru Takemitsu. The Philadelphia might still not exactly be in the forefront of the new music movement, but it at least acknowledged its existence.

Similarly, the orchestra was presenting to its subscribers a cross-section of the young conductors of the day. For many years, Ormandy had ceased undergoing periodic renewals of his contract for stated periods; instead, he operated under a permanent, continuing agreement which had no terminal date and which could be abrogated by either party only upon two years' notice. In effect, he was the Philadelphia Orchestra's musical director for life, with a salary estimated at from $75,000 to $100,000 a year.

Nevertheless, everyone was perfectly aware that some day a new conductor would be standing upon the Philadelphia podium. Every young conductor who appears as a guest with a major orchestra is in a sense prospecting for an eventual job; and it was no different with the Philadelphia. Three conductors reappeared with particular frequency in recent years, Lorin Maazel, Seiji Ozawa and Istvan Kertesz, but most of the other young names were also prominent. In 1968–'69 Claudio Abbado, Rafael Fruhbeck de Burgos and Carlo Maria Giulini made their debuts at the Academy; by now hardly anybody has been missed.

In 1968 the orchestra startled the record world by shifting its recording affiliation from Columbia to RCA Victor, thereby reversing its move of twenty-five years previously. The change was not made precipitously; after receiving and comparing propositions from both companies, a three-man subcommittee set up by the board of directors recommended a five-year contract with RCA. The subcommittee consisted of Crawford H. Greenewalt, president of du Pont; Richard C. Bond, president of Wanamaker's, and Stuart T. Saunders, president of the Pennsylvania Railroad. RCA's delegation was headed by Norman Racusin, head of the record division, who freely admits he was momentarily taken aback by the formidable array of business talent confronting him on the orchestra's side of the conference table. Roger Hall, the Philadelphia's ex-manager now with RCA, played an important part in leading the orchestra back into the company's fold.

The deal completed with RCA gave the orchestra a minimum guarantee of $2,000,000 over a five-year period, the most profitable arrangement it had ever enjoyed in its history. However, Balis, speaking for the orchestra association, maintained that other considerations besides the purely economic had influenced the change. "RCA," he explained, "simply offered us the opportunity to produce a more distinguished catalogue." It was indicated, however, that the lighter side would be by no means neglected, for RCA began to produce a series made by the musicians under the name of the "Philadelphia Orchestra Pops" with conductors such as Henry Mancini, the Hollywood maestro.

The old record contract expired May 15, 1968, and Columbia took full advantage of its expiring rights by recording the orchestra at a furious pace in the weeks before the terminal date in an effort to get as many works as possible "in the can" for later release. Victor, of course, began its recording sessions promptly. The result was that both companies would be releasing new Philadelphia recordings for some time to come, with royalties from both sides flowing into the association.

For his first release by RCA, Ormandy chose to record Tchaikovsky's *Pathétique* Symphony—a sentimental journey for him, since this had been the first recording he ever made with the orchestra back in 1936. Some eyebrows were raised in the industry when Columbia, in a rather obvious attempt to confuse purchasers, chose to re-release still another *Pathétique* made by Ormandy and the Philadelphia in 1960 without indicating its original date of issue.

Five other records were included in the first RCA Philadelphia release, which the record company put out with considerable fanfare. As a result of the switch to RCA, it now was possible for the orchestra to record with solo artists exclusive with that label, and two of these, Artur Rubinstein and Van Cliburn, were represented in the initial set. Rubinstein made a Chopin record including the Piano Concerto

No. 2 in F minor and the *Grand Fantasy on Polish Airs*, and Cliburn performed the Grieg A minor and Liszt E-flat Piano Concertos on a single record. Ormandy devoted one record to two American works, Charles Ives' Symphony No. 3 and William Schuman's *New England Triptych*. On another he conducted Bruckner's Symphony No. 7 in E in its original version.

The final record was devoted to setting forth the solo skills of the orchestra's first desk men and other outstanding instrumentalists. The vehicles selected were a bit unusual: four concertos for diverse instruments by Bach's contemporary, Georg Philipp Telemann. Among the Philadelphia players who had solo roles on this record were oboists John de Lancie, Charles Morris and Stevens Hewitt; violinists Norman Carol, David Madison and William de Pasquale; cellist Samuel Mayes; double-bassist Roger Scott; trumpeters Gilbert Johnson, Seymour Rosenfeld and Donald McComas; hornist Mason Jones, and timpanist Gerald Carlyss.

The shift to RCA brought the orchestra back to the Academy of Music as a recording site. Although the Academy's acoustics were excellent for live performances, Columbia's engineers had found that a low reverberation rate produced a certain dryness of sound that showed up in recordings. Accordingly for twelve years past, Columbia had made its recordings in a kind of union and social hall called Town Hall on North Broad Street. However, RCA's Princeton laboratories had developed a device to enhance the reverberation qualities of the Academy without affecting its otherwise first-rate acoustical qualities. The exact nature of the electronic methods used was not divulged by RCA, but all present considered the initial recording sessions a success. Said Ormandy: "Town Hall was a great hi-fi studio, but this sounds like a concert hall."

Important as recording royalties were to the orchestra (the average annual income from this source had for years been in the neighborhood of $250,000), the orchestra's basic financial underpinning always depended upon ticket sales at home and outside endowment income. Actually, thanks to its high record sales and near-sold out ticket average, the orchestra in an average year earns 80 per cent of its current costs—an unusually high ratio for a symphony orchestra. The remaining 20 per cent gap is met from its endowment funds, not overly large, and from annual membership campaigns. In 1966–'67, a typical year, the deficit from operations totaled $615,632, against which were applied $189,851 from endowment fund income and $231,354 in campaign contributions—leaving a net loss for the year of $194,427.

In 1966 the Ford Foundation created an $82,500,000 trust fund for the benefit of the nation's symphony orchestras, with money to be raised on a two-for-one matching basis. In the case of the Philadelphia Orchestra, a grant of $2,000,000 was authorized, provided that the orchestra itself raised $4,000,000 by June 30, 1971. At first the Philadelphia board was reluctant to accept the offer, generous as it was; there was a feeling among some directors that the board should order its own affairs, raise its own funds, and run its own orchestra without recourse to outside help. The Philadelphia probably was the only symphony orchestra in the United States that even entertained for a moment the idea of turning down the Ford grant; however, the challenge was finally accepted, and the directors set about campaigning among the community for the matching funds. In fact, they went even further, for the drive for $4,000,000 was expanded into a campaign to raise no less than $10,000,000 by 1976, the year of the National Bicentennial. The raising of such a sum, in the view of the Philadelphia's officials, would solve once and for all the orchestra's financial problems—except that they knew in their hearts that the financial problems of symphony orchestras are never solved.

Whatever the ultimate fate of the $10,000,000 campaign, the raising of the $4,000,000 necessary to qualify for the Ford grant proved relatively expeditious, for the target was reached by October, 1968, well in advance of the 1971 deadline. The end of 1968 also brought about a major change in the orchestra association's direction, for Balis left the presidency and became chairman of the board. He had served as president for twelve years.

Balis's successor was Richard C. Bond, chief executive officer of John Wanamaker and one of the city's leading business and civic figures. Bond said that his election to the top post of the orchestra association did not portend any basic changes in policies. Some close

observers of the scene held that Bond's accession to power typified
a growing interest of the Philadelphia business community in the
orchestra, and that it indicated a possible broadening of the board's
make-up and social outlook. In any case, on the eve of its seventieth
birthday, the Philadelphia Orchestra seemed to be developing closer
and broader ties with the community as a whole than at any
previous time in its history.

⸘ ORMANDY'S ORCHESTRA

For a man who is by nature unassuming and even retiring,
Eugene Ormandy has always been remarkably insistent and out-
spoken upon one point: the sound of the Philadelphia Orchestra is
his, and his alone. Echoing Louis XIV's *"L'Etat, c'est moi,"* he says
unabashedly: "The Philadelphia sound, it's me." And, after thirty-
three years of conducting the orchestra, it seems like a reasonable
enough statement.

For years Stokowski's awesome reputation obscured Ormandy's
achievement in Philadelphia. Long after he departed, Stokowski's
shadow remained, with skeptics contending that the orchestra he had
built would make almost any conductor sound good—for a while.
It took time and patience for Ormandy to disprove the theory, but
he succeeded. In effect, he built a new orchestra almost imperceptibly
within the framework of the old one. By the end of the 1968–'69
season only eight players who had been engaged by Stokowski still
remained in the orchestra.* For better or worse, the present-day
Philadelphia Orchestra and its sound are Ormandy's, and have been
for years.

How is that sound achieved? Part of the answer surely lies in
the simple desire to obtain it. Sound, after all, is the medium

---

* All eight were string players. Their names, with their starting dates, follow.
Violinists: Manuel Roth (1924), Louis Gesensway (1925), David Madison (1927),
Meyer Simkin (1930). Violists: Paul Ferguson (1930), Leonard Mogill (1935).
Cellist: Samuel Mayes (1936). Bassist: Carl Torello (1934). Cellist Elsa Hilger,
who began in 1935, retired at the close of the 1968–'69 season. Several other current players were with the orchestra while Stokowski was co-conductor, but they
were engaged by Ormandy.

through which music communicates, and Stokowski in the past and Ormandy in the present have concentrated upon producing tones that are unsurpassable in their purity and richness. Ormandy says he can evoke a sound highly similar to the Philadelphia's from other orchestras after several rehearsal sessions, and there are recordings which bear him out. The conductor remains the basic element in producing the Philadelphia sound, first by his own sensitivity of ear, second by his ability to evoke what he wants from the musicians.

The second element is the quality of the instruments. The Philadelphia possesses one of the finest collections of musical instruments, especially string instruments, of any organization in the world. It is a specialty of the house, and one which can be measured not only monetarily (the orchestra's instruments are insured for $500,000 when it goes on tour) but in terms of hundreds of years of craftsmanship. Amati, Gagliano, Goffriller, Guarnerius, Stradivarius—these and many other famous instrument makers' names are liberally represented in the orchestra's ranks. Most of these are the property of the orchestra, and they are not kept for special occasions but used in performances week in and week out. Some are individually owned by the players, and are often purchased with the assistance of the orchestra. Violinist Herbert Light, for example, recently obtained a Stradivarius with a value "in excess of $50,000"; the orchestra gave him an interest-free loan to help pay for it. The double-bass players of the orchestra, who seem to take an especial pride in their work as a section, make great efforts to hand their instruments down as one generation succeeds another. Ferdinand Maresh, second in the section, tells of getting a bass used previously by Vincent Lazzaro: "I fell in love with it," he says, "and he gave it to me cheap because he knew it would stay in the orchestra. I don't know of any other orchestra where that goes on."

Fine instruments, however, are useless without fine players, and it is the human element which provides the final essential of the Philadelphia sound. In a sense, the orchestra assures itself of a continuance of its tonal qualities at each auditioning of a new player, for the capacity of meeting Philadelphia standards of technique and tone is paramount. Even then, most musicians say that it takes a

new player several years to integrate himself fully into the Philadelphia tonal picture. New players often tell of being almost overwhelmed by the sound around them when they first enter the
orchestra. Says a young cellist who has been with other major
orchestras including the Pittsburgh: "This is a more demanding
orchestra than the others. It requires more physical strength—
musical strength, but also sheer force." Says a veteran violinist: "We
simply dig in and play harder than other orchestras do. Ormandy is a
string player himself and knows how to get the sound. Our sound
is essentially a string sound. Ormandy insists on depth, fullness and
richness, and we give it to him."

On the whole, Ormandy is as popular with his men as any
conductor is likely to be. Goddard Lieberson, president of Columbia
Records, once remarked: "Show me an orchestra that likes its conductor and I'll show you a lousy orchestra," and there is an element
of truth in the quip. Affection is a quality few conductors seek and
few musicians bestow; in the Philadelphia Orchestra there exists
basically a working relationship founded on amicability and mutual
respect. There are musicians in the orchestra who have played at
other times under such conductors as George Szell, Erich Leinsdorf
and the late Fritz Reiner, and while they respect these men as
musicians they regard them as martinets, and prefer Ormandy's more
relaxed and human approach. Conversely, there may well be former
Philadelphia players in other orchestras who prefer their present
conductors to Ormandy. But there is no doubt that Ormandy, who
is not basically a disciplinarian, has succeeded in establishing a
relationship with his men that gives him the results he wants. "Look,"
says a practical-minded brass-player, "no conductor is Santa Claus.
To us, picking your conductor is like picking your poison. But there
are not many of them I'd trade for Ormandy."

Although Ormandy has done a fair share of guest-conducting
both in the United States and abroad, he has remained essentially
the Philadelphia's conductor. He was totally unaffected by the trend
which developed among conductors in the mid-1960s to reducing their
workloads, curtailing their seasons, or retiring from their musical
directorships altogether. As a season-long music director taking per-

sonal responsibility for the bulk of the orchestra's concerts at home and on tour, Ormandy represents something of a musical anachronism and may possibly be the last of his line. He also is unusual in that he has never become associated as a conductor who concentrates on any particular musical era, style, or composer. He has made a specialty of being a non-specialist. He's not a Baroque man, a Beethoven man, a Berlioz man, or a modernist. He's an *orchestra* man; if a piece has been written for orchestra, and he thinks it worth playing, he will play it with a minimum of fuss and fanfare. Nor does he insist on limiting himself to masterpieces; he once quoted approvingly a reference of Francis Poulenc's to *"l'adorable mauvaise musique,"* and insisted that it, too, be given its place.

Ormandy's memory is prodigious; except in concertos and in some new works he does not conduct with a score. In his early days in Minneapolis he was asked to record a new piece, Roy Harris' overture *When Johnny Comes Marching Home.* Unfortunately, it was late in arriving, and didn't reach the conductor until the morning of the recording session. Ormandy was in a rage, but looked it over at breakfast and for a time afterwards. Then, still angry, he tossed it on the floor, went to Northrup Auditorium, where the session was being held, and recorded it forthwith—from memory. His career is studded with similar feats, though usually without the tantrum. When he was invited to conduct Johann Strauss' *Fledermaus* at the Metropolitan Opera he knew only the overture; within a few days he memorized the entire score.

Ormandy has often found himself memorizing unconsciously new scores which he had intended only to read through. He told Donald Engle, when the latter was orchestra manager, that memorizing scores required no trouble on his part, adding: "If it were any trouble I would use the notes." An American pianist tells of playing a concerto with the orchestra, then seating himself in a vacant chair in the wings to listen to Ormandy conduct the second part of the program. As Ormandy was about to enter he asked Saul Caston, then the assistant conductor, who was standing near by: "What symphony is it tonight?" "Brahms' Fourth," Caston replied. "Oh," said Ormandy, and went out and conducted. The pianist suspects the little charade may have been enacted whimsically for his benefit, but he also is sure Ormandy could have gone out and conducted any symphony in the repertory which Caston might have named.

Ormandy's enormous facility and his impeccable technique have won him the admiration and respect of professionals throughout the world; they have also led a few critics to accuse him of a tendency to remain on the surface of the music rather than penetrating its depths. It is a charge difficult to document on the basis of his massive body of recordings or the memory of dozens of magnificent concerts with the Philadelphia Orchestra. The big gesture, the spectacular "interpretation," the creation of a podium "personality" are not part of Ormandy's character and have never been among his goals. To him a successful concert is one in which the composer's music has been set forth to an audience with all the intellectual straightforwardness, professional efficiency, technical perfection and tonal beauty of which he and his orchestra are capable. And it is precisely because all compositions of all eras are equally responsive to this professionalism in the highest degree that Ormandy and his orchestra are at home everywhere in music. For versatility, virtuosity and sheer beauty of sound the Philadelphia Orchestra of today knows no equal, and none other but Eugene Ormandy could have brought it to its present state.

♭ A TALK WITH ORMANDY

(Transcript of a conversation between Eugene Ormandy and the author in Phiadelphia, October, 1968).

H.K. Could you describe to me the emotion you felt on the first occasion you conducted the Philadelphia Orchestra, the time you stepped in for Toscanini?

E.O. I wish I could! Actually, this wasn't the first time I had conducted the orchestra; I had conducted two summers at Robin Hood Dell. So I knew I would be facing friendly colleagues. Still, the thought of replacing Toscanini, whom I admired so much, was exciting and thrilling. I had only three days to prepare for the first rehearsal, and I worked at night and on the train going to and from Philadelphia for the rehearsals. It was hard, but I was young, enthusiastic and hopeful, and it was a challenge I was happy to accept. Now, when I came out on the stage for the concert, many in the audience didn't know that Toscanini had canceled out. They hadn't seen it in the papers and they hadn't looked at the program. So when I walked out I could hear a kind of "Huh?" coming from all over, as if they were wondering "Who is this boy?" I looked much younger than I was then, with a lot of reddish blond hair. But the audience gave me a wonderful welcome, the concert went off well, and the critics were more than kind.

H.K. What was the transition period between you and Stokowski like—the years from 1936 to 1941 or so, when you overlapped?

E.O. Well, so far as I was concerned it was not really a transition. Mr. Stokowski conducted six weeks out of each season and I believed and hoped that he would continue indefinitely to conduct the six weeks in each season. It was his decision not to return after 1941.

H.K. Well, after you had been given the job and were to share the podium with Stokowski, how did you and he work out who was to conduct what?

E.O. I think most conductors, stepping into a new job with an orchestra, would have said: "Now I'm going to show them how *I* conduct, how *I* approach Tchaikovsky or Beethoven or Stravinsky or anybody else." I instinctively, without talking to a single human being, said to myself: "My dear friend, you've found a marvelous orchestra, one of the greatest in the world, with an incomparable sound. Be careful to preserve that sound." So I decided to continue with the orchestra as I found it, making gradual changes according to my own ideas.

H.K. Did you and Stokowski discuss specific repertoire?

E.O. He had only six programs to make for each season while I had twenty-two, and we both had to consider what works each of us planned to record during the season. He himself told me that he preferred to concentrate on the moderns and the Russians while I concentrated on the classics. So after his programs were made I planned mine and there was no duplication. I decided it was better for him to choose what he wanted, and for me to select from the wealth of musical literature that was left. There was plenty to pick from.

H.K. You spoke of gradual changes. Can you give me an example?

E.O. Well, one criticism I heard in the old days was that the Philadelphia was a show-piece orchestra geared to the Russian literature—Tchaikovsky, Rimsky-Korsakov, Stravinsky—rather than to the classics. It was very foolish to say this, because the orchestra in those days could play anything. But when I took over I made it my business to play three or four Mozart and Haydn symphonies each season. Some of the subscribers even complained about this!

H.K. What happened after Stokowski left Philadelphia? Why did it take him so long to come back?

E.O. There was some bitterness between him and the board when he left; apparently he made some demands the board felt they couldn't fulfill and he left and went to California. I myself felt that it was a tragedy that this man who made the orchestra world-famous no longer appeared with it.

H.K. So you kept inviting him back—

E.O. No, I didn't. But I did mention it to the board, pointing out that a new generation was growing up who had never seen nor heard him. For a long time they doubted the wisdom, but at last they agreed. I wrote to Stokowski, who was living in New York by then, inviting him to conduct his former orchestra. He accepted and has returned every year since. I really was very happy to be the person who had the imagination to bring this great man back to Philadelphia again.

H.K. At various points in your career you have conducted both with and without a baton. What is the explanation?

E.O. I always used a baton when I conducted, until 1939, when I tore a ligament in my right shoulder and had to have an operation. The doctor recommended I stop using the baton then; the strain is much less without one. In 1950 when I was rehearsing *Fledermaus* at the Metropolitan Opera the singers on the stage told me they couldn't see my beat, so I borrowed a baton and the problem was solved. From then on I used the baton for operas, but not in concerts. In 1960, after talking it over with my doctor, I started to use the baton for concerts again and have been doing so ever since. It makes little difference to me, although I find that the members of the orchestra prefer to have me use the baton.

H.K. Can conducting be taught?

E.O. When I am asked this question I am reminded of a story I heard when I was a young violinist touring Germany. A young man went to Nikisch as he was getting out of his car at the Gewandhaus and said: "Maestro, please give me lessons. I want to be your pupil." Nikisch replied: "Of course, I'd be glad to. It's very easy: 1–2–3–4, 1–2–3, 1–2. The rest you have to do yourself," and left. I agree. Conducting cannot be taught. If you go into the history of great conductors you will find that none of them had conducting lessons as such. They all grew up as orchestral musicians and because of their inborn talent for conducting, when the opportunity presented itself, often unexpectedly, they were ready to step on the podium. A possible exception to this theory is Mr. Stokowski, who was a church organist before he became a conductor.

H.K. It has been said that you play less modern music than Stokowski did with the orchestra. Is this true, and if so, is it because the music being written today is not as interesting as the contemporary music of his time?

E.O. I should really answer the last question first. In my opinion, contemporary music today is not as great as in the days when Stravinsky, Schoenberg and Berg were in their prime. But aside from that, when I first came to Philadelphia in 1936 I received many letters saying: "Please don't play too many contemporary composers. Play the old masters. We come to concerts to be entertained and not to be educated." So, as a very young, inexperienced person, I decided to combine the two. I figured out that any music lover would be willing to have about 25 per cent of the program modern and 75 per cent the great eighteenth, nineteenth and early twentieth century masters. However, that has changed during my more than thirty years, and I now play very much more contemporary music. We do about twenty-eight or thirty new works a season, not all of them major. The 1968–'69 season was more heavily programmed with contemporary works than in many previous years. But I select very carefully. I feel that it is our duty as conductors of great orchestras to give the public a taste of the new works being created today. How do we know that another Beethoven, Mozart, Haydn or Bach may not be among us? We must give them a chance to be heard, and I will continue to introduce new works to our audiences.

H.K. It has been said that the symphony is dead as a musical form. Do you agree?

E.O. My opinion is just the opposite. I think the symphonic form and the symphony orchestra will be here long after *we* are dead.

H.K. But are composers going to continue writing music that can be played by symphony orchestras, that will replenish the symphonic repertory?

E.O. My answer is yes. But all of us who were trained in the standard musical language will have to learn a new form of music which is completely different from that we knew years ago. The Polish composer Penderecki, whom I consider one of the great present-day composers, created his own language, an entirely new form of writing. My colleagues and I had to learn it for performances of his *Threnody for the Victims of Hiroshima,* which we played in the 1968–'69 season, and his new *Slavic Mass,* which will receive its first American performance later on.

H.K. How has the conductor's job changed in your years with the Philadelphia Orchestra?

E.O. The answer is very simple. When I came we had a twenty-eight week season, now we have fifty-two. We tour far more, we travel abroad, we have added the four-week Saratoga season. It is much more difficult, since we have to learn and prepare many more works, new and old.

H.K. Your musical memory, which is so remarkable—does it extend to other things, such as the printed page of a book, or is it just a musical facility?

E.O. No, I cannot remember books as well. But music I do remember. For contemporary works I always use a score because I feel that the members of the orchestra are more comfortable in knowing a conductor has the score in front of him.

H.K. Have you changed in any way as a conductor in those years?

E.O. Well, thirty-three years ago when I heard something wrong I looked in that direction. Now I look the other way, as if I didn't hear it.

H.K. When did you start to do that?

E.O. When I realized that every member of the orchestra is just as human as I am. I make mistakes, too.

H.K. Young conductors today seem unwilling to settle down to a permanent musical director's post in the traditional sense. Do you approve or disapprove?

E.O. I don't approve or disapprove, but I can understand. They think they are wonderful conductors and many of them are, or we wouldn't invite them here. But their attitude often is: "I want to make a world-wide reputation in a hurry and I don't have time to sit down." Some of them have committed to memory or are prepared to play five or ten programs, and they would love to cash in on them, conducting them in various European countries. The responsibility of a major or even lesser symphony orchestra is something they don't want. This is not good for an orchestra; one of the reasons for the stature of the Philadelphia Orchestra is that it has had only two conductors in fifty-five years. It is not good for the development of a conductor, either. Conductors grow with their own orchestras.

H.K. You, more than almost any conductor, have been devoted to a single orchestra, putting in more time and labor with it than any one has done anywhere else with one orchestra. Why?

E.O. Because as time went on it became a way of life for me, and it is the only life in which I am happy. Making music with these artists is a wonderful experience, and a new experience every day. It is so easy for a conductor to communicate his ideas and wishes to them, and they play as one great Stradivarius, not as individual musicians. Every guest conductor has this same opinion.

H.K. How much thought do you give to an eventual successor in Philadelphia? What kind of conductor would you like to see come after you?

E.O. This is a difficult question to answer. First of all, the decision is up to the board. I am not ready to retire, but I do naturally think about a successor as I get older. The conductor who comes here should be an outstanding, well-rounded musician, even if he's only thirty years old. By now conductors with great talent have great experience at thirty or thirty-five. He should remember that Philadelphia is a conservative city but that it also likes to look forward. He should be able to present a variety of programs—classics, romantics, contemporaries. He should be prepared to stay—I don't think the board of directors would engage a man, even today, even with the fifty-two week season, who would want to conduct less than half the season. He should make up his mind that this is his home, this is where he belongs. He should be willing to become a leader in the community. All of that combined would make the kind of conductor who should take over the Philadelphia Orchestra.

CHAPTER V

The Life of the Orchestra

"The professional musician, as such, can have no special social status whatever, because he may be anything, from an ex-drummer boy to an artist and philosopher of world-wide reputation."
—George Bernard Shaw, *The World,* January 11, 1893

THE AMERICAN PLAYER

That orchestras are made up of people is a fact sometimes overlooked by musical commentators and historians, not to mention an occasional conductor. They are people linked by a common interest which also happens to be their profession, but they also are motivated by the same goals and purposes as others—making a living, raising a family, staying healthy, pursuing happiness.

Orchestras embody a tremendous ethnic variety. Music has always been a melting pot, and few groupings of 100 persons represent as great an admixture of racial stocks and religious backgrounds as a typical symphony orchestra. And yet the make-up of a group like the Philadelphia Orchestra has been undergoing a tremendous change in the post-World War II era, and its end is not yet in sight. It is becoming, in a word, Americanized.

The typical musician of the late nineteenth century was foreign-born and trained; indeed, in some cases he even retained his foreign citizenship. The Philadelphia Orchestra that Leopold Stokowski inherited in 1912 was almost entirely German by birth and schooling. So was the Chicago Symphony of Theodore Thomas and Frederick Stock. The Boston Symphony always had a high proportion of French players. Hungarians contributed heavily to a generation of symphonic musicians in America; when Eugene Ormandy was engaged for the Capitol Theater Orchestra it was conducted by Erno Rapee, a fellow Hungarian, and he found a good many other compatriots playing there. The violin was the traditional instrument handed to the children of Jewish families in Czarist Russia, and many of these young "fiddlers on the roof" eventually made their way to American symphony orchestras. Italians followed a similar path. The influx of foreign artists was at its height during the era of unrestricted immigration into the United States, but in the years immediately before and after World War II musicians were numerous among the refugees who found haven in this country.

But perhaps for the last twenty years, and certainly for the last ten, the Americanization of the symphony orchestra has been proceeding at a rapid pace. This process is but one facet of the slow but steady growth of musical culture in this country. High school bands and orchestras—particularly the former—are discovering incipient wind instrumentalists throughout the land. Good string players are far less common; no one has yet devised a quick and easy method of learning the violin, and the only time to begin is in early childhood. But surprising numbers of brass and woodwind players don't really get started until their early teens, and public high school bands are turning out some first-rate musicians.

Certainly their products are playing an increasing role in the make-up of the Philadelphia Orchestra. Trombonist Tyrone Brueninger began playing the baritone horn in elementary school, switched to the trombone at Upper Perkiomen High School in Pennsylvania, auditioned for the U.S. Army Band where he passed the musical test but flunked the physical, and stepped into the Philadelphia Orchestra at the age of twenty-eight. Tuba player Abe

Torchinsky first became acquainted with his massive instrument when he joined a neighborhood band as a boy in Philadelphia. Bass trombonist Robert Harper, one of the orchestra's two players of American Indian descent (the other being cellist Samuel Mayes), became a musician at the age of twelve in school in Quincy, Massachusetts, trying various instruments and finally settling on the trombone. Ferdinand Maresh played violin as a child; his high school teacher needed a double-bass player, switched him to the instrument, never thinking he was training a budding Philadelphian. The paths to a great orchestra do not always lie through a traditional conservatory.

Some authorities, such as Sol Schoenbach, former first bassoon of the orchestra and now head of the Settlement Music School in Philadelphia, believe that the next great wave of orchestral musicians is going to be Negro. The Philadelphia has already had two Negro players in the category of "extra musicians"—that is, instrumentalists who are employed on a more or less regular basis when the orchestra has to be augmented for special concerts or when there is a temporary vacancy owing to an illness or death in the ranks.

But whatever the color, race or religion of its players, there is scarcely any doubt that within a relatively few years the Philadelphia Orchestra will be virtually 100 per cent American-born and trained, and the probability is that while the great conservatories such as Curtis will supply many players, more and more are going to get their basic training in public schools.

What kind of young player is coming into the orchestra these days and is likely to continue doing so in the immediate future? A typical example might be that of a cellist named Lloyd Smith, who was born in 1942 and joined the orchestra in 1967, playing at the last stand of his section. In appearance, at least, Smith resembles a young lawyer or business man rather than presenting the traditional image of a musician; he is married, has a young child, lives in nearby Bryn Athyn, builds model trains for a hobby, and except when he gets onto the stage with a cello between his knees is indistinguishable from the mass of middle-class, suburban humanity of which he is a part.

Like many of today's newer players, Lloyd Smith is a mid-

Westerner, born in Cleveland and raised in Indianapolis, where he attended Arsenal Technical High School. After stabs at the piano and violin he settled on the cello as his preferred instrument, and played it in his school orchestra. He spent a full year in academic work as an undergraduate at Columbia University before deciding to shift to Curtis Institute and a full-time musical career.

While still a first-year man with the Philadelphia Orchestra, Smith had an experience which illustrates vividly the twin pulls on a modern musician—the responsibilities of being a family man and the challenges of being a performing artist. The conflict came about in June, 1968, when, just at the time his wife Rheta was expecting their first child, he was invited to appear as soloist in Dvorak's Cello Concerto in B minor in several summer concerts with the Indianapolis Symphony at Garfield Park in Indianapolis. No father wants to miss the arrival of his first-born; no orchestral musician wants to miss the chance of stepping forth as a soloist. Rheta Smith was not only an expectant mother but an understanding musician; she had been an oboist in the Pittsburgh Symphony when she met Lloyd. She told her husband to take care of Dvorak while she took care of the baby. Eugene Ormandy was equally co-operative: he gave the young cellist a week off to appear in Indianapolis as soloist.

And so the concerts went on. Smith was able to rush back to Philadelphia between appearances to greet a baby boy a few hours after his birth, and then to return ecstatically for his final performance in the park. The management even announced the birth to the crowd just before the concert began. Then, to provide a soggy anti-climax to the whole hectic weekend, a cloudburst hit the park at the fourth measure of the concerto, scattering the audience, the orchestra, and the still somewhat bewildered new parent.

Not all of Lloyd Smith's weekends are like that. But he, like thousands of other musicians—and their wives—have found that earning one's living playing in a symphony orchestra in the United States today makes for a life that is exciting and rewarding, exhausting and frustrating. But for all its tensions and pressures, not many of them would exchange their careers for any other.

⸮ PEOPLE AND PROBLEMS

The fact that a certain trumpeter can't eat sauerkraut because it destroys his lip control, or that many a violinist has to contend with tennis elbow or chin rash, or that a particular cellist has an aversion to the cellist at the next stand may seem like purely personal problems, but they have their effect upon the proper interpretation of a symphony by Mozart or Beethoven who, it should be remembered, had troubles of their own.

Physical fitness is a basic matter to an orchestra musician. An office worker can drag himself through a day with a bad headache; a physician usually ignores his own head cold; there are newspaper men who contend they are at their best after a night on the town. But an orchestral musician who plays at less than peak condition endangers not only his own performance but that of the orchestra. "You don't go out on a binge the night before a concert," says trumpeter Gil Johnson. "Most players place a great value on their general physical condition. It affects their breathing, their diaphragm control, their co-ordination, their alertness." Many musicians watch their pre-concert diets carefully (sauerkraut is only the beginning of a long list of spicy foods that trouble brass players), and a good many work regularly at physical conditioning. A visit to the YMHA gymnasium at Broad and Pine Streets near the Academy of Music is likely to find a number of surprising spectacles: bassoonist Bernard Garfield and bassist Gilbert Eney running laps around a track, violinist Irvin Rosen briskly punching a bag, cellist William Saputelli lying on his back pushing up a metal bar with his feet. The Friday matinee audience never saw them like that.

Not only must a successful musician be conscious of his own state of mind and body, he must also keep an eye on his neighbor's. The problem that office and industrial workers have of adjusting to one another's personalities and idiosyncracies is multiplied a hundred-fold in the human interplay of an orchestra. The ultimate objective of an orchestra's activity—the performance of music—depends upon 100 people working together in absolute and literal harmony. To withdraw or to sulk, to soldier on the job or to offer anything less than one's best, is fatal.

And yet abrasive elements are always present. Playing music is grueling and exacting work, and the better one is at it, the more demanding are the standards he is likely to set himself to meet. Playing music in close proximity to others poses special problems: in an ordinary office it's always possible to change the location of one's desk, to decamp to a corner where the light is better, to move away from the loud-mouth who's always using the phone, to take up a position with a better view of the steno pool. But a bassoonist is stuck with his fellow bassoonists and the rest of the woodwinds; a first violinist must sit with the first violins and a second with the seconds; the cymbal player has to rub shoulders with the timpanist.

In this tightly confined world in which a player spends his entire working days (and nights), personalities can grate and viewpoints clash. A great deal of attention is necessarily paid to such matters as compatability of stand partners. Most of the instrumentalists in an orchestra line up, like Noah's animals, in pairs, two players to one stand. The musician on the inside, that is, away from the audience, gets to turn the pages, which most players say they do not regard as an onerous chore, however it may seem to an onlooker.

Adjusting to one's immediate neighbor both musically and personally is essential, since musicians see their stand partners almost as much as their wives, and find them much more inescapable. "Even the positioning of the music stand can become a major issue," says violist Gabe Braverman, who for years has worked in close association with his partner Leonard Mogill. Braverman says that stand partners often develop musical ideas and interests together. Since they work from the same sheet of music they have to see to it that bowing indications, accents and other markings are clearly distinguishable. "In our orchestra," Braverman adds, "the pencil and eraser are very busy." Seeing to it that the music is in good order and on the stands for each concert is the responsibility of librarian Jesse C. Taynton, a former double-bass player.

If working with a stand partner involves one of the basic personality adjustments a player may have to make, taking his place as
a member of a section is another. A cellist may not automatically
love or admire every other member of the cello section, but he has
no other choice than to work with him closely. Markings of bowing
and phrasing are worked out by the section head, usually in co-
operation with the conductor, and passed back through the section;
here, as in so many other aspects of orchestral playing, individuality
has to be sacrificed, although any conductor who knows his trade will
listen carefully to an objection or suggestion even from the last
desk. Sometimes string players have difficulty in hearing themselves
as they play in their sections. "We're listening to the other players,
too," explains Lloyd Smith, "and your own sound always doesn't
come through. You can't tell by looking at the fingerboard or the
bow, either; you have to listen. That's what makes it difficult to
play well in an orchestra as compared to chamber or solo music."
Section loyalties are sharp in the Philadelphia Orchestra; a bass
player, for example, insists that "man for man, we have the finest
basses in the country." The Philadelphia strings in general regard
themselves as second to none. Says Francis de Pasquale, cellist who
recently collected his Swiss watch for twenty-five years of service:
"There's a shortage of string players in the United States—until the
Philadelphia Orchestra announces an audition. Then a hundred
show up."

An orchestra as a unit must also have its own *esprit de corps,* and
probably the Philadelphia works together as cohesively and amicably
as any large musical organization in the country. There seems little
division along racial or religious lines, which has not always been
the case in American orchestras. Double-bass player Carl Torello
recalls: "There was a time in Boston when if you didn't speak
Parisian French, you were just about out. There was a Bohemian
group in Chicago that operated the same way. Man, they had sharp
elbows." Says trumpeter Samuel Krauss: "We have the most homo-
geneous group in the world."

Despite the closeness of working relationships among the players
—or perhaps because of it—differences in personality, opinions and

outside interests have a way of making themselves felt once the performances are over. "When the stick comes down for a concert," says first flutist Murray Panitz, "nobody thinks of individuals. But when it's not playing, an orchestra is like any large group of people. There are cliques and groupings, feuds and friendships. Some people you're really friendly with; others you just nod to." Since approximately half the orchestra attended the Curtis Institute there are a good number of friendships that date back to student days. Union affairs also serve some members as a rallying point; as in most locals there are both militants and moderates, and the differences between them sometimes become acrimonious. Actually, the musicians in the orchestra have found it desirable to form a kind of union within a union, for although all belong to Local 77, American Federation of Musicians, they have established, with the consent of the local, an orchestra committee (headed by violinist Ernest Goldstein, who succeeded bass player Neil Courtney in 1968), which conducts most of their collective bargaining and grievance affairs directly with the orchestra association.

If there is one point upon which orchestral musicians differ from most other mortals it is in the intensity with which their job becomes part of their daily lives. A few years back there was a delightful anecdote about the wealthy Texan who flew his private plane to New York to hear his compatriot Van Cliburn play on his triumphal return from Moscow. Lost in the big city, the Texan accosted a bearded old rabbi who happened to be passing by and asked him how he could get to Carnegie Hall. The sage looked him up and down from his ten-gallon hat to his spurred boots, and replied: "Practice, practice, practice."

Exactly the same path leads to the Academy of Music, and the members of the Philadelphia Orchestra never cease following it. Not that every fiddler goes home every night and works over every part of every piece of the following weekend's programs; that's what rehearsals are for. But when musicians have an unfamiliar composition coming up or an especially difficult one, they will not hesitate to take their work home with them. And when, for any reason, there is even a slight lag in concert or rehearsal schedules, they will take out their instruments on their own just to stay in trim. Many, indeed, practice literally every day of their lives. There's an old saying that you can recognize a musician's house by two things: it looks slightly run down, and there's always music coming out of it.

⸘ THE ORCHESTRA WIFE

"In our house all we care about these days is the Walton Concerto." The speaker is an attractive blonde young woman named Barbara de Pasquale. She is married to William de Pasquale, associate concertmaster of the Philadelphia Orchestra, and her preoccupation with Walton's Violin Concerto resulted from an appearance he was to make with the orchestra as soloist in the work.

Barbara de Pasquale—who was born Barbara Sorlien of Norwegian stock in Fargo, North Dakota—is a musician herself, playing several rows behind her husband in the Philadelphia Orchestra. They were the first married couple to join the orchestra as a team.

Musicians make a practice of marrying musicians, much more so than, say, lawyers marry lawyers, or poets marry poets. But even a woman who does not play an instrument surrenders her life to music when she marries a musician. It's possible for the wife of an accountant or broker or merchant to pay little heed to her husband's business, but a musician's wife will hear music, or talk of music, all through her life. Far more than most other wives, they habitually observe their husbands at work. Saturday night at the Academy is traditionally orchestra wives' night, although there are some who go on other nights. Many wives, and children, too, journey to Saratoga with their husbands for the summer season, living in rented cottages or in the Skidmore College dorms. In recent years—unlike 1936, when the orchestra men voted to make their first cross-country tour a stag affair—wives in large numbers have been going along on the journeys to Japan and Europe.

But being an orchestra wife also makes for a life beset by problems that are numerous and vexatious. The normal processes of raising, caring for, and educating a family are complicated by being married to a man who customarily works nights as well as days, who practically never has a free weekend, who travels and tours a great deal, whose schedule is subject to sudden calls and changes, who does a great deal of studying, practicing (and often teaching) at home, who, above all, by the nature of his work operates continually under a high degree of artistic and personal tension.

Says Mrs. Ernest Goldstein, whose husband plays in the first violins: "The hours and the separation are big problems. It's hard for Ernie to get together with the kids because of the hours. And it's a strenuous life with the travel, and because the players are always giving a maximum effort."

Violist Braverman sums it up this way: "The role of the orchestra wife is a unique one. No other profession produces the same kind of domestic relationship. It's hard to find a balance between life in the orchestra and life at home. There's no regularity, never one week like another. Living is very erratic and we have to have our social obligations attuned to the orchestra schedules. This is true during the fifty-two-week season, just as it was before.

"I rarely saw my children when they were young. After all, most of our touring is done during the winter. That's when the furnace goes on the blink or the children come down with colds. So the wives have to shift for themselves. An orchestra wife has to learn to adjust herself to this kind of living."

Nevertheless, the adjustment manages to get made. There is only a handful of bachelors in the Philadelphia Orchestra, and most of the parents within its ranks say they would have no objections to their children following music as a career. In fact, many of them actively encourage the idea by giving their youngsters their first lessons themselves. Sometimes this leads to unexpected results, as when principal clarinetist Anthony Gigliotti found his young son switching to the bassoon after a few parental lessons. Considering the number of Philadelphia Orchestra children who are actively studying instruments either with their fathers or through classes at Curtis, the Settlement School or elsewhere, musical family life can't be all that bad.

♭ HOW TO SURVIVE REHEARSALS

The basic work of an orchestra is done at rehearsals. It is there that players and conductors alike get to know not only the music they are playing, but each other as well. Rehearsals serve to prepare them for specific programs ahead, and also to keep them in fighting— or, rather, playing—trim. Even when the Philadelphia Orchestra comes to New York on Tuesday nights to play a program it has already played in Philadelphia over the weekend, its Philharmonic Hall appearance is likely to be preceded by a rehearsal on the spot. At Saratoga also rehearsals are part of the routine, as they are when the orchestra is traveling abroad. Union regulations limit rehearsals to two-and-a-half hours' duration, and there usually are four a week.*

Rehearsal styles differ from orchestra to orchestra, depending upon the approach taken by the conductor. In Philadelphia, re-hearsals tend to be informal, relaxed, free from unnecessary pressure. Serious and painstaking work goes on, but it goes on without tension. That is something which is saved for concerts; the Philadelphia Orchestra has never been accused of "leaving the concert in the rehearsal hall." Ormandy customarily is a congenial boss at rehearsals; he has a great fund of stories stemming from his experiences in Europe and America alike, and he likes to tell them. Nobody stops him. Says one woodwind player: "We have a saying: 'Talking beats playing.' So when Mr. Ormandy starts with a story about some in-cident that happened which we've heard before, some one is sure to call out: 'Yes, Maestro, tell it again.'"

A similar amiability affects the entire orchestra, which at re-hearsals occasionally even undertakes to imitate the role of audiences. Sometimes the players will burst into mock applause at the end of the third movement of Tchaikovsky's *Pathétique* Symphony in imi-

* The 1966–'69 contract provided that the players may not be required to per-form more than eight "services" each week, a "service" being either a performance or a rehearsal. Ordinarily they are equally divided. At actual concerts, the rule is that players must be in their places ready to play five minutes before the starting time. Many, of course, prefer to arrive earlier and warm up longer.

tation of audiences that mistake it for the Finale. A prolonged cadenza for the harp or another solo instrument is likely to bring cries of "bravo!" and a shower of pennies and nickels tossed at the feet of the grinning performer. When mezzo-soprano Shirley Verrett rehearsed for her concert performance of *Carmen* at the Saratoga Festival she preceded her Act I entrance with an offstage operatic laugh. The orchestra stopped playing and laughed right back. Such pranks and jokes may never replace television, but they serve to keep everybody loose and guard against possible rehearsal rigors.

Sometimes, when an unfamiliar work is being rehearsed, Ormandy will sit in the back of the hall while assistant conductor William Smith plays through the score with the orchestra. This is a method used by many conductors. It enables them to size up the way a work "fits" an orchestra, and also to judge such matters as instrumental balance and sonorities. More often, though, Bill Smith will sit out in the hall while Ormandy conducts. This is invariably the case in a hall that is relatively unfamiliar to the orchestra. Smith says "I think in terms of his ears"; he gauges balances; sees how the soloist, if any, is blending with the orchestra; even checks out the humidity and weather conditions, which can have an effect on the orchestra's sound.

At a typical recent rehearsal in a "foreign" hall, Simth sat in a seat well toward the rear, while Ormandy, perched on a stool before the orchestra, rehearsed a program that included Ernest Bloch's *Schelomo* Rhapsody for Cello and Orchestra with Sammy Mayes as soloist and Aaron Copland's *Billy the Kid.* "How's the sound?" Ormandy called out. "Brass is heavy," called back Smith. Ormandy nodded: "Heavy. Always is in this place. Percussion, too. Too loud, much too loud." The orchestra listened attentively, necessary changes were made, the passage was repeated. This time Smith called out "Fine!", Ormandy saluted the orchestra without missing a beat, and the work proceeded. Finally, *Schelomo* was completed, with Mayes' fellow cellists half-jokingly tapping their bows on their stands in approval of his solo performance.

Balances seemed better in Copland's saga of the old West, *Billy the Kid,* which followed, but after a time Ormandy stopped the orchestra and turned to first harpist Marilyn Costello after a brief solo passage and remarked reflectively:

"Did you play with me when we recorded this years ago?"

"I don't think so," she replied.

"I got a marvelous effect there," he said. "Like a beer-hall piano."

"Pinetop Smith," called out a brass player.

Everybody laughed. The next time it sounded like a beer-hall piano. Pinetop Smith.

It should not be inferred from any of this that players like rehearsals. They don't. In fact, most regard the best kind as those that are called off. But by maintaining a generally pleasant atmosphere and by exercising his artistic and organizational skills quietly, Ormandy manages to cover a maximum amount of music in a minimum amount of time without bruising anybody in the process. And whatever apparent laxity or looseness may be superficially observable at rehearsals, they have completely disappeared when the orchestra seats itself on the concert stage, completely rehearsed, perfectly disciplined, every man and instrument at concert pitch. Says one player who has seen the transformation occur nightly for thirty years: "It's a little miracle every time. They say a college football team gives everything it has all the time, while the professionals pace themselves and rise to the big moments. Well, this is the only orchestra I know that's like a college team."

♎ MUSICIAN VS. CONDUCTOR

Morris Shulik, one of the first violins in the Philadelphia Orchestra, remembers vividly a trip to Europe he made as a member of the Amerita Orchestra, a fifteen-man ensemble a few years ago. "We were all strings," he recalls, "and we went without a conductor. So we fought each other all the time. Here we fight with him. A conductor is a good hate-symbol."

On the whole, the Philadelphia Orchestra has a reputation for getting along reasonably well with conductors—not only its own permanent musical director, but the guests who have occupied its podium over the years. This is not invariably so with orchestras, for musicians have a good deal of power over the man who conducts them—in some respects, almost as much as he has over them. They have been known to use that power against him. Experienced musicians can recognize in a few moments how much expertise and technical proficiency a conductor brings to his work. "He's nude up there," says first violinist Frank Costanzo, who has been watching conductors for twenty-seven years. "You can tell in the first minute if he's good, bad or indifferent." Players, like audiences, are responsive to a conductor's interpretive ideas and nuances. Musicians actually enjoy certain performances and dislike others, just as non-professional listeners do; each member of the orchestra can talk about memorable concerts almost as if he had been sitting in the hall listening, rather than on the stage playing.

Whether because they do not like a guest conductor's methods or personality, orchestral musicians can make life difficult for him. An incorrect note, a missed cue, a late entrance can work havoc with a conductor's interpretation, and although few instrumentalists will acknowledge deliberate malfeasance, certain orchestras have gained a reputation for being especially tough on newcomers. The Philadelphia is not one of them. Many guest conductors are so impressed by its rich sound and technical expertness that they begin by complimenting the players. That always helps. But any conductor who shows respect for the instrumentalists before him even as he asserts his own proper authority from the podium is likely to find the Philadelphia as responsive and co-operative as any ensemble in the world. Some years back Paul Paray, on a guest-conducting stint with the orchestra, slipped on the ice and broke his arm. He appeared on the podium wearing a sling and a cast. "This orchestra," he said, "I could conduct with my nose."

Nevertheless, there have been a few unpleasant incidents. Musicians don't like conductors who challenge them, and a Viennese-born conductor who some years ago stood over an oboist instructing him in the art of his instrument did not evoke a very favorable response from the orchestra. Another conductor, now dead, who came to this country with an extensive reputation based largely on European recordings, made some disparaging remarks about women in general and women musicians in particular, and soon found that the orchestra could develop feedback without benefit of hi-fi.

Nobody enjoys working for a sharp-tongued or nasty-tempered conductor; there are plenty of musicians who, no matter how much they respect certain conductors, don't wish to play for them. Musicians can uproot themselves from orchestras for a variety of reasons, but it's a fair assumption that, if no other cause is obvious, the departure of a musician, especially if he's a first-desk man, means that he isn't seeing eye-to-eye—or hearing ear-to-ear—with the conductor.

Conductors have lost most of the power they used to hold over orchestral musicians; no longer is it possible for a musician to be summarily dismissed, a condition which used to be prevalent in many cities. In the old days, even Philadelphia wasn't immune. "With Stokowski," says a long-time violinist, "every rehearsal was a war, and you never knew who the casualties would be." But even though altercations are still possible, musicians are treated much more deferentially nowadays, and no one can be discharged except for "just cause," and then only after a hearing in which the union and orchestra membership are well represented. Such confrontations have become infrequent in Philadelphia. "Ormandy lets you play your instrument without fear," is the way a bass-player puts it.

Personal empathy and musical knowledge are, of course, important elements in a conductor's make-up, but they can be considerably impaired if he hasn't got the ability to convey them to an orchestra and elicit the effects he wants—if he lacks what musicians call "stick technique." As almost every Philadelphia concert attests, Ormandy is one of the greatest orchestral technicians who ever lived, a fact which is appreciated by no one more keenly than a musician.

"Conductors must be able to communicate," says a cellist. "Without it, they're dead. It's done with words, with the stick, with personality. Sometimes I think it's more important for a conductor to manipulate people than to possess musical ability. He's after you all the time to work your best. You have to watch the hands, the face, the eyes. Sometimes you feel almost a chemical reaction. There's a half-humorous theory that so many cellists end up as conductors themselves because they don't have as many notes to play as violinists and so can spend more time watching and studying the conductor.* But actually we all watch. There's always something to learn. When a guest conductor comes here who is versed in a particular specialty, such as French music, it can be pleasant and enlightening to work with him. Just the same, musicians naturally complain about conductors. It's part of the temperament."

Sums up associate concertmaster David Madison: "The job of a conductor is to lead, to watch, to keep everybody on his toes. When you've got a gang like this where everybody is on his toes, you've got something."

℔ THE VIRTUOSO INSTINCT

Says Samuel Mayes, the first cellist of the Philadelphia Orchestra: "The life of a solo virtuoso is one of the most lonesome I know of. Here, in an orchestra, I am never alone, never a stranger in town. When we get to a city we go out in a group, we're friends together. There's always somebody to play golf with." Adds concertmaster Norman Carol: "It may sound trite to say it, but an orchestra is a family, it has a camaraderie of its own, it gives you a great feeling of people that you simply do not have when you try to make your way as a soloist."

Nevertheless, a good many musicians concede privately that many—probably the majority—of string players in an orchestra, especially of the quality of the Philadelphia Orchestra, are frustrated soloists. This is less true of wind-players, for though there have been a handful who have been able to make successful careers as solo clarinetists or flutists, the natural habitat of a great wind player, such as a Kincaid or a Tabuteau, a Mason Jones or a John de Lancie, is a great orchestra.

For a string player, especially a violinist, however, the normal

* A full range of conductors have emerged from the ranks of the Philadelphia Orchestra. They include Rosario Bourdon, Anshel Brusilow, Saul Caston, Max Goberman, Alexander Hilsberg, Hans Kindler, Arthur Bennett Lipkin, Frank Miller, Daniel Saidenberg, Jan Savitt, Fabien Sevitzky, Jacques Singer and Henry C. Smith.

objective of those who show outstanding promise is at least a stab at a solo career. In the Philadelphia Orchestra, as in other orchestras, there are those who have actually made such an attempt and fallen back, not necessarily for lack of superior ability, but simply because they did not have the time, the finances or—that most vital but elusive element—the luck to assist them toward their highest desire. Within the ranks of any great orchestra may be a half-dozen string players who could hold their own against the acknowledged solo masters of their instruments. "It's the back-row people who make this orchestra," says violinist Herb Light. "They're capable of being up front. Our second violin section has many fine players." Light himself, one of the younger players, started with the seconds, now plays with the firsts.

To play a violin, a viola, a cello for a lifetime in an orchestra has its satisfactions, but also its disappointments. Especially in classical symphonic music, much of the time is spent in playing repeated patterns or figurations as an accompaniment to the melodic line in some other instrument, usually in the winds or brasses. String players suffer an additional loss of individual identity simply because they are members of the largest body by far of orchestral components. In the Philadelphia Orchestra there are thirty-four violinists, twelve violists, twelve cellists, and nine double-bassists—well over half the orchestra. Musically, it's hard for a string player to excel individually in a crowd like that; economically he is less likely than a wind or a brass player to be able to negotiate a personal salary increase.

As a matter of fact, there inevitably is a certain amount of professional hostility between string players and the rest of the orchestra. Violinists play almost continuously, from the moment the conductor raises his baton to the moment he gives the final beat. Winds, brass and percussion play much more sporadically, in some cases being excused altogether. A tuba player, a third or fourth trombone, a harpist or a piccolo player, can miss a whole week of concerts and still receive a regular paycheck.

Brass and woodwind players argue that they have their problems, too. Economically, some of them miss out on recording fees, for only those who actually perform at a recording session are paid, although every one is assured the yearly minimum guarantee of $2000. They also point out that lay-offs present dangers of their own. "It's true I have my nights off," first harpist Marilyn Costello says. "But it's hard to maintain top form that way. A violinist plays every day and can stay in form; I have to do it myself."

But the main contention of brasses, winds and percussion in the unending battle of the sections is that while they may not play as continuously as the strings, when they do play they are almost always in an exposed position. An ancient and no doubt apocryphal story tells of a kettledrummer who suddenly went berserk during a concert conducted by Walter Damrosch. In the middle of a gentle, barely audible portion of Mendelssohn's *Midsummer Night's Dream* music he inexplicably began beating out a savage rat-tat-tat on his instrument. Startled, Damrosch whirled around on the podium and said: "Who did that?" A violinist can make a mistake during a concert and never be heard except by his stand partner; he can even stop playing altogether for a few measures and not spoil the over-all effect. But let a trumpet crack on a note, or a timpanist miss a cue, and the whole world knows it. "Just the first note of the *Rienzi* Overture, a pianissimo swelling up, can be just as difficult and dangerous as the entire Bach Brandenburg Concerto No. 2," says first trumpeter Gilbert Johnson. Associate first horn Nolan Miller, who partners his former teacher Mason Jones (in a symphony orchestra two horns pair off to play the high notes, two others the low), maintains that the more familiar a passage is, the more difficult it becomes to play. "The slower the tempo and the softer the dynamic quality, the harder," he adds. "In long solos I sometimes get nervous —but after I've played it rather than before."

Nevertheless, many of the string players remain unconvinced. Says one of the younger and more ambitious violinists in the orchestra: "The strings are overworked and underpaid; there's considerable envy of the brasses for their time off. I admit that to be paid for playing music is a wonderful thing. But a violinist in an orchestra ceases to be an individual, although you have to have initiative and personality just to play in a first-class orchestra. The conductor does your thinking for you, and that can have a disastrous effect. The repertory is not always stimulating; artistically the music is gratifying, but it still has to be routine. There's an inescapable element of boredom."

One member of the orchestra, cellist Marcel Farago, in a spirit of inquiry, sent his fellow-members a questionnaire asking them to name (a) the five composers they liked most to play, (b) the five compositions they liked most, (c) the five composers they liked least, and (d) the five compositions they liked least. Heaven knows what light might have been shed on the darker recesses of musicians' minds had Farago's colleagues responded to his survey in a scientific spirit. Alas, they did not. Most declined to answer at all, and some who did took the whole affair as a joke, such as the tuba player who solemnly said that he liked most of all to play the symphonies of Mozart! Farago himself, a fourteen-year veteran, says he prefers to play new pieces rather than routine repertory.

Still another view is given by Elsa Hilger, associate first cellist, whose retirement in 1969 ended a thirty-three year career with the orchestra. Miss Hilger, whose musical devotion and determination haven't prevented her from being happily married to a dentist and raising a son to be a doctor, says she never worried either about losing her individuality or the problem of routine.

"I was warned about it," she says. "I began life as a prodigy at the age of eleven in Vienna, and when I went into the orchestra I was told: 'Elsa, you'll never be a soloist again.' It's not true. I kept up my solo playing; I've played works like Haydn's Cello Concerto and Tchaikovsky's *Rococo Variations* with the orchestra. I started out on the last stand of the cellos and I played there just as if I were on the first stand. I play every concert as if it were a solo recital, and every concert excites me, even after all these years. For me, it is never routine."

Nevertheless, most string players—and other instrumentalists as well—seek supplemental outlets for their skills in addition to playing in the orchestra. The chance to earn extra money is only part of the lure; even more important is the psychological need felt by many players to assert their musical and personal individuality.

Such outside activities take an astonishing variety of forms.

Teaching is the most obvious and universal. Many members of the Philadelphia Orchestra teach at such nearby institutions as Curtis Institute, Temple University, and the Settlement Music School. Oftentimes players will continue to teach after their retirement. The post-MacArthur saying that "old musicians never die, they just fake away" is not necessarily true; several, like trumpeter Sigmund Hering, are on the faculty of the Settlement School, a remarkable institution catering largely to underprivileged children and, with an enrollment of 3500, said to be the largest music school in the world.

Of course, many Philadelphia musicians have private pupils, and not a few have seen their students actually join them in the ranks of the Philadelphia Orchestra. Violinist Frank Costanzo taught four members of the orchestra; violist Leonard Mogill three. The constant training of replacements in this way has helped provide the orchestra with its unique constancy and continuity of sound.

Essentially, though, the musicians are performers rather than pedagogues. The violinist who earns his living playing four concerts a week with the orchestra finds his gratification in playing more music for himself, either in a chamber music session with friends or through a modest recital of some sort. Where the wife is a musician, sometimes the recital becomes a family affair; cellist Joseph Druian, for example, has given concerts with his wife Yvonne, a pianist whom he met at Curtis. More likely, the orchestral musician is likely to find his outlet in a string quartet or similar chamber group; there have been many formed in the orchestra through its history, including that of the four de Pasquale brothers. Not all of these groups have played together commercially; like amateurs in the pristine sense of the word they get together for their own pleasure and love of their art. The orchestra schedule prevents these sessions from occurring as often as some of these players would like, but there nevertheless are several groups which meet perhaps once a month. During the summer festival in Saratoga, informal chamber music sessions may be observed going on at the Skidmore College dormitories where the orchestra is housed. Occasionally an outsider drops in, as is the case with a music-loving dentist in Norfolk, Virginia, who makes it a point to visit Washington, D.C. when the orchestra comes there, to join three of his orchestra friends in playing through a quartet or two. In addition, first-desk men of the orchestra have banded together to form such groups as the Philadelphia Woodwind Quintet and the Philadelphia Brass Ensemble. Composition is an outlet for several players, such as violinist Louis Gesensway.

Quite a few of the Philadelphia musicians have become leaders or advisers of musical groups in their home communities. Frank Costanzo every October conducts the Sisters of Mercy Symphony Orchestra, a musical organization of nuns in Merion, Pennsylvania, and in addition has been active in the affairs of the Amerita Orchestra, a string group devoted to the performance of Italian and American music. Another group that attracted the interest of the orchestra members was the Philadelphia Concerto Players, directed by the Philadelphia's trombonist Henry C. Smith, which enabled back-desk men and front-desk men alike to step forward to the center of the concert platform.

It is in activities like this that an instrumentalist will often find his most abiding satisfaction, and a wise management will do its utmost to encourage him; for just as each of Napoleon's soldiers carried in his knapsack the baton of a field-marshal, so does each orchestral player worth his salt carry in his case the instrument of a virtuoso.

THE PRIDE OF PHILADELPHIA

No one can spend time with the people connected with the Philadelphia Orchestra without being struck by an all-pervasive feeling of pride in the organization. The musicians grumble and gripe in the immemorial manner of musicians; they have run-ins with each other and with the management; they have conducted stoppages and strikes in the past and it is not impossible that they will do so again. Yet all share a feeling of personal loyalty and involvement which few other musical organizations can command. Their pride is not belligerent or assertive, but it is plain to behold. Few Philadelphia men will publicly proclaim in so many words that theirs is the greatest orchestra in the world, but all play as if it were.

Several string players say that they have over the years declined offers of first-desk positions in other orchestras, preferring to remain in second or third chairs of the Philadelphia rather than becoming section heads in orchestras even of the quality of Minneapolis or Detroit. Partially this is a matter of economics; Philadelphia is regarded in the trade as a "good job," with a superior labor contract, and likely to remain in the forefront of whatever improvements are negotiated in the future. In addition, the proximity of Curtis, Temple, the Settlement School, the Philadelphia Musical Academy, the University of Pennsylvania and other institutions affords the possibility of academic and teaching outlets which might not be available elsewhere.

But the matter goes beyond the question of remuneration, either regular or supplementary. The Philadelphia musicians maintain a certain disdain for what they regard as the "commercialism" of players elsewhere, the orchestra most frequently mentioned in this connection being the New York Philharmonic. Says trumpeter Sam Krauss: "This is not a secondary job for anybody." Admittedly, this may be making a virtue of necessity; New York, as the center of television and other entertainment media, offers greater opportunity for extra work than Philadelphia does. It might also be noted that the Philadelphia, with 213 concerts a year and concommitant rehearsal sessions, has the kind of schedule that discourages too many outside engagements. Nevertheless there is no doubt that to the bulk of the Philadelphia players, a permanent job in the orchestra represents the ultimate in musical employment. Says a viola player: "I was born and raised in Philadelphia and went to Curtis. My goal since I was thirteen or fourteen years old was to be a member of the Philadelphia Orchestra. My father was a violinist from the old country; he used to take me to the concerts. To me, paradise was to play in the Philadelphia Orchestra."

With a turnover rate of only two or three a year, the orchestra is one of the most stable in personnel in the entire country—as might be expected from an orchestra that has had only two conductors since 1912. Were it not for the inflexible policy of retirement at age sixty-five, the turnover would be even lower. Even when over-age players leave the orchestra, they continue a lively interest in its affairs. The orchestra has a policy of providing free admission, when seats are available, for its alumni, and one of the more pleasant duties of assistant manager Joe Santarlasci is to stand in the lobby of the Academy before concerts, distributing tickets to former players as they arrive.

New players in the orchestra say they encounter active co-operation and assistance from the older members; according to veteran violinist Isadore Schwartz it may take five to seven years before a new string player becomes fully assimilated into the orchestra's tonal fabric. Most new players acknowledge feeling a sense of challenge when they enter the Philadelphia Orchestra that they have not encountered previously. Tympanist Gerald Carlyss, who joined the orchestra in 1967 at the age of twenty-five, describes his first actual experience as a player with the orchestra almost in terms of awe: "When I heard the sounds at the first rehearsal, I just went 'Wow!' It's difficult at first to play with this orchestra. You just want to listen."

To most of the personnel of the orchestra, living in or near Philadelphia is part of the attractiveness of their jobs. They know all the ancient Philadelphia jokes, and take them good-humoredly, even adding a few of their own. But they like the city, the people, the audiences; there is about them that sense of quiet satisfaction and outward contentment that is the hallmark of the perfect Philadelphian, no matter what his calling, as he heads for home, hearth and family after the daily mission abroad has been accomplished. If they wanted to be anywhere else they surely could, for musicians of this talent, skill and devotion would be welcome anywhere in the world where there is music. But they don't want to be elsewhere; they want to be in Philadelphia.

For all these reasons, the Philadelphia Orchestra still manages to attract fine players, even string players, who are in short supply throughout the country. And, of course, it is upon the continuing presence of such players that the future of the orchestra depends. It is true that the Philadelphia Orchestra could never have become what it is if Stokowski hadn't virtually created it, if Ormandy hadn't

completely renewed it, if Scheel and Pohlig hadn't laid a foundation
for it, perhaps deeper and truer than they knew. Yet neither would
it be a great orchestra if it were not composed of great musicians from
the first desk to the last, a company of artists blending their skills
and personalities to produce some of the sublimest sounds this
strident century has heard.

It may be, as some authorities insist, that the symphony orchestra
has passed its zenith as an institution. After all, the orchestra is now
some 300 years old and for nearly 200 of those years has reigned
unchallenged as the supreme medium of musical expression. Music,
once regarded as the speech of angels, is lately becoming the province
of the machine; the voice of the synthesizer and the electronic console
is being heard increasingly in the land. But the symphony orchestra
in America shows no sign yet of losing its hold upon the great mass
of the musical public; for the great orchestras and the great conductors audiences never seem to be lacking. Even the immortals die;
we may be on the verge of a new musical era with as yet undreamed-of
sounds and devices. But perhaps it is not too much to hope that as
long as there are those to play music and those to listen, the symphony
orchestra will continue to hold an honored place, and that in its
foremost ranks will always be the Philadelphia Orchestra.

Members of the Philadelphia Orchestra
1900-1969

Following is a list of members of the Philadelphia Orchestra from its inception to the present, with dates of service. Current members (1969) are indicated by an asterisk (*).

Abas, S., Violin—1901-02
Abbas, Philip, Cello—1916-17
* Abel, Alan D., Battery—1959-
Aleinikoff, Harry, Violin—1915-60
Alemann, Paul, Clarinet—1904-30
Altman, B., Violin—1942-43
Angeloty, Louis, Violin—1908-22
* Angelucci, Adelchi L., Bassoon—1944-45, 1950-
Antonelli, P., Horn—1920-23
* Arben, David, Violin—1959-
Arey, Rufus M., Clarinet (Principal)—1923-24
Argiewicz, Bernard, Cello—1917-19
Arian, Edward W., Bass—1947-1967
Arkless, William L., Violin—1900-01; Viola—1915-18
Aronoff, Max, Viola—1944-45
Aschke, J., Piccolo—1901-02
Asen, Simon, Viola—1936-44
Asenmacker, Anton, Cello—1917-19
Atkinson, Burnett F., Flute—1944-52
Ayala, J., Trumpet—1916-17

Badollet, F. V., Flute—1901-04
Bailiff, Jill, Harp (extra)—1947-1952
Baker, Harry J., Battery—1923-24
Bancroft, Irving J., Violin—1916-41
(Principal II 1929)

Bansbach, Philip, Viola—1919-22
Barchewitz, W., Violin—1901-04
* Barnes, Darrell, Viola—1965-
* Barnes, Edward, Stage Hand—1956-
Baronne, Clemente, Flute and Piccolo—1900-01, 1904-10
(Principal 1907-10)
Barone, Richard, Violin—1923-24
Basse, Herman, Trumpet—1904-05, 1914-17
(Principal 1904-05; 1914-15)
* Batchelder, Wilfred, Bass—1951-
Battles, Gus, Flute—1906-09
Bauer, J. K., Viola—1936-58
Baumel, Herbert, Violin—1942-45
Bay, Victor, Violin—1922-23
Beck, Jacob, Trumpet—1900-01
Beck, William J., Violin—1906-09
Beimel, George, Violin—1925-45
Belenko, Samuel, Cello—1925-64
Belgiorno, Simone, Trombone
(Principal 1930-31)
Belinski, Mirko, Cello—1904-09
Bellois, J. F., Violin—1900-01
Belov, Joel, Violin—1912-20, 1923-24, 1927-31
Belov, Samuel, Viola—1908-20
(Principal 1919-20)
Benavente, Joseph, Cello—1917-18
Bender, August, Trumpet—1901-03

Beneter, F., Violin–1901-02
Benfield, Warren, Bass–1942-49
Bennett, Harold, Flute–1940-44
Berv, A. Isadore, Horn–1923-38
    (Principal 1930-38)
Bettoney, Frederick, Bassoon–1917-20
Betz, Marshall, Librarian and Stage Hand–
    1912-18, 1921-56
Bianculli, P., Violin–1913-14
* Biava, Luis O., Violin–1968-
Bielo, Henry, Bassoon–1920-22
Bielo, Julius, Bass–1920-22
* Black, Norman, Violin–1950-
Blaha, Antonin, Violin–1906-08, 1909-12
Bleyer, Max, Trumpet–1903-08
    (Principal 1903-04)
Bloom, Robert, Oboe and English Horn–
    1930-36
Blumenfeld, Max, Violin–1904-06
Bobell, H., Violin–1903-04
Boehm, Gustav, Violin–1900-01
Boehse, Louis, Bass–1904-07, 1908-31
* Bogdanoff, Leonard, Viola–1955-
Bonade, Daniel, Clarinet–1917-22, 1924-30
* Bookspan, Michael, Percussion and
    Timpani–1953
Bornstein, Milton, Violin–1921-25
Bourdon, Rosario, Cello–1904-08
Bov, Domenico, Violin–1917-23, 1924-57
Branski, Isador, Viola–1919-20
* Braverman, Gabriel, Viola–1938-
Brennand, Charles, Cello–1956-1967
* Breuninger, Tyrone, Trombone–1967-
Britt, Horace, Cello (Principal)–1907-08
Britt, Roger, Violin–1914-20
Brodo, Joseph, Violin–1918-24, 1943-60
Broeckaert, Leopold, Flute–1904-05
Broiles, Melvyn L., Trumpet (Assoc. Prin-
    cipal)–1957-58
Brown, H. I., Violin–1921-25
Brown, Keith, Trombone–1959-62
Brusilow, Anshel, Concertmaster–1959-66
Bukay, Anne, Harp (extra)–1946-47
Burkartmaier, J. H., Violin–1900-01

Cahan, Nathan, Bass–1900-24
Cahon, P., Cello–1901-02
Cailliet, Lucien, Clarinet–1916-38
Callot, André, Violin–1925-31
Campowsky, H., Violin–1903-17
Caputa, Domenico, Horn (Principal)–
    1929-31
* Carlyss, Gerald, Timpani (Principal)–
    1967-
* Carol, Norman, Concertmaster–1966-

Carow, Herman, Violin–1916-18
Carow, Hugo, Viola–1900-04
* Caserta, Santo, Cello–1956-
Caston, Saul, Trumpet–1918-45
    (Associate Conductor 1936-45)
Cauffman, S. H., Cello–1901-02, 1903-04
Cerminara, Napoleon, Clarinet–1913-44
Chambers, James, Horn–1941-46
Chazin, Harry, Violin–1919-23
Cheifetz, S., Viola–1924-25
Chudnowsky, Josef, Violin–1913-24
Cianciarulo, John A., Violin–1900-01,
    1903-05
Cimino, Guiseppe, Horn–1918-19
* Clauser, Donald, Viola–1966-
Cole, Howard, Trombone–1948-68
Cole, Lucius, Violin–1905-19
Cole, Robert, Flute and Piccolo–1949-62
Coleman, David, Violin–1918-25
Cook, Frederick W., Violin–1906-24
Cooley, Carlton, Viola–1919-20, 1954-63
    (Principal, 1956-63)
Conrad, William, Bassoon–1921-22
Cortadella, S., Bass–1923-24
Cortese, Francesco, Harp–1900-01
* Costanzo, Frank, Violin–1941-
* Courtney, Neil, Bass–1962-
* Curtiss, Sidney, Violin–1960-
* Costello, Marilyn, Harp–1945-
    (Principal, 1946-)
Cras, R., Horn–1919-20
* Csonka, Margarita, Harp–1963-
Czaplinski, Henri, Violin–1924-27

Dabrowski, S., Violin–1923-57
* Dalschaert, Cathleen, Violin–1967-
* Dalschaert, Stephane, Violin–1967-
D'Amelio, Benjamin, Violin–1919-24
Dandois, Marcel, Oboe–1928-29
Deak, Stephen, Cello–1925-27
DeBoer, J., Violin–1901-02
Dechert, George, Trombone–1901-04
De Clerck, George, Viola–1912-19
De Cray, Marcella, Harp–1952-63
De Gomez, Victor, Cello–1916-19
* de Lancie, John, Oboe–1946-
    (Principal, 1954-)
Delli Gatti, Frank, Viola–Violin–1920-21;
    1921-23
Del Negro, F., Bassoon–1922-62
* de Pasquale, Joseph, Viola (Principal)–
    1964-
* dePasquale, Barbara, Violin–1963-
* de Pasquale, Francis, Cello–1943-
* de Pasquale, William, Violin–1963-
* de Pasquale, Robert, Violin–1964-

De Santis, Louis, Clarinet (Principal)–
 1930-31
Devaux, Eugene, Oboe–1910-11
* Di Camilla, Armand, Violin–1946-
Diestel, William, Viola (Principal)–1908-15
Dieterichs, Fritz, Clarinet (Principal)–
 1901-12
Di Fulvio, Louis, Oboe–1925-59
Di Natale, Joseph, Violin–1917-18
Dodge, William F., Violin–1906-07
* Dodson, Glenn, Trombone (Principal)–
 1968-
Doell, Carl, Concertmaster–1900-01
Donatelli, P. A., Tuba–1923-48
Donath, Frederick, Viola and Celesta–
 1923-24
Donath, Paul, Violin–1903-04, 1907-17
Donner, Max, Violin–1907-08
D'Orio, John, Horn–1910-18, 1921-28,
 1931-32
Doucet, Alfred, Oboe (Principal)–1902-13
* Dreyfus, George, Violin–1953-
* Druian, Joseph, Cello–1944-
Druian, Raphael, Violin–1949
Dubinsky, David, Violin–1900-01; Viola–
 1901-02; Violin 1908-29;
 (Principal II 1912-29)
 (Personnel Manager 1915-29)
Dubinsky, Vladimir, Cello (Principal)–
 1906-07
Dupuis, A., Oboe–1916-18

Ebann, W. B., Cello (Principal)–1901-02
Eckstein, Sol, Bass Clarinet–1900-01
Eiler, Oscar, Cello–1912-14
Einhorn, Bruno, Cello–1913-17
Eisenberg, Benjamin, Violin–1918-19
Eisenberg, Irwin, Violin–1946-67
Eisenberg, Maurice, Cello–1917-19
Elkan, Henri, Viola–1920-28
Elkind, S., Bass–1921-22
Elst, Otto, Trombone (Principal)–1906-16
Emery, Kenneth B., Flute–1943-
* Eney, F. Gilbert, Bass–1943-
Engel, Rudolph, Viola and Trumpet–
 1904-31
Epstein, David, Viola–1922-38
Epstein, Leonard, Viola–1920-24, 1945-60
Epstein, Meyer B., Violin–1923-24
Ezerman, D. H., Cello–1901-02

Fabris, Pasqual, Violin–1924-27
Fahsbender, Rudolph, Bass–1920-23
Falk, Julius, Violin–1900-03
Fanelli, Vincent Jr., Harp–1913-30
* Farago, Marcel, Cello–1955-

Farnham, Allen, Violin, Piano and Celesta–
 1931-41
Fasshauer, Carl, Violin–1912-18
Fasshauer, John, Bass–1900-05, 1907-21
* Fawcett, James W., Viola–1962-
Fearn, Ward, Horn–1941-65
Feher, Milton, Violin–1930-36
Fehling, Henry W., Violin (Principal)–
 1900-01
Feldman, Harry, Violin–1923-24
Fenstel, W., Cello–1900-01
* Ferguson, Paul, Viola–1930-
Ferir, Emile, Viola (Principal)–1918-19
Ferrara, Antonio, Violin–1916-20, 1921-23,
 1924-28
Ferrara, Luigi, Violin–1917-18, 1919-29
Fillsack, Paul, Violin and Clarinet–1901-24
Fischer, John A., Flute and Piccolo–1909-59
Fischer, R., Cello–1902-03
Fisher, Philip, Trumpet–1945-46
Fishzohn, Louis, Violin–1925-29
Fisner, John, Bassoon–1922-50
Fogg, Clarence, Viola–1900-02, 1903-04,
 1906-08
Folgmann, Emil, Cello–1919-20, 1921-27
Franke, C., Violin–1901-02
Frantz Leonard, Viola–1944-60
Frazer, John H., Cello–1925-29
Frengut, Leon, Viola–1931-36
Frey, George O., Tuba–1921-23; Trombone
 and Euphonium–1923-24
Frey, Nathan, Viola–1921-24
Fries, Robert, Horn (co-Principal)–1963-65
Friese, A., Battery–1901-05
Froelich, Max, Cello–1918-20
Fruncillo, John, Viola–1900-01
Fuchs, Paul, Bassoon–1902-08

Gabowitz, Louis, Violin–1928-39
Garaffoni, Mario, Bass–1924-29
* Garfield, Bernard H., Bassoon (Principal)–
 1957-
Gastel, Edgar A., Violin–1900-01
Gastel, Erwin, Cello–1900-01
Gauthier, Roger, Oboe–1925-26
Geib, Fred, Tuba–1904-05
Geffert, Edward W., Trombone–1917-21
Geoffrion, Victor, Bass–1922-27
Gerhard, C. E., Trombone–1900-01,
 1904-09, 1921-46
Gershman, Paul, Violin–1931-32
* Gesensway, Louis, Violin–1925-
Gibson, William, Trombone–1940-42
Giese, Waldemar, Bass–1929-43
* Gigliotti, Anthony, Clarinet–1949-
 (Principal 1951-)

Jakob, Joseph A., Horn–1909-10
*Janson, Glenn E., Horn–1962-
*Janson, Julia, Violin–1964-
Jarrow, Sol E., Viola–1905-06
Jocher, Lewis C., Bass–1900-01
*Johnson, Gilbert, Trumpet (Principal)–
1958-
*Jones, Mason, Horn–1938-
(Principal, 1946-)
(Personnel Manager, 1963-)
Jordan, Clarence, Violin–1924-25

Kaehler, Ernest, Violin–1900-01, 1907-13
Kahn, Gordon, Viola–1925-62
Kaplan, Maurice, Viola–1920-32
*Kaplow, Maurice, Viola–1956-
Karella, Clarence, Tuba–1948-49
Kastner, Alfred, Harp–1901-02, 1903-04
Kaufman, Schima, Violin–1925-62
Kayaloff, Yasha, Violin–1925-48
Kearney, Joseph E., Viola–1903-04
Keller, Oscar, Clarinet–1902-04
Kent, Leonard, Horn–1949
Keyser, George William, Viola–1908-19
Kihlman, Carl, Violin–1903-19
Kincaid, William M., Flute (Principal)–
1921-60
Kindler, Hans, Cello–1914-20
(Principal, 1916-20)
Kliachko, Samuel, Cello–1920-22
Klupp, Karl, Horn–1901-04
Kneisel, Carl, Cello–1908-17, 1919-22
Knorr, F. H., Bass–1900 01
Koch, Henry, Horn–1900-01
Koehler, A., Trumpet– 1903-04
Koenig, H., Violin–1903-04
Koert, Jan, Violin–1900-02; Viola
(Principal)–1902-08
Kohon, Benjamin, Bassoon (Principal)–
1912-15
Korb, A., Violin–1901-06
Kosman, Elkan, Concertmaster–1901-02
Koutzen, Boris, Violin–1924-27
Krachmalnick, Jacob, Concertmaster–
1951-58
*Krauss, Samuel, Trumpet–1944-
(Principal, 1945-58)
Kravk, Stefan, Violin–1946-47
Kreisler, Hugo, Cello–1906-07
*Krell, John C., Piccolo–1952-
Kresse, Emil, Violin, Timpani and Battery–
1901-45
Kresse, George, Violin–1901-03, 1906-07
Kriens, Christian, Viola–1902-04
Krueger, Richard, Bassoon (Principal)–
1901-12, 1915-22

Kruger, E., Violin–1903-05
Kruger, Otto, Violin–1905-17
Krummeich, Paul, Violin–1903-07
Kruse, William, Jr., Bassoon–1920-21
Kudisch, Alexis, Violin–1918-19
Kumme, Julius G., Viola–1900-01

Lachmuth, Max, Oboe and English Horn–
1900-01
Lambert, Robert, Trombone–1946-55
La Monaca, Joseph, Flute–1910-40
Lannutti, Arthur, Bassoon–1945
Lannutti, Charles, Horn–1942-63
*Lanza, Joseph, Violin–1958-
*Lanza, Louis, Violin–1964-
Lapetina, F. M., Viola–1900-01
Lapitino, Frances J., Harp–1911-13
Latisch, Emile, Bass–1910-17
Lazzaro, Vincent, Jr., Bass–1921-64
Leavitt, Earl, Trombone–1945-48
Le Barbier, H. C., Trumpet (Principal)–
1909-14
Lehnhoff, Sheppard, Viola–1929-30
Lein, Morris, Trumpet–1923-25
Leman, J. W. F., Viola–1908-18
Lemisch, Miln, Viola–1900-01
Lennartz, Alfred, Cello–1902-16
Leoncavallo, A. Victor, Oboe–1926-28
Lester, Leon, Clarinet–1938-66
Leventhal, B. F., Viola–1911-23
Levy, Harry, Violin–1918-19
Lewin, Morris, Cello–1928-52
Lewis, Arthur, Viola–1967-68
Lifschey, Samuel, Viola (Principal)–
1925-55
*Light, Herbert, Violin–1960-
Lindemann, Robert, Clarinet (Principal)–
1913-17
Lipkin, A., Violin–1922-49
Livoti, George, Violin–1923-24
Loeben, Gustave A., Viola and Celesta–
1919-54
Lorenz, Alfred, Violin–1901-02, 1903-17;
Viola (Principal)–1917-18; Violin–
1918-43
Lorenz, Franz, Cello–1909-17
Lotz, Paul P., Trombone–1900-01, 1909-45
(Personnel Manager, 1929-45)
Lucas, H., Viola–1901-02
Luck, Arthur, Bass–1914-18
*Ludwig, Irving, Violin–1949-50, 1954-
*Lusak, Owen, Violin–1944-

*McComas, Donald, Trumpet–1964-
McGinnis, Robert, Clarinet–1930-40
(Principal, 1931-40)

McLane, Ralph, Clarinet (Principal)–
1943-51
Mackey, C. Stanley, Tuba–1900-04;
1905-15
*Madison, David, Violin–1927-
(Concertmaster, 1958-59)
Madler, Robert, Bass–1902-07
Maestre, E., Cello–1922-24
Malach, E., Bass–1918-19
Mansfelt, Theodore, Cello–1904-05
Maquarre, André, Flute (Principal)–
1918-20
Maquarre, Daniel, Flute (Principal)–
1910-18
Marchetti, Attillio, Oboe (Principal)–
1913-15
*Maresh, Ferdinand, Bass–1948-
Marquardt, John, Concertmaster–1902-03
Marquardt, Mrs. John, Harp–1902-03
Martonne, Herman, Violin–1917-20
Mayer, Clarence, Horn–1926-65
Mayer, Gustav, Battery–1916-23
Mayer, Henry, Jr., Battery–1907-23
*Mayes, Samuel H., Cello (Principal)–
1936-48, 1964-
*Mayes, Winifred W., Cello–1964-
Mear, Sidney, Trumpet–1946
Meichelt, Albert, Trumpet–1902-04
Melatti, Nicola, Violin–1922-24
Meriz, Emilio, Violin–1917-18
Mertz, Herbert, Violin–1919-20
Messias, J., Cello–1901-02
Meyer, Harry W., Violin–1904-15
Meyer, John A., Violin–1900-01
Meyer, Paul, Violin–1914-21
Michaux, Henry J., Viola–1915-40
(Principal, 1915-17)
Miller, Charles S., Violin–1918-19, 1943-64
*Miller, Max, Violin–1962-
*Miller, Nolan, Horn–1965-
Miller, Frank, Cello–1930-35
Minsel, Robert, Horn–1901-04
(Principal 1901-02)
Minsker, John, English Horn–1936-59
Mischakoff, Mischa, Concertmaster–1927-29
Modess, Oskar, Bassoon (Principal)–
1900-01
*Mogill, Leonard, Viola–1935-
Mollenhauer, Bernhard, Violin–1900-01
Molloy, John W., Violin–1920-48
Monasewitch, Grisha, Violin–1927-36
*Montanaro, Donald, Clarinet–1957-
Moret, Albert R., Violin–1902-20
*Morris, Charles M., Oboe–1954-
Morton, Frank S., Violin–1906-07
Mueller, Herman, Viola and Bassoon–

1910-17; Bassoon–1917-37
Mueller, Matthew I., Violin–1922-53
Mueller, Otto, Violin–1907-14, 1921-24
Muller, C. H., Bass–1900-01
Munroe, Lorne A., Cello (Principal)–
1951-64
Munsch, G., Clarinet–1901-02
Murphy, Charlton L., Violin–1900-01
Murray, Edward, Viola–1924-35, 1936-38

Nast, Ludwig, Cello–1902-04
Nava, Gennaro M., Viola–1922-23
Neeter, Philip, Viola–1925-29
Nicoletta, F. A., Harp–1923-31
Nowinski, David., Violin–1906-17

Oberstein, Bram, Cello–1923-24
Oesterreich, W., Flute and Piccolo–1903-04
Olanoff, Max, Violin–1918-19
Olk, Gustav, Viola–1903-04
Olk, Hugo, Violin (Principal)–1902-04
Ollstein, Samuel, Violin–1920-22
Olefsky, Paul, Cello–1946-54
(Principal, 1948)
*Owen, Charles E., Percussion–1954-

Paepke, Gustav, Violin–1902-05, 1922-23
*Panitz, Murray W., Flute (Principal)–
1961-
Parme, F., Clarinet–1925-27
Pauli, Matyas, Bass–1918-23, 1926-42
Pellegrini, L., Violin–1919-20
Pellerite, James, Flute (Principal)–1960-61
Penha, Michel, Cello (Principal)–1920-25
Pepper, Joseph, Violin–1948-51
Pfannkuchen, William, Bassoon–1906-07
Pfeiffer, Walter, Violin–1910-19
*Pfeuffer, Robert, Bassoon–1962-
Pfouts, Earl, Violin–1911-18
*Phillips, Bert, Cello–1959-
Phillips, Edna, Harp (Principal)–1930-46
Pick, Hanns, Cello (Principal)–1925-26
*Pierson, Herbert, Horn–1938-42, 1946-
Pieschel, Paul, Bassoon (Principal)–1908-09
Pillishcer, Stephen, Violin–1924-25
Pitowsky, Paul, Violin–1921-25
Planert, Paul, Bass–1901-05
Podemski, Benjamin, Battery–1923-54
Pollikoff, Max, Violin–1929-30
Popoff, Alexander, Violin–1923-25
Popperl, P., Violin–1901-02
Portnoy, Bernard, Clarinet (Principal)–
1940-43, 1949
Pottag, M., Horn–1901-02
Price, Erwin L., Trombone–1942-43
Prinz, Milton, Cello–1924-30

Primavera, Joseph P., Jr., Viola–1951-67
Pulis, Gordon M., Trombone–1939-42,
   1945-46
Putlitz, Lois P., Violin–1936-62

Querengaesser, Karl, Bass–1901-15
* Querze, Raoul, Clarinet–1962-

Rahmig, Paul, Bass–1901-17, 1919-20,
   1924-26
   (Principal 1901-14)
Raho, Edward, Oboe–1913-30
Raho, Lewis, Oboe–1918-24
Raper, Wayne, Oboe–1960-65
Rattay, Howard F., Violin–1905-06
Rehrig, Harold W., Trumpet–1923-63
Reiter, Joseph, Horn (Principal)–1900-01
Rensch, A., Oboe–1901-02
* Reuben, Ronald, Bass Clarinet–1967-
Reve, Kalman, Violin–1923-24
Reynolds, Veda, Violin–1943-67
Rhodes, J., Viola–1901-02
Rice, L. M., Viola–1902-03
Rich, Thaddeus, Concertmaster–1906-26
Richardson, John, Violin–1929-31
Riese, Albert, Horn–1904-31
Rietzel, Herman, Oboe–1911-13
Ritter, Albert, Timpani–1902-03
Ritzke, A., Clarinet–1900-01
Rodemann, August H., Flute (Principal)–
   1902-07
Rodenkirchen, C. H., Trumpet–1907-09,
   1911-15
   (Principal)–1907-09
Roelofsma, Edmond, Clarinet–1902-20
Roens, Samuel, Viola–1919-20, 1921-54
Roeschmann, B., Violin–1900-01, 1903-04
Rogister, Jean, Viola–1923-24
* Rosen, Irvin, Violin–1945-
* Rosenblatt, Louis, Oboe and English Horn–
   1959-
* Rosenfeld, Seymour, Trumpet–1946-
* Roth, Manuel, Violin and Battery–1924-
Rowe, George D., Clarinet–1944-57
Rozanel, E., Trumpet–1917-18
Ruden, Sol, Violin–1929-53, 1956-68
   (Principal II 1941)
Rykmans, R., Bass–1901-02

Saal, Alfred, Cello (Principal)–1904-06
* Saam, Frank, Violin–1958-
Saidenberg, Daniel, Cello–1925-29
Sandby, Herman, Cello (Principal)–
   1902-04, 1908-16
* Saputelli, William, Cello–1952-
Sargeant, Emmet R., Cello–1929-44

Sauder, Adolph, Oboe–1900-01
Savitt, Jan, Violin–1925-34
Saylor, Herbert F., Violin–1904-05
Schaefer, Fritz, Viola–1904-05
Schaeffer, John A., Bass–1949-51
Scheel, Julius, Concertmaster–1901-12
Scheele, Paul, Viola–1904-15
Schewe, Reinhold, Violin–1900-01, 1907-16
Schinner, K., Horn–1901-02
Schlechtweg, William, Trombone–1904-15
Schlegel, Hans, Flute and Piccolo–1916-40
Schmidt, Alexander, Violin–1908-12
Schmidt, Emil, Viola–1900-01
Schmidt, Emil F., Violin–1900-01, 1903-04,
   1908-23
Schmidt, George, Viola–1902-11
Schmidt, Henry, Violin–1920-63
   (Personnel Manager 1944-63)
Schmidt, Richard, Viola (Principal)–
   1900-01
Schmidt, William A., Cello–1903-04,
   1911-12, 1914-46
Schmitz, Charles M., Cello–1900-01
Schmitz, Philipp, Cello–1903-13, 1919-25
Schoen, William, Viola (Principal)–
   1963-64
Schoenbach, Sol, Bassoon (Principal)–
   1937-44, 1946-57
Schoenthal, Charles F., Flute–1900-01,
   1909-10
   (Principal 1900-01)
Schon, Gerold, Cello–1918-20
Schon, John G., Bassoon–1916-20
Schott, George, Cello–1912-18
Schrader, Fred, Trombone (Principal)–
   1904-06
Schreibmann, B., Trumpet–1921-23
Schuch, B., Violin–1901-02
Schuecker, Edmund, Harp–1904-09
Schuecker, Joseph, Harp–1909-11
Schulman, Julius, Violin–1937-44
Schulman, Leonard, Timpani–1945-53
Schulz, Max, Violin–1902-05
Schurig, Richard, Bass (Principal)–1900-02
Schwar, Oscar, Timpani–1903-46
* Schwartz, Isadore, Violin–1945-
Sciapiro, Michel, Violin–1914-15
* Scott, Roger, Bass–1947-
   (Principal, 1948)
* Scutt, Kenneth E., Flute–1962-
Seder, Theodore, Horn–1939-42
* Segall, Irving, Viola–1963-
Selinski, Max, Violin–1907-14
Seltzer, Frank, Trumpet–1907-11
Serly, Tibor, Viola–1928-35
Serpentini, Ernest, Oboe–1924-26

Serpentini, Jules J., Clarinet–1920-62
Sevitzky, Fabien, Bass–1923-30
* Shahan, Michael, Bass–1964-
Schaievitch, David, Flute–1905-06
* Shamlian, John, Bassoon–1951-
Shannon, J. Byron, Bass–1920-24
Sharlip, Benjamin, Violin–1935-68
Sharp, Sidney, Violin–1945-46
Sherbow, Marcus, Violin–1900-04
Sherman, Joseph, Violin–1923-25
* Shulik, Morris, Violin–1947-
Shure, Paul C., Violin–1941-42, 1945-46
Siani, S., Bass–1924-47
Siegel, Adrian, Cello–1922-59
Siegert, Bernard, Cello–1920-21
Siekierka, Israel, Violin–1924-43
Silberman, Harry, Violin–1917-18
Silverstein, Joseph, Violin–1953-54
Simkins, Jascha, Violin–1920-23, 1924-61
* Simkin, Meyer, Violin–1930-
Simon, Emile, Cello–1907-14
* Simonelli, John, Horn–1965-
Simons, Gardell, Trombone–1915-30
Sinatra, Frank, Timpani and Battery–
    1945-46
Singer, Jacques, Violin–1930-38
Singer, Samuel, Viola–1940-44
Small, J. C., Piccolo–1900-01
Smit, Josef, Cello–1924-25
Smit, Kalman, Violin–1926-31
Smith, Henry C., III, Trombone
    (Principal)–1955-1967
* Smith, Lloyd, Cello–1967-
* Smith, William R., Assistant Conductor–
    1952-
Snader, Nathan, Violin–1946-50
Sokoloff, Isador, Cello–1914-18
Sottnek, Max, Violin–1909-13
Speckin, Willy, Bass–1903-10
Speil, Alfred, Violin–1901-03
Spoor, S., Violin–1919-20
* Stahl, Jacob, Violin–1950-
Stange, Gustav, Trombone–1902-04
Starzinsky, L., Viola–1901-10
Steck, V. William, Violin–1961-1964
Stein, Robert, Cello–1902-03
Steinke, Bruno, Cello–1919-20
Sterin, J., Cello–1927-58
* Stewart, M. Dee, Trombone–1962-
Steyer, Bruno, Viola–1924-25
Stiegelmayer, Karl, Oboe–1901-10
Stobbe, Walter H., Battery–1900-01
Stobbe, William R., Timpani–1900-01
Stockbridge, A. F., Violin–1906-07
Stokking, William, Jr., Cello–1960-66
Stoll, Fred C., Trombone–1942-46

Stoll, Leon, Viola–1900-01
Stoll, William, Jr., Violin–1900-01
Storch, Alfons, Violin–1904-06
Strahlendorf, P., Violin and Bass Clarinet–
    1901-02
Strassenberger, Max, Bass–1927-62
Streuber, K., Bass–1901-02
Stringer, Edward A., Violin–1900-01
Stroble, Jacob, Violin–1900-01
Sturm, Julius, Cello–1902-04
Svedrofsky, Michael, Violin
    (Concertmaster)–1904-06
* Sweeney, James J., Stage Personnel–1958-
Szulc, Bronislaw, Horn–1923-33

Tabuteau, Marcel, Oboe (Principal)–
    1915-54
Tak, Eduard, Violin–1905-06
Tartas, Morris, Viola–1919-20
* Taynton, Jesse C., Librarian–1946-
* Terry, Kenton F., Flute–1943-
Thiede, Alexander J., Violin–1920-29
Thomae, Andrew, Tuba–1915-21
Thor, Marius, Violin–1928-30
Thurmond, James M., Jr., Horn–1931-32
Tiedge, Hans, Violin and Battery–1902-17
Tipton, Albert, Flute–1940-1942,
    1945-1946
Tomei, A. A., Horn–1938-54
* Torchinsky, Abe, Tuba–1949-
Torello, Anton, Bass (Principal)–1914-48
* Torello, Carl, Bass–1934-
Torello, William, Bass–1936-38, 1940-1942,
    1952-54
Trein, Ludwig, Cello–1900-04, 1907-11
Tung, Ling, Violin–1958-64
Tung, Juan, Cello–1959-60
Tyre, Marjorie, Harp–1934-41, 1942-45

Unger, R., Cello–1901-02
Unglada, G., Violin–1908-12
Urbash, Emil, Flute and Piccolo–1902-03

Valerio, James, Battery–1924-1959
Van Amburgh, F. W., Clarinet–1912-13
Van den Beemt, Hedda, Violin–1901-07,
    1911-20; Celesta–1920-24
    (Principal 1906-07)
van den Burg, Willem, Cello (Principal)–
    1926-35
Van Leuwen, August, Flute–1901-02
Van Sciver, Israel S., Battery–1900-01
Van Stratum, Albert, Violin–1905-06
Vergnaud, Amédée, Viola–1924-32
Verney, Romain, Viola (Principal)–1920-25
Viek, Max, Horn–1929-32

Villani, A., Bass—1922-23
Vogel, Adolph, Cello—1921-25
Vogel, J., Trombone—1901-02
Vogelgesang, Frederick, Violin—1939-42,
   1945-46
Volmer, Henry F., Viola—1900-01
Volmer, Louis, Cello—1900-01

Wagner, Ernst, Trombone—1901-04
Wagner, Frederick E., Trumpet—1900-01,
   1917-21
   (Principal 1900-01)
Wagner, Lawrence, Bass Clarinet—1966-67
Wainwright, Lynne, Harp—1941-42
Waldman, Josef, Violin—1912-16
Walter, Robert, Violin—1903-06
Wardle, George, Horn—1928-38
Warner, Henry, Violin—1900-02
Waschek, Emil, Viola—1905-06
Watson, Frank S., Cello—1918-25
Watson, Nelson J., Bass—1923-24
Weinberg, Herman, Violin—1919-60
Weinelt, Karl, Horn—1904-05
Weinstein, Max, Oboe—1930-32
Weissenborn, H., Clarinet—1900-01
Welker, William, Violin—1900-01
Wells, Daniel R., Viola—1900-02
Wells, Norman C., Jr., Oboe—1958-1959
Wells, William M., Cello—1900-04
Wenning, M. F., Violin and Bassoon—
   1901-03
Wenzel, Charles R., Cello—1904-06

Werner, Florenz, Violin—1901-03
Wertheim, L., Viola (Principal)—1901-02
Whitaker, Carl, Bass—1900-01
Whitenack, Irven A., Bass—1938-40
Whitfield, Edw. J., Trombone—1943
Wiemann, Heinrich, Bass—1924-25; Bass
   and Tuba—1926-53
* Wigler, Jerome, Violin—1951-
Williams, Ernst S., Trumpet—1917-23
Winterstein, Benjamin H., Violin—1916-18
Wittman, Florian, Viola—1922-23
Wittmann, H., Bass—1900-01
Witzemann, John K., Violin—1900-17
Wolfe, Joseph, Oboe and English Horn—
   1929-30
Wollenberg, M., Bass—1906-07
Wulf, John, Bass—1907-19

Zalstein, Max, Violin—1925-45
Zaratzian, Harry, Viola (Principal)—1954-56
Zapp, G., Violin—1901-02
Zawisza, Leon, Violin—1949
Zeise, Karl W., Cello—1922-24, 1928-32
Zeitzew, Leon, Violin—1920-21
Zelig, Tibor, Violin—1944-45
Zenker, Alexander, Violin—1916-58
Zierold, Paul, Cello—1905-07
Zimmerman, Oscar, Bass—1930-36
Ziporkin, L., Bass—1917-19
Zoellner, Albert, Horn—1900-01
Zungolo, Anthony, Violin—1937-46

APPENDIX B

First Performances
(PARTIAL LIST)

Following is a list, compiled by the Philadelphia Orchestra, of some of the first performances it has given since 1900, with dates and names of conductors and soloists.

Composer	Title and Date of Premiere	Conductor Soloist	First Performance
ANTHEIL	Symphony No. 5 Dec. 31, 1948, Jan. 1, 1949	Eugene Ormandy	World
AURIG	Nocturne Jan. 26–27, 1923	Darius Milhaud	United States
BARBER	Violin Concerto Feb. 7–8, 1941	Eugene Ormandy Albert Spalding	World
BARBER	Ballet Suite, Medea, Op. 23 Dec. 5–6, 1947	Eugene Ormandy	World
BARBER	Toccata Festiva Sept. 30–Oct. 1, 1960	Eugene Ormandy Paul Callaway, organ	World
BARRYMORE	In Memoriam, Tone-Poem April 22, 1944	Eugene Ormandy	World
BARTÓK	Piano Concerto No. 3 Feb. 8–9, 1946	Eugene Ormandy Gyorgy Sandor	World
BARTÓK	Violin Concerto No. 1 Dec. 2, 1959	Eugene Ormandy Yehudi Menuhin	United States
BARTÓK	Five Songs for Mezzo-Soprano and Orchestra, Op. 15 Oct. 7, 1961	Eugene Ormandy Carolyn Stanford	United States
BEREZOWSKY	Harp Concerto, Op. 31 Jan. 26–27, 1945	Eugene Ormandy Edna Phillips	World
BERG	Wozzeck Mar. 21, 1931	Leopold Stokowski Philadelphia Grand Opera Company	United States

Composer	Title and Date of Premiere	Conductor Soloist	First Performance
BLISS	Melée Fantasque Feb. 27–28, 1925	Leopold Stokowski	United States
BLITZSTEIN	Freedom Morning Apr. 14–15, 1944	Saul Caston	United States
BLOCH	Suite Symphonique Oct. 26–27, 1945	Pierre Monteux	World
BRITTEN	Cantata Misericordium Feb. 26–27, 1965	Eugene Ormandy	United States
BRITTEN	Diversions on a Theme for Piano for Left Hand Jan. 16–17, 1942	Eugene Ormandy Paul Wittgenstein	World
BRITTEN	Variations and Fugue on a Theme of Purcell Dec. 13, 1947	Eugene Ormandy	United States
CARPENTER	A Pilgrim Vision Nov. 26–27, 1920	Leopold Stokowski	United States
CHASINS	Piano Concerto No. 1, Op. 14 Jan. 18, 1929	Ossip Gabrilowitsch Abram Chasins	World
CHAVEZ	Soli, No. 3 May 16, 1966	Eugene Ormandy	Western Hemisphere
CONVERSE	The Mystic Trumpeter, Op. 19 March 3–4, 1905	Fritz Scheel	United States
COPLAND	Dance Symphony Apr. 15, 1931	Leopold Stokowski	World
COWELL	Concerto for Koto and Orch. Dec. 18–19, 1964	Leopold Stokowski Kimio Eto (Koto)	World
CRESTON	Symphony No. 3, Op. 48 Oct. 27, 1950	Eugene Ormandy	World
DE FALLA	El amor brujo Apr. 15–17, 1922	Leopold Stokowski	United States
DE SABATA	Night of Plato Jan. 25, 1968	Lorin Maazel	United States
DIAMOND	Elegies for Flute, English Horn and Strings Sept. 23, 1965	Eugene Ormandy Murray Panitz Louis Rosenblatt	World
DIAMOND	Symphony No. 7 Jan. 26–27, 1962	Eugene Ormandy	World
DUTILLEUX	Ballet Suite from Le Loup Sept. 23, 1965	Eugene Ormandy	United States
DVORAK	Heldenlied, Op. 111 Dec. 27–28, 1901	Fritz Scheel	United States
VON EINEM	Nachtstück for Orchestra Op. 29 Feb. 4–5, 1966	Eugene Ormandy	United States
VON EINEM	Philadelphia Symphony Nov. 9–10, 1962	Eugene Ormandy	United States

Composer	Title and Date of Premiere	Conductor Soloist	First Performance
ENESCO	Orchestra Suite (2nd) Feb. 19–20, 1926	Leopold Stokowski	United States
FARWELL	Once I Passed Through A Populous City Mar. 30–31, 1928	Pierre Monteux	World
FINNEY	Symphony No. 2 Nov. 13–14, 1959	Eugene Ormandy	World
FITELBERG	Polish Rhapsody Nov. 4–5, 1921	Leopold Stokowski	United States
FOSS	Concerto for Improvising Solo Instruments and Orchestra Oct. 7–8, 1960	Eugene Ormandy	World
FOSS	Ode (Revised version) Oct. 17–18, 1958	Eugene Ormandy	World (revised version)
FRANÇAIX	L'Horloge de Flore, for Solo Oboe and Orchestra Mar. 31–April 1, 1961	Eugene Ormandy John de Lancie	World
GESENSWAY	Flute Concerto Nov. 1–2, 1946	Eugene Ormandy William Kincaid	World
GESENSWAY	Suite: Three Movements for Strings and Percussion Mar. 9–10, 1945	Eugene Ormandy	World
GESENSWAY	The Four Squares of Philadelphia Feb. 25–26, 1955	Eugene Ormandy	World
GINASTERA	Concerto per Corde May 14, 1966	Eugene Ormandy	World
GINASTERA	Harp Concerto Feb. 18, 1965	Eugene Ormandy Nicanor Zabaleta	World
GINASTERA	Psalm 150 for Mixed Chorus Boys' Chorus and Orchestra August 1, 1968	Eugene Ormandy	North America
GLAZOUNOV	Scènes de Ballet, Op. 52 Feb. 24–25, 1905	Fritz Scheel	United States
GLUCK	Iphigenia in Aulis Feb. 22–23, 1935	Alexander Smallens	United States
GOULD	Show Piece for Orchestra May 7, 1954	Eugene Ormandy	World
GRANADOS	Excerpts (Intermezzo, Epilogue from Goyescas) Mar. 10–11, 1916	Leopold Stokowski	World
GRETCHANINOFF	Symphony No. 5 Apr. 5, 1939	Leopold Stokowski	World
GROFÉ	Trick or Treat—Halloween Fantasy for Strings Mar. 2, 1963	André Kostelanetz	World
GRUENBERG	Violin Concerto, Op. 47 Dec. 1–2, 1944	Eugene Ormandy Jascha Heifetz	World

Composer	Title and Date of Premiere	Conductor Soloist	First Performance
HANSON	Pastorale for Solo Oboe, Strings and Harp Oct. 20–21, 1950	Eugene Ormandy Marcel Tabuteau	World
HANSON	Sinfonia Sacra (Symphony No. V) Feb. 18–19, 1955	Eugene Ormandy	World
HARRIS	Symphony No. 9–1963 Jan. 18–19, 1963	Eugene Ormandy	World
HARTMANN	Symphony No. 6, for Large Orchestra Mar. 27–28, 1959	Eugene Ormandy	United States
HINDEMITH	Ballet Overture, Cupid and Psyche Oct. 29–30, 1943	Eugene Ormandy	World
HINDEMITH	Clarinet Concerto Dec. 11, 1950	Eugene Ormandy Benny Goodman	World
D'INDY	Second Symphony in B Flat Dec. 30–31, 1904	Fritz Scheel	United States
D'INDY	Trilogy after Wallenstein Schiller's Dramatic Poem, Op. 12, Dec. 19–20, 1902	Fritz Scheel	United States
KODALY	Peacock Variations Nov. 22–23, 1946	Zoltán Kodály	United States
KOUTZEN	Violin Concerto Feb. 22–23, 1952	Eugene Ormandy Nadia Koutzen	World
KRENEK	Concerto for Harp and Chamber Orchestra Dec. 12–13, 1952	Eugene Ormandy Edna Phillips	World
MAHLER	Das Lied von der Erde Dec. 15–16, 1916	Leopold Stokowski Tilly Koenen Johannes Sembach	United States
MAHLER	Symphony No. 8 Mar. 1–2, 1916	Leopold Stokowski	United States
MAHLER	Symphony No. 10 in F sharp major (Deryck Cooke version) Nov. 5–6, 1965	Eugene Ormandy	United States
MALIPIERO	Concerti Jan. 4–5, 1929	Ossip Gabrilowitsch	United States
MALIPIERO	San Francesco d'Assisi Jan. 4–5, 1929	Ossip Gabrilowitsch	United States
MARTINU	Concerto for Two Pianos Nov. 5–6, 1943	Eugene Ormandy Luboshutz and Nemenoff	World
MARTINU	Symphony No. 4 Nov. 30–Dec. 1, 1945	Eugene Ormandy	World
McDONALD	Violin Concerto Mar. 16–17, 1945	Eugene Ormandy Alexander Hilsberg	World

Composer	Title and Date of Premiere	Conductor Soloist	First Performance
McDonald	Rhumba Symphony Oct. 4, 1935	Leopold Stokowski	World
McDonald	Santa Fe Trail Nov. 16, 1934	Leopold Stokowski	World
McDonald	Saga of the Mississippi Apr. 9–10, 1948	Eugene Ormandy	World
McDonald	Suite, From Childhood, for Harp and Orchestra Jan. 17–18, 1941	Eugene Ormandy Edna Phillips	World
Medtner	Piano Concerto in C minor Oct. 31–Nov. 1, 1924	Leopold Stokowski Nicholas Medtner	United States
Menotti	Apocalypse Jan. 18–19, 1952	Victor de Sabata	World (of entire suite)
Menotti	Violin Concerto in A minor Dec. 5–6, 1952	Eugene Ormandy Efrem Zimbalist	World
Menotti	The Consul (concert version) Jan. 14, 1926	Thomas Schippers	World (of concert version)
Miaskowsky	Symphony No. 5, in D major Jan. 2–4, 1926	Leopold Stokowski	United States
Miaskowsky	Symphony No. 6 Nov. 26–27, 1926	Leopold Stokowski	United States
Milhaud	Suite for Violin and Orch. Nov. 16–17, 1945	Eugene Ormandy Zino Francescatti	World
Nabokov	Cello Concerto, Les Hommages Nov. 6–7, 1953	Eugene Ormandy Lorne Munroe	World
Nabokov	Solitude, Four Moods for Orchestra Oct. 27–28, 1961	Eugene Ormandy	World
Persichetti	Fables, for Narrator and Orchestra Apr. 20–21, 1945	Eugene Ormandy	World
Persichetti	Symphony No. 3 Nov. 21–22, 1947	Eugene Ormandy	World
Persichetti	Symphony No. 4 Dec. 17–18, 1954	Eugene Ormandy	World
Piston	Symphony No. 7 Feb. 10–11, 1961	Eugene Ormandy	World
Prokofiev	Piano Concerto for Left Hand Op. 53 Mar. 28–29, 1958	Eugene Ormandy· Rudolf Serkin	United States
Prokofiev	Ode to the End of the War Oct. 29, 1946	Eugene Ormandy	United States
Prokofiev	Le Pas d'acier (staged) Apr. 10–11, 1931	Leopold Stokowski	United States (of staged version)
Prokofiev	Symphony No. 4, for Large Orchestra, Op. 47/122 Sept. 27–28, 1957	Eugene Ormandy	Western Hemisphere

Composer	Title and Date of Premiere	Conductor Soloist	First Performance
RABAUD	Symphony No. 2 in E minor Oct. 24–25, 1913	Leopold Stokowski	United States
RACHMANINOFF	Piano Concerto No. 4 in G minor March 18–19, 1927	Leopold Stokowski Sergei Rachmaninoff	World
RACHMANINOFF	Rhapsody on a Theme by Paganini Nov. 7, 1934	Leopold Stokowski Sergei Rachmaninoff	World
RACHMANINOFF	Symphonic Dances Jan. 3–4, 1941	Eugene Ormandy	World
RACHMANINOFF	Symphony No. 1 in D minor, Op. 13 Mar. 19–20, 1948	Eugene Ormandy	United States
RACHMANINOFF	Symphony No. 3 in A minor, Op. 44 Nov. 6–7, 1936	Leopold Stokowski	World
RACHMANINOFF	Symphony, The Bells Feb. 6–7, 1920	Leopold Stokowski	United States
REGER	Totenfeier, Op. 145A (Original Version) Apr. 8–9, 1966	Eugene Ormandy	United States
RIMSKY-KORSAKOV	Excerpts from Invisible City of Kitezh October 26–27, 1923	Leopold Stokowski	United States
RIVIER	Symphony No. 6 ("Les Présages") Mar. 3–4, 1967	Georges Prêtre	United States
ROREM	Eagles Oct. 23–24, 1959	Eugene Ormandy	World
ROSENTHAL	Christmas Symphonies Dec. 23–27, 1948	Eugene Ormandy	World
ROSENTHAL	Saint Francis of Assisi Oct. 29, 1946	Eugene Ormandy	United States
ROZSA	Notturno Ungherese, Op. 28 Apr. 17–18, 1964	Eugene Ormandy	World
ROZSA	The Vintner's Daughter, (Twelve variations on a French folksong) Mar. 23–24, 1956	Eugene Ormandy	World
SAINT-SAËNS	March Héroïque March 24, 1920	Leopold Stokowski	United States
SCALERO	The Divine Forest Dec. 20–21, 1940	Eugene Ormandy	United States
SCHELLING	A Victory Ball Feb. 23–24, 1923	Leopold Stokowski	World
SCHMIDT	Symphony No. 2 in E flat major Jan. 17–18, 1941	Eugene Ormandy	United States

Composer	Title and Date of Premiere	Conductor Soloist	First Performance
SCHOENBERG	Die glückliche Hand (staged) Apr. 11–12, 1930	Leopold Stokowski	United States (of staged version)
SCHOENBERG	Gurrelieder Apr. 8–9, 1932	Leopold Stokowski	United States
SCHOENBERG	Violin Concerto Dec. 6–7, 1940	Leopold Stokowski Louis Krasner	United States
SCRIABIN	Divine Poem (Symphony No. 3) Op. 43 Nov. 19–20, 1915	Leopold Stokowski	United States
SESSIONS	Symphony No. 5 Feb. 7–8, 1964	Eugene Ormandy	World
SHOSTAKOVICH	Cello Concerto in E flat Op. 107 Nov. 6–7, 1959	Eugene Ormandy Mstislav Rostropovich	United States
SHOSTAKOVICH	Symphony No. 1, Op. 10 Nov. 2–3, 1928	Leopold Stokowski	United States
SHOSTAKOVICH	Symphony No. 4, Op. 43 Feb. 15–16, 1963	Eugene Ormandy	United States
SHOSTAKOVICH	Symphony No. 6, Op. 54 Nov. 29–30, 1940	Leopold Stokowski	Outside Russia
SIBELIUS	Symphony No. 5 in E flat major Oct. 21–22, 1921	Leopold Stokowski	United States
SIBELIUS	Symphony No. 6, Op. 104 Apr. 23–24, 1926	Leopold Stokowski	United States
SIBELIUS	Symphony No. 7, Op. 105 Apr. 3–5, 1926	Leopold Stokowski	United States
SIEGMEISTER	Dick Whittington and his Cat (A Symphonic Story for Children)	William Smith	World
STRAUSS	Alpensymphonie, Op. 64 Apr. 28–29, 1916	Leopold Stokowski	United States
STRAVINSKY	Firebird (staged) April 11, 1930	Leopold Stokowski Martha Graham	United States (of staged version)
STRAVINSKY	Monumentum pro Gesualdo Jan. 13–14, 1961	William Smith	United States
STRAVINSKY	Mavra Dec. 28–29, 1934	Alexander Smallens	United States
STRAVINSKY	Oedipus Rex (staged) Apr. 10–11, 1931	Leopold Stokowski	United States (of staged version)
STRAVINSKY	Le Sacre du printemps Mar. 3–4, 1922	Leopold Stokowski	United States
STRAVINSKY	Song of the Nightingale Oct. 19–20, 1923	Leopold Stokowski	United States
STRAVINSKY	Symphonies of Wind Instruments Nov. 23–24, 1923	Leopold Stokowski	United States

Composer	Title and Date of Premiere	Conductor Soloist	First Performance
SZYMANOWSKI	Violin Concerto No. 1, Op. 35 Nov. 18–19, 1924	Leopold Stokowski Angel Reyes	United States
SZYMANOWSKI	Symphony No. 3, Chant de la Nuit Nov. 19–20, 1926	Leopold Stokowski	United States
TANSMAN	Viola Concerto Dec. 29–30, 1939	Eugene Ormandy Samuel Lifschey	United States
TCHAIKOVSKY	"Symphony No. 7 in E flat major" Feb. 16–17, 1962	Eugene Ormandy	Western Hemisphere
THOMPSON	A Trip to Nahant, Fantasia for Orchestra	Eugene Ormandy	World
THOMPSON	Fugues and Cantilenas May 2, 1959	Virgil Thomson	World
THOMSON	Louisiana Story, Suite for Orchestra Nov. 26–27, 1948	Eugene Ormandy	World
THOMSON	Suite for Orchestra Nov. 17–18, 1944	Virgil Thomson	World
VARÈSE	Amériques Apr. 9–10, 1926	Leopold Stokowski	World
VAUCLAIN	Symphony in One Movement Apr. 18–19, 1947	Eugene Ormandy	World
VAUGHAN WILLIAMS	Symphony No. 8 Oct. 5–6, 1956	Eugene Ormandy	United States
VILLA-LOBOS	Harp Concerto Jan. 14–15, 1955	Heitor Villa-Lobos Nicanor Zabaleta	World
VILLA-LOBOS	Sinfonia No. 8 (1950) Jan. 14–15, 1955	Villa-Lobos	World
VILLA-LOBOS	Sinfonia No. 9 May 16, 1966	Eugene Ormandy	World
VINCENT	Symphonic Poem after Descartes Mar. 20–21, 1959	Eugene Ormandy	World
WEBERN	Im Sommerwind Idyll for Large Orchestra May 25, 1962	Eugene Ormandy	World
WEBERN	Three Pieces for Orchestra Apr. 14–15, 1967	Eugene Ormandy	World
YARDUMIAN	Piano Concerto Jan. 3–4, 1958	Eugene Ormandy Rudolf Firkusny	World
YARDUMIAN	Violin Concerto Mar. 30–31, 1951	Eugene Ormandy Anshel Brusilow	World
YARDUMIAN	Symphony Dec. 1–2, 1961	Eugene Ormandy	World
YARDUMIAN	Symphony No. 2 (Psalms) for Orchestra and Contralto Nov. 13–14, 1964	Eugene Ormandy Lili Chookasian	World

Composer	Title and Date of Premiere	Conductor Soloist	First Performance
ZADOR	Elégié Nov. 11–12, 1960	Eugene Ormandy	World
ZADOR	Five Contrasts for Orchestra Jan. 8–9, 1965	Eugene Ormandy	World
ZIMBALIST	Violin Concerto in C sharp minor Nov. 28–29, 1947	Eugene Ormandy	World
ZIMBALIST	Tone Poem: Portrait of an Artist Dec. 7–8, 1945	Eugene Ormandy	World

APPENDIX C

Discography

Following is a list of available recordings by the Philadelphia Orchestra on the Columbia and RCA labels. Each major work is listed individually; for record couplings compare numbers. Where multiple numbers are given, the recording is available in more than one packaging.

COLUMBIA RECORDS

Conducted by Eugene Ormandy

ALFVEN	Swedish Rhapsody	MS 6196
J. C. BACH	Sinfonia for Double Orchestra, Op. 18, No. 1	MS 6180
J. S. BACH	Air on the G String	MS 6081
	Concerto in D Minor for Three Pianos and Orchestra (R. G. and J. Casadesus)	MS 6495
	Easter Oratorio (Raskin, Forrester, Lewis, Beattie, Temple University Concert Choir)	MS 6539
	Mass in B Minor (Steber, Elias, Verreau, Cross, Temple University Choirs)	M3S 680
	Passacaglia and Fugue in C Minor	MS 6180
	Toccata, Adagio and Fugue in C Major	MS 6180
	Toccata and Fugue in D Minor	MS 6180, MGP 7
BARBER	Adagio for Strings	MS 6224
	Toccata Festiva (Biggs)	MS 6398
BARTÓK	Bluebeard's Castle (Elias, Hines)	MS 6425
	Concerto for Orchestra	MS 6626
	Deux Images	MS 6789
	The Miraculous Mandarin Suite	MS 6789
	Two Portraits (Brusilow)	MS 6789
	Violin Concerto No. 1 (Stern)	MS 6277
BEETHOVEN	Christ on the Mount of Olives (Raskin, Lewis, Beattie, Temple University Choirs)	MS 6841
	Piano Concerto No. 1 (Serkin	MS 6838, D4S 740
	Piano Concerto No. 2 (Serkin)	MS 6839, D4S 740
	Piano Concerto No. 4 (Istomin)	MS 7199
	Piano Concerto No. 4 (Serkin)	MS 6745, D4S 740

	The Nine Symphonies (Ninth with Amara, Chook-	
	asian, Alexander, Macurdy, Mormon Tabernacle	
	Choir, Condie)	D7S 745
	Symphony No. 3, "Eroica"	MS 6266
	Symphony No. 8	M2S 738
	Symphony No. 9 "Choral" (Same as above)	MS 7016
	Triple Concerto (Stern, Rose, Istomin)	D2S 720
BERG	Lulu Suite	MS 7041
BERLIOZ	Requiem (Temple University Choirs, Page)	M2S 730
	Symphonie Fantastique	MS 6248
BIZET	Carmen Suite	MS 6051
	L'Arlésienne Suites Nos. 1 and 2	MS 6546
BLOCH	Schelomo (Rose)	MS 6253
BORODIN	In the Steppes of Central Asia	MS 6073
	Nocturne	MS 6224
	Polovtsian Dances	MS 6073
BRAHMS	A German Requiem (Curtin, Hines, Mormon Taber-	
	nacle Choir)	M2S 686
	Double Concerto (Stern, Rose)	MS 7251, D2S 720
	Piano Concerto No. 1 (Serkin)	MS 6304, D3S 741
	Piano Concerto No. 2 (Istomin)	MS 6715
	Piano Concerto No. 2 (Serkin)	D3S 741
	Symphony No. 1	MS 6067
	Variations on a Theme by Handel	MS 7298, M2S 686
	Variations on a Theme by Haydn	MS 7298
	Violin Concerto (Stern)	MS 6153, D3S 721
BRITTEN	The Young Person's Guide to the Orchestra	MS 6027
BRUCH	Violin Concerto No. 1 (Stern)	MS 7003
BRUCKNER	Symphony No. 5	M2S 768
	Te Deum (Stader, Vanni, Kolk, Gramm, Temple	
	University Choirs)	M2S 768
CASELLA	Paganiniana	MS 6205
CASTELNUOVO-TEDESCO	Guitar Concerto in D Major (Williams)	MS 6834
CHOPIN	Les Sylphides	MS 6508
	Piano Concerto No. 1 (Brailowsky)	MS 6252
	Piano Concerto No. 1 (Gilels)	MS 6712
COPLAND	Fanfare for the Common Man	MS 6684
	Lincoln Portrait (Stevenson)	MS 6684
CORELLI	Concerto Grosso No. 8	MS 6081
	Suite for Strings	MS 6095
DEBUSSY	Danse	MS 6697
	La Mer	MS 6077
	Nocturnes (Temple University Women's Choir)	MS 6697
	Prelude to The Afternoon of a Faun (Kincaid)	MS 6077, M2S 738
DE FALLA	Nights in the Gardens of Spain (Entremont)	MS 6629
DELIBES	Coppelia Ballet Suite	MS 6508
	Sylvia Ballet Suite	MS 6508

DELIUS	A Dance Rhapsody No. 2	MS 6376
	Brigg Fair	MS 6376
	In a Summer Garden	MS 6376
	On Hearing the First Cuckoo in Spring	MS 6376
DVORAK	Cello Concerto (Rose)	MS 6714
	Romance (Stern)	MS 6876
	Violin Concerto (Stern)	MS 6876
ENESCO	Roumanian Rhapsodies Nos. 1 and 2	MS 6018
FRANCK	Symphonic Variations (R. Casadesus)	MS 6070
	Symphony in D Minor	MS 6297
GERSHWIN	An American in Paris	MS 7258
	Concerto in F Major (Entremont)	MS 7013
	Porgy and Bess—A Symphonic Picture (Arr: Bennett)	MS 7258
	Rhapsody in Blue (Entremont)	MS 7013
	Rhapsody in Blue (Levant)	CS 8461
GLINKA	Russlan and Ludmilla Overture	MS 6092
GRIEG	Piano Concerto (Entremont)	MS 6016, D3S 715
	Peer Gynt Suite No. 1	MS 6196
GROFÉ	Grand Canyon Suite	MS 6003
HANDEL	The Messiah (Farrell, Lipton, Cunningham, Warfield, Mormon Tabernacle Choir)	M2S 607
	The Royal Fireworks Suite	MS 6095
	The Water Music Suite	MS 6095
HAYDN	Sinfonia Concertante in B-flat Major	MS 6061
	Symphony No. 96, "Miracle"	MS 6812
	Symphony No. 101, "Clock"	MS 6812
HINDEMITH	Symphonic Metamorphoses	MS 6562
	Symphony Mathis der Maler	MS 6562
IBERT	Divertissement	MS 6449
D'INDY	Symphony on a French Mountain Air (R. Casadesus)	MS 6070
IVES	Symphony No. 1	MS 7111, D3S 783
	Three Places in New England	MS 6684, MS 7015, MS 7111
KODÁLY	Concerto for Orchestra	MS 7034
	Dances of Galanta	MS 7034
	Dances of Marosszék	MS 7034
	Hary Janos Suite	MS 6746
LALO	Symphonie Espagnole (Stern)	MS 7003
LISZT	Hungarian Rhapsodies Nos. 1 and 2	MS 6018
	Piano Concerto No. 1 (Entremont)	MS 6071
	Piano Concerto No. 2 (Entremont)	MS 6071
	Totentanz (Brailowsky)	MS 6252
MAHLER	Das Lied von der Erde (Chookasian, Lewis)	MS 6946, D3S 774
	Symphony No. 10	M2S 735, D3S 774
MENDELSSOHN	A Midsummer Night's Dream—Incidental Music	MS 6628
	Capriccio Brillante (Serkin)	MS 7183

	Concerto in A-flat Major for Two Pianos (Gold and Fizdale)	MS 6681
	Concerto in E Major for Two Pianos (Gold and Fizdale)	MS 6681
	Piano Concerto No. 1 (Serkin)	MS 6128, MS 7185, D3S 741
	Piano Concerto No. 2 (Serkin)	MS 6128
	Scherzo from Octet for Strings	MS 6081
	Symphony No. 4	MS 6628
	Violin Concerto (Stern)	MS 6062, D3S 721
MOZART	Bassoon Concerto (Garfield)	MS 6451
	Clarinet Concerto (Gigliotti)	MS 6452
	Concerto in E-Flat Major for Two Pianos (R. and G. Casadesus)	MS 6274
	Concerto in F Major for Three Pianos (R. G. and J. Casadesus)	MS 6495
	Eine Kleine Nachtmusik	MS 6081
	Flute Concerto No. 1 (Kincaid)	MS 6451
	Four Horn Concertos (Jones)	MS 6785
	Oboe Concerto (de Lancie)	MS 6452
	Piano Concerto No. 27 (Serkin)	MS 6839
	Sinfonia Concertante in E-flat Major for Winds	MS 6061
	Symphony No. 30	MS 6722
	Symphony No. 31, "Paris"	MS 6722
MUSSORGSKY	Night on Bald Mountain	MS 6073, MS 7148
	Pictures at an Exhibition	MS 7148
NIELSEN	Helios Overture	MS 7004
	Overture to Masquerade	MS 6882
	Pan and Syrinx	MS 7004
	Prelude to Act II of Masquerade	MS 6882
	Rhapsodic Overture	MS 7004
	Symphony No. 1	MS 7004
	Symphony No. 6	MS 6882
OFFENBACH	Gaité Parisienne (arr. Rosenthal)	MS 6546
ORFF	Carmina Burana (Harsanyi, Petrak, Rutgers University Choir)	MS 6163
	Catulli Carmina (Blegen, Kness, Temple University Choirs)	MS 7017
PAGANINI	Violin Concerto No. 1 (Francescatti)	MS 6268
POULENC	Organ Concerto (Biggs)	MS 6398
PROKOFIEV	Classical Symphony	MS 6545, MGP 7
	The Love for Three Oranges—Suite	MS 6545
	Lieutenant Kijé Suite	MS 6545
	Peter and the Wolf (Ritchard)	MS 6027
	Piano Concerto No. 4 (Serkin)	MS 6405
	Symphony No. 4	MS 6154
	Symphony No. 5	MS 6004
	Symphony No. 6	MS 6489
	Violin Concerto No. 1 (Stern)	MS 6635
	Violin Concerto No. 2 (Stern)	MS 6635
RACHMANINOFF	Piano Concerto No. 1 (Entremont)	MS 6517
	Piano Concerto No. 4 (Entremont)	MS 6517

	Rhapsody on a Theme of Paganini (Entremont)	MS 6016, D3S 715
	Symphonic Dances	MS 6205
	Symphony No. 1	MS 6986, D3S 813
	Symphony No. 2	MS 6110, D3S 813
	Symphony No. 3	MS 7081, D3S 813
	Vocalise	MS 7081, D3S 813
RAVEL	Alborada del Gracioso	MS 6169
	Bolero	MS 6169, MS 6478, MGP 7
	Concerto for the Left Hand (R. Casadesus)	MS 6274
	Daphnis and Chloe, Suite No. 2	MS 6077
	La Valse	MS 6478, M2S 738
	Le Tombeau de Couperin (de Lancie)	MS 6169
	Piano Concerto in G Major (Entremont)	MS 6629
	Rapsodie Espagnole	MS 6697
RESPIGHI	The Birds	MS 7242
	Church Windows	MS 7242
	Feste Romane	MS 6587
	The Fountains of Rome	MS 6587
	The Pines of Rome	MS 6587, MPG 7
RIMSKY-KORSAKOV	Capriccio Espagnole	MS 6917
	Le Coq d'Or–Bridal Procession	MS 6917
	Le Coq d'Or–Suite	MS 6092
	Russian Easter Overture	MS 6092
	Scheherezade (Brusilow)	MS 6365
RODRIGO	Concierto de Aranjuez for Guitar and Orchestra (Williams)	MS 6834
ROUSSEL	Bacchus et Ariane	MS 6267
SAINT-SAENS	Piano Concerto No. 2 (Entremont)	MS 6778
	Piano Concerto No. 4 (Entremont)	MS 6778
	Symphony No. 3, "Organ" (Biggs)	MS 6469
SCHOENBERG	Theme and Variations	MS 7041, M2S 767
SCHUBERT	Symphony No. 9, "Great"	MS 7272
SCHUMANN	Introduction and Allegro Appassionata (Serkin)	MS 6688
	Introduction and Concert Allegro (Serkin)	MS 7183
	Piano Concerto (Serkin)	MS 6688, MS 7185, D3S 741
SHOSTAKOVICH	Cello Concerto (Rostropovich)	MS 6124
	Symphony No. 1	MS 6124
	Symphony No. 4	MS 6459
	Symphony No. 5	MS 7279
SIBELIUS	En Saga	MS 6732
	Finlandia (Mormon Tabernacle Choir)	MS 6196, MS 6732
	The Swan of Tuonela (Rosenblatt)	MS 6157, MS 6732
	Symphony No. 1	MS 6395
	Symphony No. 2	MS 6024
	Valse Triste	MS 6196, MS 6732
	Violin Concerto (Oistrakh)	MS 6157
STRAUSS	Also Sprach Zarathustra	MS 6547
	Burleske (Serkin)	MS 7183

	Death and Transfiguration	MS 6324
	Der Rosenkavalier–Suite	MS 6678
	Don Juan	MS 6324
	Don Quixote (Munroe, Cooley)	MS 6515
	Ein Heldenleben (Brusilow)	MS 6249
	Salome–Dance of the Seven Veils	MS 6678
	Till Eulenspiegel	MS 6678
STRAVINSKY	Petrouchka Suite	MS 6746
TCHAIKOVSKY	Capriccio Italien	MS 6917, MGP 7
	Eugene Onegin–Waltz	MS 6917
	Nutcracker Ballet (Excerpts)	MS 6621, D3S 706
	Nutcracker Ballet Suite	MS 6807
	Overture "1812"	MS 6073
	Piano Concerto No. 2 (Graffman)	MS 6755
	Piano Concerto No. 3 (Graffman)	MS 6755
	Romeo and Juliet–Overture–Fantasy	MS 6942, M2S 738
	Serenade for Strings	MS 6224
	Sleeping Beauty Ballet (Excerpts)	MS 6279, D3S 706
	Sleeping Beauty Ballet Suite	MS 6942
	Swan Lake Ballet (Excerpts)	MS 6437, D3S 706
	Swan Lake Ballet Suite	MS 6807
	Symphony No. 4	MS 6756, D3S 727
	Symphony No. 5	MS 6109, D3S 727
	Symphony No. 6, "Pathetique"	MS 7169, D3S 727
	"Symphony No. 7" (arr. Bogatyrev)	MS 6349
	Variations on a Rococo Theme for Cello and Orchestra (Rose)	MS 6714
	Violin Concerto (Oistrakh)	MS 6298
	Violin Concerto (Stern)	MS 6062, D3S 721
VAUGHAN WILLIAMS	Fantasia on Greensleeves	MS 6224
VERDI	Requiem (Amara, Forrester, Tucker, London, Westminster Choir)	M2S 707
VIOTTI	Violin Concerto No. 22 (Stern)	MS 6277
VIVALDI	Concerto in C Minor for Two Violins (Oistrakh, Stern)	MS 6204
	Concerto in D Major for Two Violins (Oistrakh, Stern)	MS 6204
	Concerto in D Minor for Two Violins (Oistrakh, Stern)	MS 6204
	Concerto in G Minor for Two Violins (Oistrakh, Stern)	MS 6204
	The Seasons (Brusilow)	MS 6195
WAGNER	Die Meistersinger–Dance of the Apprentices and Entrance of the Meistersingers	MGP 7
	Die Meistersinger–Prelude to Act III, Dance of the Apprentices and Entrance of the Meistersingers	MS 6442
	Lohengrin–Prelude to Act III	MS 6442
	Siegfried–Forest Murmurs	MS 6442
	Tannhauser–Overture and Venusberg Music	MS 6442
	Tristan and Isolde–Prelude and Love Death	M2S 738
WALTON	Belshazzar's Feast (Cassel, Rutgers University Choir)	MS 6267
	Facade	MS 6449
	Violin Concerto (Francescatti)	MS 6201

WEBERN	Im Sommerwind	MS 7041
	Three Pieces for Orchestra	MS 7041
YARDUMIAN	Chorale Prelude	MS 6859
	Symphony No. 1	MS 6859
	Symphony No. 2 (Chookasian)	MS 6859

CONDUCTED BY LEOPOLD STOKOWSKI

DE FALLA	El Amor Brujo (Verrett)	MS 6147
WAGNER	Tristan und Isolde–Love Music from Acts 2 and 3	MS 6147

CONDUCTED BY CHARLES MUNCH

BERLIOZ	Damnation of Faust (Excerpts)	MS 6523
FAURÉ	Pelléas et Mélisande	MS 6523
RAVEL	Valses Nobles et Sentimentales	MS 6523

COLLECTIONS

CONDUCTED BY EUGENE ORMANDY

AMERICA—Stars and Stripes Forever; Variations on "America" (Ives); MS 7289
On the Trail, etc.

*ANVIL CHORUS—Favorite Opera Choruses from *Faust, Aida, Carmen,* etc. MS 7061

*THE BELOVED CHORUSES—Jesu, Joy of Man's Desiring; Hallelujah Chorus; MS 6058
Sheep May Safely Graze, etc.

*THE BELOVED CHORUSES, VOL. II—Holy Art Thou (Handel); Father in Heaven MS 6679
(Bach-Gounod's Ave Maria); How Lovely Is Thy Dwelling Place (Brahms)

*BLESS THIS HOUSE—The Lord's Prayer; The Palms, Panis Angelicus, etc. MS 6835

THE BLUE DANUBE—Emperor Waltz; Voices of Spring; Tales from MS 6217
the Vienna Woods, etc.

THE BLUE DANUBE—Emperor Waltz; Vienna Blood; Waltz of the Flowers; etc. D3S 789

CARNIVAL IN VIENNA—1001 Nights Waltz; Gold and Silver Waltz; MS 6352
Tristch-Trastch Polka; etc.

**A CHRISTMAS FESTIVAL—Favorite Carols MS 6639

CLAIR DE LUNE—Traumerei; The Swan; Barcarolle; etc. MS 6883

DANCES FOR ORCHESTRA—Habanera; Anitra's Dance; Danse Macabre, etc. MS 6457

FAVORITE ROMANTIC WALTZES—Waltz of the Flowers, Waltz from Serenade in C; MS 6687
Grand Valse Brillante; etc.

A FESTIVAL OF MARCHES—March of the Toreadors; *Aida* Grand March; MS 6474
Funeral March of a Marionette; etc.

FIREWORKS—Ride of the Valkyries; Comedian's Gallop; Sabre Dance; etc. MS 6624

FIRST CHAIR ENCORES, VOL. 1—Virtuoso works featuring first-chair players from MS 6791
the Philadelphia Orchestra

* With the Mormon Tabernacle Choir of Salt Lake City, Richard Condie, Director.
** With the Temple University Choir.

First Chair Encores, Vol. 2—See above   MS 6977

**The Glorious Sound of Christmas—More Favorite Carols   MS 6369

*God Bless America—America, the Beautiful; The Star-Spangled Banner;   MS 6721
Battle Hymn of the Republic

Greatest Hits—Sabre Dance; Clair de Lune; Blue Danube Waltz; etc.   MS 6934

**Greatest Christmas Hits—Deck the Halls; Little Drummer Boy; The Twelve   MS 7161
Days of Christmas; O Come All Ye Faithful; etc.

Greatest Hits, Vol. 3—Air on G String; Anitra's Dance; *Aida*   MS 7072
Grand March, etc.

Greatest Hits, Vol. 4—Traumerei; Wedding March; When Johnny Comes   MS 7267
Marching Home; etc.

Greensleeves—Londonderry Air; Schubert's Serenade; Meditation from *Thais;* etc.   MS 7103

*Hallelujah Chorus—Favorite Handel Choruses from *Messiah, Israel in Egypt,*   MS 7292
Judas Maccabaeus, etc.

Holiday for Orchestra—Camptown Races; When Johnny Comes Marching Home;   MS 6757
Paderewski's Minuet; etc.

Hora Staccato—Flight of the Bumble Bee; Pizzicato Polkas (Delibes and Strauss);   MS 7146
Perpetual Motions (Paganini and Novacek); etc.

Invitation to the Dance—Danse Macabre; Russian Sailors Dance;   MS 6241
Mephisto Waltz; etc.

*The Lord's Prayer, Vol. 1—Battle Hymn of the Republic; Come, Come Ye Saints;   MS 6068
Londonderry Air; etc.

*The Lord's Prayer, Vol. 2—Hallelujah, Amen; A Mighty Fortress; Come,   MS 6367
Sweet Death; etc.

Magic Fire Music—*Tannhauser* Fest March; Ride of the Valkyries; *Lohengrin*—   MS 6701
Act III Prelude

Magnificent Marches—March of the Boyars; Trumpet Voluntary;   MS 6979
Wedding March; etc.

Marche Slav—Russian Easter Overture; *Russlan and Ludmilla* Overture; etc.   MS 6875

More Greatest Hits—Barcarolle; Reverie, Ave Maria; etc.   MS 6993

*The Mormon Tabernacle Choir's Greatest Hits—Hallelujah Chorus;   MS 6951
Battle Hymn of the Republic; God Bless America; etc.

*The Mormon Tabernacle Choir's Greatest Hits, Vol. 2—This is My Country;   MS 7086
Land of Hope and Glory; Beautiful Dreamer; etc.

Ports of Call—Bolero; La Valse; Clair de Lune; etc.   MS 6478

Reverie—Greensleeves; Pavane for a Dead Princess; Polovtsian Dance No. 2, etc.   MS 6575

The Richest Sound on Earth—Pines of Rome; Toccata and Fugue in D Minor;   MGP 7
Bolero; etc.

Ritual Fire Dance—Dance of the Comedians; Dance of the Hours; etc.   MS 6823

Sabre Dance—Russian Sailor's Dance; Polovtsian Dances; etc.   MS 6958

Spectaculars—Offenbach Can-Cans; Fire Bell and Tristch-Trastch Polkas; etc.   MS 6739

That Philadelphia Sound—20 Orchestral Favorites   M2X 786

*This Is My Country—Finlandia; Marseillaise; Land of Hope and Glory;   MS 6419
O Columbia the Gem of the Ocean

*This Land Is Your Land—Home on the Range; Shenandoah; Down in   MS 6747
the Valley; etc;

Those Fabulous Philadelphians—Landmarks and Legends conducted by   MGP 17
    Ormandy and Stokowski; includes Wagner: Love Music from *Tristan und Isolde*
    Acts 2 and 3, *Rosenkavalier* Suite; etc.

Waltz of the Flowers—Sleeping Beauty and Swan Lake Waltzes; etc.   MS 7133

Wine, Women and Song—Skater's Waltz; Estudiantina Waltz;   MS 7032
    1001 Nights Waltz; etc.

RCA RECORDS

Conducted by Eugene Ormandy

Brahms	Double Concerto (Heifetz, Feuermann)	LCT 1016
Bruckner	Symphony No. 7	LSC 3059
Chopin	Piano Concerto No. 2 (Rubinstein)	LSC 3055
	Grand Fantasy on Polish Airs (Rubinstein)	LSC 3055
Dvorak	Scherzo Capriccioso	LSC 3085
Grieg	Piano Concerto (Cliburn)	LSC 3065
Ives	Symphony No. 3	LSC 3060
Liszt	Piano Concerto No. 1 (Cliburn)	LSC 3065
	Hungarian Rhapsodies Nos. 1 and 2	LSC 3085
Mahler	Symphony No. 1	LSC 3107
Mendelssohn	Elijah (Marsh, Verrett, Lewis, Krause, Singing City Choir, Columbus Boychoir)	LSC 6190
Mozart	Symphony No. 41, "Jupiter"	LSC 3056
Rachmaninoff	The Four Piano Concertos and Rhapsody on a Theme by Paganini Rachmaninoff with Ormandy and Stokowski conducting)	LM 6123
Schubert	Symphony No. 8, "Unfinished"	LSC 3056
Schuman	New England Triptych	LSC 3060
Smetana	Bartered Bride, Overture and Polka Furiant	LSC 3085
Tchaikovsky	Symphony No. 6, "Pathetique"	LSC 3058
Telemann	Four Concertos for various instruments	LSC 3057

Conducted by Leopold Stokowski

Rachmaninoff	The Four Piano Concertos and Rhapsody (see listing above)	LM 6123

Conducted by Arturo Toscanini

Schubert	Symphony No. 9 in C, "Great"	LD 2662

Philadelphia Orchestra "Pops" conducted by Henry Mancini

Mancini	Beaver Valley '37; Dream of a Lifetime; Strings on Fire; etc.	LSC 3106

INDEX

ILLUSTRATION ACKNOWLEDGMENTS

Cartoon by Emidio "Mike" Angelo, *Someone Drops a Handkerchief During a Performance of The Philadelphia Orchestra*

The portrait of Leopold Stokowski is reproduced by kind permission of Mr. Stokowski. PHOTO BY MORRIS WARMAN

Time cover by V. Perfilieff; © *Time, Inc.*, 1930

Fantasia photograph © Walt Disney Productions

All other pictures from the archives of the Philadelphia Orchestra Association, including:

Karl Pohlig. PHOTO BY HAESELER, PHILADELPHIA

Studio portrait of Stokowski. PHOTO BY VANDAMM, NEW YORK

Overhead shot of the Orchestra, Philharmonic Hall, Lincoln Center, New York. PHOTO BY COLUMBIA RECORDS: DON HUNSTEIN

Advertisement on Tokyo street announcing the Orchestra's tour of Japan. COURTESY, WAYNE SHILKRET

The Orchestra in concert at the Saratoga Performing Arts Center. COURTESY, SARATOGA PERFORMING ARTS CENTER

Ormandy with Alexander Hilsberg, William Kincaid and Marcel Tabuteau. PHOTO BY JULES SCHICK

The Orchestra in concert at the Academy; Ormandy with Rachmaninoff; Robin Hood Dell; Ormandy with Sibelius, Finland, 1955; Ormandy with Stokowski in 1965; Ormandy at rehearsal; Ormandy with John Pfeiffer during a recording session; Close-up of Ormandy conducting; Close-up of Stokowski conducting; Exterior view of the Academy of Music; Interior view of the Academy; Matinee crowds outside the Broad Street entrance to the Academy; Stage view during a children's concert; A youthful audience in rapt attention; Frances Wister and Orville Bullitt with Ormandy; Cellists at rehearsal; Ormandy goes over a point with the Orchestra during rehearsal; Horns, Mason Jones and others; Harpists, Marilyn Costello and Margarita Csonka; First-desk woodwinds; The Orchestra on stage at the Academy; Brothers, The de Pasquale Quartet; Husbands and wives of the Orchestra; Guest soloist, Fritz Kreisler with Ormandy and others; Pierre Monteux; Lauritz Melchior, Kirsten Flagstad and Charles O'Connell; Marian Anderson with Ormandy; Tabuteau and Toscanini in 1941; Isaac Stern and others at rehearsal; Ormandy with Dimitri Shostakovitch; Adlai Stevenson with the Orchestra; Van Cliburn with the Orchestra; Arthur Rubinstein performing at the Academy; Stravinsky at rehearsal; Ormandy and composer Krzysztof Penderecki; Ormandy conducting. PHOTOS BY ADRIAN SIEGEL